THE PURPOSE
AND POWER OF
LOVE
& MARRIAGE

MYLES MUNROE

THE PURPOSE
AND POWER OF
LOVE
& MARRIAGE

Destiny Image® Publishers, Inc.

P.O. Box 310
Shippensburg, PA 17257-0310

*"Speaking to the Purposes of God for This Generation
and for the Generations to Come"*

ISBN 0-7684-2251-5

Previously Published as:
ISBN 0-7684-2154-3: Understanding Love™ Marriage, Still a Great Idea
ISBN 0-7684-2155-1: Understanding Love™ and the Secrets of the Heart
ISBN 0-7684-2156-X: Understanding Love™ For a Lifetime

Bahamas Faith Ministry

P.O. Box N9583
Nassau, Bahamas

For Worldwide Distribution
Printed in the U.S.A.

2 3 4 5 6 7 8 9 10 / 10 09 08 07 06 05

This book and all other Destiny Image, Revival Press,
MercyPlace, Fresh Bread, Destiny Image Fiction,
and Treasure House books are available
at Christian bookstores and distributors worldwide.

For a U.S. bookstore nearest you,
call **1-800-722-6774**.

For more information on foreign distributors,
call **717-532-3040**.

Or reach us on the Internet:
www.destinyimage.com

Dedication

$\mathcal{T}$o my beautiful, fantastic, awesome, wonderful, sensitive wife, Ruth—your support, respect, commitment, dedication, patience, and prayers for me make me look like a good husband and father. Thank you for making the principles in this book a practical reality. Thank you for making our marriage all I expected this adventure in human relations to be. I love you.

To my precious daughter, Charisa, and my beloved son, Chairo. May your marriages be built on the principles and precepts inherent in the distilled wisdom of the time-tested truths of the Word of God. May this book become my greatest wedding gift to you and your children as you embrace its precepts.

To my father and late mother, Matthias and Louise Munroe. Your marriage of over 50 years became the living model and standard for me as I observed the beauty and benefit of a marriage built on the foundation of the Word of God. Thank you for teaching me how to love my wife and children.

To all the unmarried singles who desire to have the successful marriage the Creator originally intended. May the wisdom of this book contribute to this desire.

To all married couples whose desire it is to improve and enhance their relationship. May you apply the principles of this book to assist in fulfilling your vows and to experience the marriage the Creator originally intended for mankind.

To the source of all wisdom, knowledge and understanding, the Creator of the institute of marriage, my Lord and Redeemer, Jehovah Shalom, Yeshua.

Contents

PART ONE
Understanding Love™ *Marriage, Still a Great Idea*

PART TWO
Understanding Love™ *and the Secrets of the Heart*

PART THREE
Understanding Love™ *For a Lifetime*

Preface

The greatest source of human joy and pain is found in the drama of love and relationships. Marriage has always been the most common context for this drama. Today, many question the viability and validity of marriage and openly wonder if it should continue to be esteemed as the bedrock of modern social development.

The epidemic and explosive rise of the divorce rate adds further fuel to the fear, hopelessness, disillusionment, and despair people feel with regard to marriage. Many are skeptical and question their chances at success in marriage. The situation is so serious that some have opted for co-habitation without any formal contract or legal agreement, with the understanding that no commitment is involved—no strings attached. In essence, we are producing a generation whose appreciation and respect for the institution of marriage is disintegrating.

Many victims of these failed marriages and divorced families develop resentment and suppressed anger, which manifest themselves in a generational transfer of broken relationships and emotional dysfunction. Because of the fear of failure, some have plainly stated that they neither believe in marriage nor intend ever to marry. The negative press given to high profile individuals in sports, entertainment, politics and, sadly, the church, whose marriages have also fallen victim to the demise of relationships, has not helped. It has served only to further erode the respect, confidence and the high position the marriage institution once held in the social structure of our communities.

Where is this all headed? Where do we go from here? Will the institution of marriage survive the onslaught of negative reports, horror stories, and the proponents of radical society change who promote the idea that marriage has outlived its usefulness and value to human society?

I am curious: If we do away with the traditional institution of marriage, what will we replace it with? What more effective and efficient arrangement could we find to secure the level of commitment, loyalty, support, sense of community, and love necessary to meet the basic needs of the human spirit, needs such as love, a sense of belonging and importance, security and mutual respect? Over the past six thousand years no civilization or culture has produced a better concept for orderly social development than that of the traditional institution of marriage. Every society and culture has recognized an instinctive desire and need for a formal arrangement for the healthy development of families.

It is my belief that no matter how advanced man may become in science, technology, systems, and knowledge, he can never improve on the foundational precepts of marriage as the bedrock of social development. It is my conviction *that marriage is such a good idea, only God could have thought of it.*

In spite of the many failed marriages, broken homes, divorce cases and disillusioned products of failed relationships, marriage is still a good idea. In fact, it is the best idea.

~PART ONE~

Understanding Love™
Marriage, Still a Great Idea

CHAPTER ONE

Marriage Is Like a Precious Gem

A lot of people are confused about marriage these days. In the eyes of many, the institution of marriage has become irrelevant, an archaic relic of a simpler and more naïve time. They question whether marriage is still a good idea, particularly in today's more "liberated" and "enlightened" culture. Concepts such as honor, trust, faithfulness, and commitment seem old-fashioned and out of touch with modern society. Many people change partners as easily as they change shoes (and almost as frequently!).

This confusion over marriage should not surprise us, considering the bewildering barrage of worldly attitudes and philosophies that hits us at every turn. Every day books, magazines, movies, and television soap operas, sitcoms, and prime-time dramas bombard us with images of wives cheating on their husbands and husbands cheating on their wives. Unmarried men and women hop into bed with each other at the drop of a hat, and just as quickly hop out again to find their next partner.

People today shop for relationships the way they shop for clothes. They "try something on for size," and if it does not fit they simply try something else. When they find something that suits them they wear it for awhile until it fades or goes out of style. Then they throw it out or hang it up in the back of their closet and rush out to replace it.

We live in a disposable, "cast-off-and-throw-away" society that has largely lost any real sense of permanence. Ours is a world of expiration dates, limited shelf life, and planned obsolescence. Nothing is absolute. Truth exists only in the eye of the beholder and morality is the whim of the moment. In such an environment, is it any wonder that people ask, "Doesn't *anything* last anymore? Isn't there *something* I can depend on?"

One major symptom of a sick society is when we attach to our human relationships the same attitude of impersonal transience that we display toward the inanimate and disposable items that we use in everyday life. Marriage is the deepest and most intimate of all human relationships, yet even it is under assault. Is marriage still viable in modern society? Does it still make sense in our transitory world? Is marriage still a good idea?

Marriage Is God's Idea

The answer is *yes*. Marriage *is* still a good idea because it is *God's* idea. He created it. He designed it. He established it and defined its parameters. Contrary to much contemporary thought and teaching, marriage is not a human concept. Mankind did not simply dream up marriage somewhere along the line as a convenient way of handling relationships and responsibilities between men and women or dealing with childbearing and parenting issues. Marriage is of divine origin.

 Marriage is still a good idea because it is GOD'S idea.

God Himself instituted and ordained marriage at the very beginning of human history. The second chapter of Genesis describes how God, taking a rib from the side of the man He had already created, fashioned from it a woman to be a "suitable helper" (Gen. 2:20) for the man. Then God brought the man and the woman together and confirmed their relationship as husband and wife, thereby ordaining the institution of marriage.

From the outset, God established marriage as a permanent relationship, the union of two separate people—a man and a woman—into "one flesh." When Adam first laid eyes on Eve he exclaimed, "This is now *bone of my bones* and *flesh of my flesh*; she shall be called 'woman,' for she was taken out of man" (Gen. 2:23, emphasis added). God's design for marriage is found in the very next verse: "For this reason a man will leave his father and mother and be united to his wife, and they will become one flesh" (Gen. 2:24).

"One flesh" is not simply the "gluing" of two people together but rather the "fusion" of two distinct elements into one. If I glue two pieces of wood together, they are bonded but not fused. They remain two separate pieces of wood, and sufficient heat or pressure will break the bond. In the world of chemistry, different elements are linked to each other by chemical bonds that allow them to work together in a particular manner. If that bond is broken, those elements are released and go their separate ways.

It is different with fusion. When two elements are fused into one they become inseparable. A force of sufficient magnitude may *destroy* them, but it can never *disjoin* them. A man and a woman who have become "one flesh" under God's design for marriage cannot be separated without suffering great damage or even destruction. It would be the spiritual equivalent of having an arm or a leg torn from their bodies.

When God ordained that the man and the woman should "become one flesh" He plainly had a permanent, lifelong relationship in mind. Jesus, the great Jewish rabbi and teacher, made this abundantly clear during a discussion with some Pharisees over the question of divorce. The Pharisees asked Jesus if it was lawful for a man to divorce his wife, pointing out that Moses had permitted it in the law.

> *"It was because your hearts were hard that Moses wrote you this law," Jesus replied. "But at the beginning of creation God 'made them male and female.' 'For this reason a man will leave his father and mother and be united to his wife, and the two will become one flesh.' So they are no longer two, but one. Therefore what God has joined together, let man not separate"* (Mark 10:5-9).

"What therefore God has joined together, let no man separate." If marriage were of human origin, then human beings would have the right to set it aside whenever they chose to do so. Since God is the one who instituted marriage, He alone has the authority to determine its standards and set its rules. He alone has the authority to do away with it. This He will not do, for the Scriptures are clear: Marriage is a God-ordained institution that involves the joining of a man and a woman as "one flesh" in a lifelong relationship. This institution will last as long as human life lasts on earth. Only in the life to come will marriage be dispensed with.

Marriage Is a Foundational Institution

Another important truth about marriage is that God established it as the first and most fundamental element of human society. While the family is the basic foundation of any healthy society, marriage is the foundation of the family. Marriage is a foundational institution that predates all other institutions. Before there were nations or governments; before there were churches, schools, or businesses; there was the family; and before the family there was marriage.

 While the family is the basic foundation of any healthy society, marriage is the foundation of the family.

Marriage is foundational because it is on this relationship that God began to build society. When God brought Adam and Eve together in the garden, marriage was the framework for the development of their social interaction as they grew together. It was in the context of marriage that they learned their responsibilities toward each other and lived out their commitments to each other.

Human society in all its forms depends on marriage for its survival. That is why the current low regard for marriage in the minds of so many is so dangerous. With all traditional values and foundations being assaulted at every turn, is it any surprise that marriage is under attack as well? With so many people so confused about marriage, is it any wonder that society in general is in such disarray? The adversary's global attack on marriage is actually an attack on society itself, and ultimately an attack on God, the creator and manufacturer of society and marriage. The adversary knows that if he can destroy marriage he can destroy families; if he can destroy families he can destroy society; and if he can destroy society he can destroy humanity.

Marriage is also the foundation upon which the Church, the community of believers and God's special society, rests. The New Testament describes the relationship between Christ and His Church as being like that of a bridegroom to his bride. This analogy has significant implications for understanding how husbands and wives are to relate to each other. For example, in his letter to the church in Ephesus the first century Jewish apostle Paul wrote:

> *Submit to one another out of reverence for Christ. Wives, submit to your husbands as to the Lord. For the husband is the head of the wife as Christ is the head of the church, His body, of which He is the Savior....Husbands, love your wives, just as Christ loved the church and gave Himself up for her...."For this reason a man will leave his father and mother and be united to his wife, and the two will become one flesh." This is a profound mystery— but I am talking about Christ and the church* (Ephesians 5:21-23,25,31-32).

The relationship between Christ and His Church is a model for that which should exist between husband and wife: a relationship of respect, mutual submission, and sacrificial love.

From Genesis to Revelation the Bible often uses the word *house* to refer to the smallest and most basic unit of society—the family. The "house" is the foundation of society, and marriage is the foundation of the "house." The health of a marriage determines the health of a "house," and the health of a nation's "houses" determines the health of the nation.

 A healthy "house" is the key to both a healthy church and a healthy society.

Misconceptions of Marriage

It is the same in the Church. A church's health depends on the health of the "houses" of its members, particularly those in leadership. Good family management is a fundamental requirement for church leaders. Paul made this clear when he wrote to Timothy, "Here is a trustworthy saying: If anyone sets his heart on being an overseer, he desires a noble task" (1 Tim. 3:1). Among other things, "He must manage his own family well and see that his children obey him with proper respect. (If anyone does not know how to manage his own family, how can he take care of God's church?)" (1 Tim. 3:4-5)

A healthy "house" is the key to both a healthy church and a healthy society. The measure of a healthy "house" is a healthy marriage. Marriage is a foundational institution.

Procreation Is Not the Primary Purpose of Marriage

One misconception many people have, both inside and outside the Church, is that the primary purpose of marriage is the propagation of the human race. The Bible indicates otherwise. Although in Genesis 1:28 God issued the charge to man to "be fruitful and multiply," and although He defined marriage as the parameters in which reproduction should take place, procreation is not the primary purpose of marriage.

God's command had to do with creation and subduing the created order. "God blessed them and said to them, 'Be fruitful and increase in number; fill the earth and subdue it. Rule over the fish of the sea and the birds of the air and over every living creature that moves on the ground' " (Gen. 1:28). God created man—male and female—and He expected them to procreate and fill the earth with other humans, all of whom would rule over the created order as His vice-regents. Marriage was essentially a *companionship covenant*, the relational structure through which men and women—husbands and wives—would join and become one flesh and *together* rule the earthly dominion God had given them. Procreation is a function of marriage but it is not the main focus.

As contemporary society plainly shows, marriage is not necessary for procreation. Unmarried men and women have no trouble at all making babies. In many parts of the world the number of out-of-wedlock births exceeds the number of babies born to married women. That is one reason why many scientists and sociologists are concerned that at the current rate, within one or two generations the global population will grow beyond the earth's capacity to sustain it.

Contrary to the common idea that marriage is mainly about making babies, marriage actually serves as a deterrent to rampant reproduction. There are at least two reasons for this. First, the social and moral requirement of being married before having children is still very strong in many, many places. Most people are still sensitive to the respectability of marriage, and that respect holds back a lot of procreation that would otherwise take place. Were it not for the institution of marriage, human beings would be even more prolific than they already are. Second, married couples who take their responsibilities seriously are careful not to conceive and give birth to more children than they can adequately love and care for. Paul had some strong words on this subject. "If anyone does not provide for his relatives, and especially for his immediate family, he has denied the faith and is worse than an unbeliever" (1 Tim. 5:8).

There is nothing sinful or unbiblical about careful *advance* family planning. (Let me make it clear that abortion is *not* "family planning," nor is it "health care." Abortion is the termination of life and the premeditated destruction of potential. It is the death of destiny and the interference of divine protocol. Abortion is rebellion against the known will of God.) On the contrary, true family planning is mature, responsible stewardship.

Sex Is Not the Primary Purpose of Marriage

Another common misunderstanding is that marriage exists for the purpose of legitimizing sexual relations. Marriage should never be equated with sex because sex is not the primary purpose of marriage. Sexual union is not and never has been the same thing as marital union. Marriage is a union that implies and involves sexual union as the establishment of a blood covenant, a central obligation, and a pleasure (see 1 Cor. 7:3-5), but the three are not the same.

First of all, marriage involves commitment. Sex has very little to do with commitment; it is a 100-percent physical response to physiological and biochemical stimuli. Sex is one expression of commitment in marriage, but it never creates commitment. By itself, sex neither *makes* nor *breaks* a marriage. Marriage is broader and deeper than sex, and transcends it. Marriage is perhaps one percent sex; the rest is ordinary, everyday life. If you marry for sex, how are you going to handle the other 99 percent?

For many years it has been a common belief that adultery breaks a marriage. That is simply not true. Sex does not create a marriage, so how can it break a marriage? Adultery is sin and, according to the Bible, the only legitimate grounds for divorce for a believer. Even then it is not automatic. Divorce is not mandatory in such instances. Adultery does not break the marriage. Breaking the marriage is a *choice*.

Recognizing that sexual union and marital union are not the same is absolutely essential to any proper understanding of marriage. It is also essential in understanding divorce and remarriage. Marriage is bigger than, distinct from, but inclusive of sexual union. Absence of sexual activity will never unmake a marriage, nor will its presence alone turn a relationship into a marriage. Marriage and sex are related but they are not the same.

A "Gem" of a Marriage

How then should we define marriage? If marriage is not primarily for sex or procreation, then what is it? As always, we can find the answer in the Bible. God's Word is truly amazing; nothing we read there is there by accident. The basic Greek word for "marry" or "marriage" is *gameo*, which derives from the same root as our English word "gem." That root word literally means to "fuse together." Fusion of different elements into one describes the process by which precious gems are formed deep in the earth. That process is also an apt description of marriage.

Precious gems such as diamonds, rubies, emeralds, and sapphires are formed far underground out of ordinary elements that are subjected to great heat and massive pressure over an extended period of time. Heat, pressure, and time working together can transform even the most common material into something extraordinary. Take coal for example. Coal is formed when partially decomposed wood or other plant matter is combined with moisture in an airless environment under intense heat and pressure. This process does not happen overnight, but requires centuries.

Although coal is basically a form of carbon, its constituent elements can still be distinguished under chemical analysis. Coal that remains in the earth long enough—thousands of years longer—under continuous heat and pressure eventually is transformed into diamond. Chemically, diamond is *pure carbon*. The distinct elements used in its formation can no longer be identified. Pressure has *fused* them into *one* inseparable element. Heat gives diamond its luster.

 It takes only a few minutes to get married, but building a marriage requires a lifetime.

Marriage as God designed it is like a precious gem. First of all, it develops over time. Diamonds don't form in ten years; they require millennia. It takes only a few minutes to *get* married, but *building* a marriage requires a lifetime. That's one reason why God established marriage as a permanent, lifelong relationship. There must be sufficient time for two people with separate and distinct backgrounds and personalities to become *fused* together as one flesh.

Secondly, godly marriage becomes stronger under pressure. A diamond is the hardest substance on earth. Millions of tons of pressure over thousands of years fuse and transform carbonized matter into a crystal that can withstand any onslaught. A diamond can be cut only under certain conditions and using specially designed tools. In a similar way, external pressures temper and strengthen a godly marriage, driving a husband and wife closer together. Just as pressure purifies a diamond, so the everyday problems and challenges of life purify a godly marriage. A husband and wife face the pressure together. The harder things get, the stronger their union grows. Marriage fuses two different people into one so that under pressure they become so hard and fast that nothing can break them.

Godly marriages and worldly marriages respond differently to pressure. In the world, when the going gets tough, partners split up. Like those two pieces of wood glued together, they are bonded but not fused. The heat and pressure of life break them apart. That same heat and pressure fuse a godly couple together so that their marriage grows ever stronger, until they become inseparable and unbreakable.

Collision of Histories

Marriage is never just the coming together of two people, but a collision of their histories. It is a clash of cultures, experiences, memories, and habits. Marriage is the beautiful accommodation of another lifetime.

Building a strong marriage takes time, patience, and hard work. One of the hardest adjustments anyone faces is moving from single life to married life. Let's be honest: People do not change overnight. When you marry someone, you marry more than just a person; you "marry" an entire family, a complete history of experiences. That's why it is often so hard at first to understand this person who is now sharing your house and your bed. Both of you bring into your marriage 20 or 30 years of life experiences that color how you see and respond to the world. Most of the time you quickly discover that you see many things quite differently from each other. Difference of viewpoint is one of the biggest sources of stress and conflict in young marriages. Adjusting to these differences is critical to marital survival. Unfortunately, many marriages fail on precisely this point.

All of us filter what we see and hear through the lens of our own experiences. Personal tragedy, physical or sexual abuse, quality of family life when growing up, educational level, faith or lack of faith—any of these affect the way we view the world around us. They help shape our expectations of life and influence how we interpret what other people say or do to us.

None of us enter marriage "clean." To one degree or another, we each bring our own emotional, psychological, and spiritual baggage. Whatever our spouse says, we hear through the filter of our own history and experience. Our spouse hears everything we say the same way. Understanding and adjusting to this requires a lot of time and patience.

Over time and under the pressures of daily life, a husband and wife come to understand each other more and more. They begin to think alike, act alike, and even feel alike. They learn to sense each other's moods and often recognize what is wrong without even asking. Gradually, their personal attitudes and viewpoints shift and move toward each other so that their mentality is no longer "yours" and "mine," but "ours." This is when the gem-like quality of marriage shines most brilliantly. Fusion creates oneness.

A godly marriage is like a precious gem in another way as well. Normally, we don't find gems simply by walking along looking on the surface of the ground as we would searching for seashells on the beach. To find gems, we have to dig deep into the earth and chisel through hard rock. In the same way, we will never obtain God's kind of marriage simply by going along with the crowd, doing what everybody else does. We have to dig deep into the heart of God to discover His principles. Precious gems are rare and so is a genuine marriage. There are no shortcuts, no easy "1-2-3" formulas. We have only God's Word to instruct us and His Spirit to give us understanding and discernment, but that is all we need.

 We will never obtain God's kind of marriage simply by going along with the crowd, doing what everybody else does. We have to dig deep into the heart of God to discover His principles.

Rarely will we find anything of true value simply lying on top of the ground. The "good stuff" is most often found deep down where we have to work to get at it. A good marriage is something we have to work at; it doesn't happen by accident. Just as a precious diamond is the final result of a long and intensive process, so is marriage.

So what is marriage? Marriage is a God-ordained institution, a lifelong relationship between one man and one woman. Over time and under the heat and pressure of life, two people under the covenant of marriage come together and are lost in each other to the point where it becomes impossible to tell where one leaves off and the other begins. Marriage is a *process*, a *fusion* of two distinct and different elements into one—a sparkling jewel of love, faithfulness, and commitment that shines brightly in a world of short-lived fads and impermanence.

PRINCIPLES

1. Marriage is still a good idea because it is God's idea.
2. Marriage is a foundational institution that predates all other institutions.
3. Procreation is not the primary purpose of marriage.
4. Sex is not the primary purpose of marriage.
5. Marriage as God designed it is like a precious gem: a fusing of two different elements into one.
6. Godly marriage develops over time.
7. Godly marriage grows strong under pressure.
8. Godly marriage is a fusion that creates oneness.

~ CHAPTER TWO ~

Marriage Is Honorable

*S*ome time ago during a trip to Germany I had the opportunity to counsel a married couple who were on the verge of divorce. The husband picked me up at the airport, and during the two-and-a-half-hour drive to their home he and I had plenty of time to talk. He began pouring his heart out to me about how much he loved his wife, and yet nothing seemed to be working out right. Continual pressure and friction in their relationship had brought them to the point of being ready to call it quits. Things had gotten so bad that they were not even sleeping in the same bed. This troubled husband could not understand what had gone wrong between him and his wife. He was begging me for some answers. I told him that I couldn't talk to him by himself because two people are involved in marriage. I would have to talk to the two of them together.

It was very late when we arrived at the house, but instead of going to bed the three of us sat down and began to talk. By the time we finished, it was 4:00 A.M. As they unfolded to me the troubles they were facing, I shared with them the most basic cause of marital failure, which is when people do not understand that marriage itself is honorable, more so than those who are involved in it.

 Success in marriage does not depend on spouses committing themselves to EACH OTHER as much as it does to their committing themselves to MARRIAGE, the unchanging institution that they have MUTUALLY entered into.

Marriage is a steady, unchanging institution entered into by two people who are constantly changing as they grow and mature. Those changes can be unnerving and frustrating and can easily ignite conflict. Respect for the honorableness and stability of marriage can give a husband and wife a solid anchor that enables them to weather the storms of change as they grow toward oneness. Recognizing the unchanging nature of marriage as an institution can encourage them during times of conflict to seek alternatives to ending their marriage. Success in marriage does not depend on spouses committing themselves to *each other* as much as it does to their committing themselves to *marriage*, the unchanging institution that they have *mutually* entered into.

It's Not Who You Love, but What You Love

The Bible presents marriage as an institution that should be highly respected and esteemed above all other institutions. Hebrews 13:4 says, "Marriage should be honored by all, and the marriage bed kept pure, for God will judge the adulterer and all the sexually immoral." The King James Version reads, "Marriage is honorable in all…" "Honorable" translates the Greek word *timios*, which also means "valuable, costly, honored, esteemed, beloved, and precious." *All* means "all": The Greek word is *pas*, meaning "all, any, every, the whole, thoroughly, whatsoever, and whosoever." Marriage, then, should be valued and esteemed, and held in highest honor at all times in all things by all people everywhere. That is God's design.

Notice that the verse says, "*Marriage* should be honored by all"; it says nothing at all about the people *in* the marriage. A common notion with most people is that the parties in a marriage—the husband and wife—should honor each other and hold each other in high esteem. This is certainly true, but ultimately it is not what makes a marriage work. What is more important is that they honor and esteem *marriage itself*. Let's face it, none of us are lovable all the time. There are times when we say something hateful or do something foolish, leaving our spouse hurt or angry. Maybe he or she has done the same to us. Either way, holding our marriage in high honor and esteem will carry us over those bumpy times when one or the other of us is unlovable or difficult to honor.

One of the keys to a long and happy marriage is understanding that it's not *who* you love, but *what* you love that's important. Let me explain. Consider an average couple; we'll call them John and Sarah. John and Sarah meet at a party and begin talking. John is 22, handsome, dark-headed, athletic, and has a good-paying job. Sarah is 20, attractive, intelligent, has beautiful hair, and also has a good job. Attracted to each other right off the bat, John and Sarah start going out together. Their relationship continues to grow until one night John says, "Sarah, I love you," and Sarah replies, "I love you, too, John."

Since John and Sarah have fallen in love, they decide to get married. John gives Sarah a ring and they begin planning their wedding. John and Sarah are so happy in their love that they feel it will sustain them forever.

Somewhere along the way, however, they both had better figure out *what* they love about each other, or they are headed for trouble in their marriage.

John needs to ask himself, "Why do I love Sarah? What is there about her that causes me to love her? Do I love her because of *who* she is, or for some other reason? Do I love her because of her attractive figure or her beautiful hair or her good job?" Sarah at 20 is all of those things, but what about when she is 40? What if at 40 Sarah has put on some weight and lost her slim figure because she has borne three or four children? What if she no longer has that good job because she stayed home to raise those children? If John loves all of the things Sarah is when she is 20, how will he feel about her when she is 40?

Sarah needs to ask herself the same questions about John. At 22, John may be everything Sarah has dreamed about in a man, but what about when he is 42 and has started losing his hair? What if he has lost much of his youthful athletic build because he has worked in an office day after day for 20 years? What if the company he worked for went bankrupt and the only job he has been able to find is as a mason's helper making half the amount of money he did before?

It is not enough just to know *who* we love; we need to know *what* we love. We need to know *why* we love the person we love. This is critically important for building a happy and successful marriage.

 The person we marry is not the person we will live with, because that person is changing all the time.

The point I am trying to make is this: The person we marry is not the person we will live with, because that person is changing all the time. Today, my wife is not the same woman I married, nor am I the same man she married. Both of us have changed in many ways and continue to change every day. If we who are constantly changing trust solely in each other to keep our marriage going, we are in real trouble. No matter how much we love, honor, and esteem each other, that alone might not be enough in the long run. Respecting and esteeming the honorability of marriage as an unchanging institution helps bring stability to our ever-changing relationship.

The person we marry is not the person we will live with. That is why marriage itself is to be honored and esteemed more than the people who are in it. People change, but marriage is constant. We must love marriage more than our spouse.

Marriage Is Bigger Than the Two People in It

If marriage itself is to be honored and esteemed even above the people involved in it, what does that mean in practical terms? For purposes of illustration it may help to compare marriage to working at a job. Let's imagine that you and I go to work for the same company. The company is a form of institution, and we have joined that institution by accepting employment there. We have committed ourselves to the *institution*.

Suppose we end up working side by side at adjacent desks. We build a good working relationship and get along fine for awhile. Then, one day we have a sharp disagreement over something and exchange heated words. We both decide that we are not talking to each other anymore.

What happens next? Do we quit our jobs simply because we had a falling out? I hope not. (Some people quit over this kind of thing, but it is almost always a sign of immaturity.) No, instead we both go home, still angry and at odds, but the next day there we are again, back at our desks. Why? Because we are committed to the *institution* more than we are to the people *in* the institution. A week passes, and even though we still are not talking, there we are, continuing to work side by side. There may be conflict between us, but we are both still committed to the institution.

Another week passes, and one day you suddenly ask, "Could I borrow your eraser?" and I say, "Okay." Slowly, our disagreement is passing and we are starting to communicate again. Before many more days go by we're talking and laughing like old friends, going to lunch together, and everything is back to normal. We make up after our disagreement because we regard the institution as more important than our personal feelings. This kind of thing happens all the time in institutions. People have conflict, but eventually reconcile their differences because the institution is bigger than their conflict.

This truth is a key to properly understanding marriage. The institution of marriage is more important than our personal feelings. There will be times when we will not be in agreement with our spouse, but that has nothing to do with the marriage. We must never confuse our personal feelings or conflicts with the institution of marriage. Marriage is honorable, respectable, and unchanging, while we at times are dishonorable or unrespectable, and we are always changing. Marriage is perfect, while we are imperfect.

Commitment to the marriage, rather than commitment to the person, is the key to success. No matter what my wife says or does to me, I'm hanging in there, and I know that regardless of what I do, she will still be there. We are committed to our marriage even more than we are committed to each other. When we disagree or argue or have other conflict, we work it out because it is only temporary. We don't break up the institution over it, because the institution is bigger than we are.

When you have a conflict with a fellow employee on your job, you work it out for the sake of the institution—the company—which is bigger than both of you. Since you have to work together you might as well solve your problem. The same attitude should apply in marriage. When a husband and wife are in conflict, they should come together and agree, "Sure, we have our differences, and we're always changing, but this marriage is bigger than both of us. We're in it for the long haul, so let's make up. Let's do whatever we need to do to make this thing work."

Marriage is bigger than the two people in it, which is the way it should be. God instituted marriage; it belongs to Him, not us. *Marriage is two imperfect people committing themselves to a perfect institution, by making perfect vows from imperfect lips before a perfect God.*

A Perfect Vow and Imperfect Lips

A vow is different from a promise. A promise is a pledge to do or not do a specific thing, such as a father promising to take his son to the zoo. A vow, on the other hand, is a solemn assertion that binds the vow maker to a certain action, service, or condition, such as a vow of poverty. As I wrote in my earlier book, *Single, Married, Separated, and Life After Divorce:*

> A promise is a commitment to do something later, and a vow is a binding commitment to begin doing something now and to continue to do it for the duration of the vow. Some vows, or contracts, are for life; others are for limited periods of time.[1]

> God takes vows very seriously:

> A vow is unto death, which is why God said, "Don't make it if you are not going to keep it"....

> "Unto death" does not mean "until your natural death." It means giving God the right to allow you to die if you break the vow. Under the Old Covenant, if they broke vows and God's mercy did not intervene, something serious happened.

> A vow is not made to another person. Vows are made to God or before God; in other words, with God as a witness.[2]

God's attitude toward vows is revealed plainly in the Scriptures. "When you make a vow to God, do not delay in fulfilling it. He has no pleasure in fools; fulfill your vow. It is better not to vow than to make a vow and not fulfill it" (Eccles. 5:4-5).

Marriage is a vow and breaking that vow is a serious matter because it also breaks one's fellowship with God. The old testament prophet Malachi expressed God's perspective on faithfulness to the marriage vow in the following words:

> *Another thing you do: You flood the Lord's altar with tears. You weep and wail because He no longer pays attention to your offerings or accepts them with pleasure from your hands. You ask, "Why?" It is because the Lord is acting as the witness between you and the wife of your youth, because you have broken faith with her, though she is your partner, the wife of your marriage covenant* (Malachi 2:13-14).

 Marriage is bigger than the two people in it.

Because marriage is a perfect vow made before a perfect God by two imperfect people, only God can make it work. Don't expect perfection from your spouse. **Marriage** is perfect, but **people** are imperfect. If you don't believe that, just take a look in the mirror. The institution of marriage is constant; it never changes. People change all the time. If you want success in your marriage, commit yourself to that which does not change. Commit yourself to the institution of marriage. It will become your center of gravity and help keep you solid.

Changing Institutions Is Not the Answer

Once we understand that marriage is an institution to be respected and esteemed, the thought of divorce never enters our minds. Respect for the institution of marriage helps carry us through those times when either our spouse or we act in an unrespectable manner. We don't abandon the institution because of conflicts or problems that arise.

One of the problems that many people in our society have is a tendency to move frequently from job to job, quitting whenever something does not go their way. Not only is this a sign of immaturity and of an unwillingness to resolve issues, it quickly erodes their credibility in the eyes of potential employers. Consider this: You go in for a job interview and they ask you, "Where did you last work?" After you answer, they ask, "Why did you leave?" The purpose of these questions is to assess your credibility. This employer wants to know what kind of person you are and whether or not you will be an asset to the company.

Suppose you answer, "I left because I didn't like my boss," or "I left because of problems I had with some fellow workers." Don't be surprised if this employer does not hire you. Why should he think that you would be any different working for him? If he finds out that you have had ten jobs over the last three years, he certainly won't hire you. He doesn't want to become number eleven on your list.

Changing institutions is not the solution to the problem. The key to growth and maturity is to hang on during the tough times and work through the problems. This is just as true in marriage as it is on the job. When problems arise in a marriage relationship, a lot of people think that their problems will go away if they simply divorce and then marry someone else. This is simply not the case. Marital difficulties are almost *never* one-sided. If you bail out of the marriage before resolving the issues, then what-ever problems *you* brought into that relationship you will carry into the next one. They may take a different shape, but they will be the same problems.

Changing institutions is not the solution to the problem. The key to growth and maturity is to hang on during the tough times and work through the problems.

There was a time not too many years ago when traditional views of mar-riage and the family were held in highest honor and respect in Western society. Divorce was virtually unheard of and, when it occurred, carried a heavy social stigma. Not anymore. Biblical concepts of marriage and the family have come under strong attack over the past couple of generations. The humanistic philosophies so prevalent today have helped remove the social and moral stigma from divorce. As a result, divorce and remarriage have become not only commonplace, but also acceptable, even in the eyes of many believers. Some people have even gone so far as to suggest that the measure of one's manhood or womanhood is determined by how many dif-ferent sex partners they have. That concept is completely twisted. It is sick and satanic, yet reflects what is currently happening in our society.

Because of the pervasiveness of worldly philosophies regarding mar-riage and family, many believers are ignorant of God's standards. We need to look again at the words of Jesus when He said, "But at the beginning of creation God 'made them male and female.' 'For this reason a man will leave his father and mother and be united to his wife, and the two will become one flesh.' So they are no longer two, but one. Therefore what God has joined together, let man not separate" (Mk. 10:6-9).

These verses reveal two important truths to understand about God's kind of marriage. First, God will join together only that which He can allow. God cannot and will not sanction sin in any form. Can you imagine God taking two sinners, joining them together, and blessing them? To do so would be to bless and encourage sin. At "the beginning of creation," when God brought them together, Adam and Eve were pure and holy, unsullied and uncorrupted by sin. Prior to the fall, their marriage was the model of everything God intended. God cannot and will not bless a sinful relationship. No God-sanctioned union can possibly exist between unbelievers or between anyone who "marries" with unresolved sin in their lives or who come together under circumstances that are sinful or otherwise contrary to God's standards.

The second truth in Mark 10:6-9 is that what God *has* joined together, man must not separate. Human civil government possesses neither the authority nor the power to disjoin a God-ordained marriage between two believers. In the natural, "civil" marriages established by civil law may also be disestablished by civil law. People who get married outside of God can also get unmarried outside of God. In the spiritual, marriage that God has sanctioned cannot be broken by the decree of men. This raises an important question. *If believers come to the marriage altar for God to join them together, why then do so many of them go to the court to get "un-joined"?*

Human courts have no power to separate what God has joined. God-style marriage is a fusion, not a bonding. What God has joined, He alone can put asunder. He won't do it, however, because to do so would violate His own standards. For believers, changing institutions is not the answer.

A Successful Marriage Depends on Knowledge

Knowledge is the answer. A successful marriage has little to do with love. Love does not guarantee success in marriage. Love is very important for *happiness* in marriage, but by itself it cannot make a marriage work. The only thing that makes a marriage work is knowledge. As a matter of fact, the only thing that makes *anything* work is knowledge. Success depends on how much we *know* about something, not how we *feel* about it.

Most married people love and feel good about each other, but many do not know how to communicate effectively or relate well to each other. There is a huge difference between recognizing feelings and knowing how to deal with conflict. Some people define intelligence as the ability to solve complex problems. More accurately, intelligence is the ability to face reality and deal with problems while maintaining one's sanity. Dealing with problems is not necessarily the same as solving them. Some problems can't be solved. An intelligent person is someone who can maintain his stability and sense of self-worth under any circumstances, evaluate the situation, deal effectively with the problem, and come out intact on the other side.

There is a great need today for intelligence and knowledge regarding marriage to offset widespread ignorance on the subject. Even the Christian Church, which should be the voice of authority on the subject of marriage, is suffering because many believers, including leaders, are biblically illiterate where marriage and the family are concerned. In this day when all the old values are being challenged left and right, both within and without the Church, many people are confused, uncertain of what to believe anymore. The root cause of this confusion is lack of knowledge.

Knowledge is critical for success and survival in anything. In Hosea 4:6a God says, "My people are destroyed from lack of knowledge." "My people" refers to the children of God. Even Christians need knowledge. The greatest knowledge of all is to know God. Proverbs 1:7 says, "The fear of the Lord is the *beginning* of knowledge, but fools despise wisdom and discipline" (emphasis added). It doesn't matter how often we come to church or how often we worship the Lord; without knowledge, we have no guarantee of success.

One of the things that really bothered me as a young Christian was hearing about so many other Christians getting divorced. If followers of Christ were failing in their marriages, what hope was there for anybody else? Here were people who supposedly were filled with the Holy Spirit, who supposedly knew the Holy God, and yet they couldn't seem to live together and get along. If that was true, we might as well forget the whole thing!

It took me a little while to learn that success in marriage depends on more than just being saved. It takes more than just being in love. Being a believer and being in love are both important in marriage, but they carry no automatic guarantee of marital success. We need knowledge of biblical principles; the design parameters that God Himself established. Biblical principles never change. The principles for a successful marriage and family that God gave Adam and Eve still work today. They are universally applicable in every age and in every culture. Trouble comes when we violate or ignore those principles.

Ultimately, marriage will not survive on love alone, or on feelings. By itself, just being born again is not enough to guarantee success. *A successful marriage hinges on knowledge—knowing and understanding God's principles.*

 God designed marriage for success, and only His counsel can make it successful.

Marriage is honorable. God instituted marriage, and He alone has the right to dictate its terms. The institution of marriage is subject to the rules, regulations, and conditions that God has set down, and He has revealed them in His Word.

God designed marriage for success, and only His counsel can make it successful. No one is better at making something work than the person who designed it. It would be a mistake to use Toyota parts to repair your Ford automobile. Toyota parts are designed for Toyotas, not Fords. Instead, you should take your Ford automobile to a licensed Ford service dealer. No one knows Ford cars better than the Ford Motor Company. Would you take your Mercedes-Benz to a Ford dealer for repairs? Not if you're smart. Only a Mercedes dealer could guarantee to repair it properly. Guaranteed success means using the right "service man." It means referring back to the designer.

Marriage is the same way. Success in marriage means using the right "service man" or "authorized dealer"—referring back to the designer for guidance. No one knows a product like the manufacturer. No one understands marriage better than God does. He created it, He established it, He ordained it, and He blesses it. Only He can make it work. Marriage is honorable because it is of divine rather than human origin. If we want *our* marriage to be honorable and successful, we must know, understand, and follow the principles that God has set out in His "manual," the Bible. That is the only sure corrective for the ignorance and misinformation that characterizes so much of the world's view of marriage.

PRINCIPLES

1. Marriage is a steady, unchanging institution entered into by two people who are constantly changing as they grow and mature.

2. The institution of marriage is more important than our personal feelings.

3. Commitment to the marriage, rather than commitment to the person, is the key to success.

4. Marriage is two imperfect people committing themselves to a perfect institution, by making perfect vows from imperfect lips.

5. God will join together only that which He can allow.

6. What God *has* joined together, man must not separate.

7. Success depends on how much we *know* about something, not how we *feel* about it.

8. A successful marriage hinges on knowledge—knowing and understanding God's principles.

Endnotes

1. Myles Munroe, *Single, Married, Separated, and Life After Divorce.* (Shippensburg: Destiny Image Publishers, Inc., 1992) p. 91.

2. Ibid.

CHAPTER THREE

Why Get Married, Anyway?

*P*eople get married for lots of reasons, some good, others not so good. Many marriages today fail because the couple does not understand either the purpose or the principles of successful marriage. They lack *knowledge*. Modern society's confusion about marriage results in many couples' marrying for the wrong reasons—reasons that are insufficient for sustaining a healthy, lifelong relationship.

No one should ever get married without first carefully and clearly answering the question, "Why?" Deliberate and thoughtful consideration in advance will prevent a lot of problems, heartache, and regret later on. Knowing why you want to marry can confirm you in a good decision and help you avoid making a bad decision.

Because knowledge is critical to success, it is important first of all to recognize some of the most common *unhealthy* reasons people use in choosing to get married. I have listed ten. This list is based not on guesswork but on evidence drawn from studies of countless failed marriages. We are not talking fiction here, but real life.

Ten Unhealthy Reasons for Getting Married

1. To spite parents.

Believe it or not, some people get married in order to spite or get back at their parents. "I'm so sick and tired of having to do everything they tell me! I'll show them! I don't have to stay around here anymore!" They may resent their parents' rules or chafe under their parents' discipline. They may be angry over their parents' disapproval of their friends, particularly that special boyfriend or girlfriend. That anger or resentment may drive them to do something foolish, like getting married without thinking it through. Even though they may know nothing about marriage, they jump at the chance because they see it as a quick way to get out from under their parents' restrictions.

Marrying to spite one's parents is a crazy reason to get married. That marriage is headed for trouble right away. The overriding emotion is negative—anger, resentment, bitterness—and not conducive for a healthy long-term relationship. Qualities essential to success, such as love, commitment, and faithfulness, are either absent or take a secondary role behind the primary motivation of spite. A person who marries out of spite sees his or her spouse not as a lover, companion, and friend, as much as a means of escape from dominating parents. That is insufficient grounds upon which to build a happy and successful marriage.

2. To escape an unhappy home.

This is similar to the first unhealthy reason. Some people grow up in unhappy or difficult home situations, and all they want to do is escape. There may be physical, verbal, or sexual abuse involved. One or both parents may be addicted to alcohol or drugs. Home life may be a constant litany of anger, shouting, cursing, and quarreling. Whatever the reason, some young people are dying to get away from home, and often see marriage as their way out. This is extremely foolish and unwise. The desire to escape an unhappy home life is no reason to get married. If you simply *must* get away, then go out and find a job, get an apartment, and move out on your own. People who marry in order to escape rarely find what they are looking for. In the end, they simply exchange one kind of unhappiness for another.

3. A negative self-image.

Unfortunately, some people get married in the hope that it will make them feel worthwhile and give meaning to their life. Their self-image is so low that they constantly need someone else to affirm their worth and tell them that they are all right. A marriage begun on this basis is in trouble before it even gets rolling.

A spouse who enters marriage with a negative self-image comes into that relationship as only half a person. If *both* people have self-image problems, they are really in for a rough time. A healthy marriage brings two wholes together, not two halves, forming a union that is greater than the sum of its parts. Two people who come together and who are confident of their own self-worth and comfortable in their personal identities can build a happy, successful, and meaningful marriage.

Marriage will not solve the problem of a negative self-image. Marriage magnifies the defects in our character and exposes our self-concept. It will only make it worse. We all must find our sense of self-worth in our relationship with Christ, in our identity as beloved children of God and heirs to His Kingdom:

Precious souls created in God's image for whom Jesus died. Truly understanding that we are members of the "royal family" will affect how we think, feel, and act. That is the cure for a negative self-image.

4. Marrying on the rebound.

This reason is closely related to the last one. People who have been hurt in a former relationship or marriage often feel discouraged and depressed, with their self-esteem lying in the dirt. They are quick to jump headlong into a new relationship with the first person who comes along offering sympathy or concern. By this they hope not only to ease their hurt but prove to themselves that there is nothing wrong with them. You don't have to get married to prove that you are all right; there are other ways to do that. It gets back to the self-image issue. If you're okay, you're okay; marriage won't change that one way or the other.

The problem with marrying on the rebound is that it is not a marriage of love, but of convenience. You're hurting and doubting yourself, and along comes someone who sympathizes with you and shows compassion. Both of you may mistake this for true love and make a quick decision to get married. In reality, however, no love is involved. For you it is only a marriage of convenience, a "quick and easy" way out of your dilemma. Don't fall for it. A "rebound" marriage is destined for trouble.

5. Fear of being left out.

This fear affects both men and women, but tends to hit women harder than men, particularly as they get older. Even in our modern society, a woman's sense of worth is linked to marriage, home, and family more so than is a man's. Many women start to get worried if they reach the age of 30 and still are not married. Sometimes panic sets in. "What am I going to do? Everybody's getting married except me! All of my friends are married. I'm the only one out of my graduating class who isn't married. What's wrong with me?"

With this mindset, some women will grab the first guy who comes along and shows any interest in her. He may not be any good for her, but that doesn't matter. He may be a defective character destined to be a deficit to her life, but she doesn't see that. She's desperate! All she sees is that he is interested in her. Even if he is only taking advantage of her, she convinces herself that he loves her and that she loves him. When he pops the question, she says, "Thank God!" and accepts eagerly. The only problem is that God had nothing to do with it. Her panic and fear of becoming an "old maid" have pushed her into a bad decision.

Men make the same mistake. Fearing the thought of being a bachelor all their lives, some men marry women who are not right for them. Fear of being left out causes many men and women to settle for a marriage that is less than what they could have had if they had been patient and trusted God.

When a person marries out of fear of being left out, one of two things usually happens. Either the marriage breaks up, or they "grin and bear it," too embarrassed to admit to the world, and especially to their friends and family, that they made a mistake. Either way, the happiness they sought eludes them, and all they know is sorrow instead.

6. Fear of independence.

Some people grow up so dependent on their parents that when they become adults, and face the prospect of being out on their own, they get married in order to have someone else to depend on. Many times the parents bear the responsibility for their children's dependency. Whether deliberately or not, they insist on doing everything for their children, never teaching them how to think or act for themselves. Some parents have a tendency to always think of their children as "my baby," and try to hold onto them forever.

Children who grow up dependent on their parents often enter marriage expecting their spouse to take care of them and provide the same security they have always known. The first time they have to stand up and be independent, they crumble, because they never learned how. Once they are faced with the necessity of handling responsibilities they never had to worry about before, some of them can't deal with it.

No one who is afraid of independence is ready to get married. Successful marriage requires that both husband and wife be comfortable and capable with independence.

7. Fear of hurting the other person.

This happens more often than we would like to admit. Let's say a young man and a young woman have been dating for awhile. She begins to talk marriage but he isn't so sure. Even though he realizes that he does not love her and knows that marriage is not the answer, he's afraid of what will happen if he breaks up with her. Maybe she has said more than once, "If you leave me, I'll just die!" or even more ominously, "If you ever leave me, I'll kill myself!" Since he doesn't know how to let her down easily and doesn't want to hurt her, he offers to marry her. These roles could just as easily be reversed, with the man putting pressure on his girlfriend who isn't sure what to do.

One reason this problem crops up is because some people do not understand the different levels of friendship. Just because a guy takes a girl out for ice cream does not mean they are ready to get married. They are just friends. Everything might be fine until one or the other of them gets carried away and starts reading more into their relationship than is really there. That person starts applying pressure until the other one begins to feel guilty and obligated.

No marriage stands a chance if it is based on fear of any kind. Don't get married simply because you are afraid of hurting the other person. It is much better for both of you to go through temporary pain now than to get married and set yourselves up for a lifetime of pain.

8. To be a therapist or a counselor for the other person.

It may sound crazy, but this is why some people get married. They feel a sense of responsibility for someone who needs the benefit of their wisdom, counsel, and advice. Be careful. Don't get carried away. Men, just because a young lady comes to you for counsel doesn't mean you should marry her. Ladies, just because a young man may seek out your advice doesn't mean he should become your husband. Marriage is not the proper forum for therapy. There are other avenues.

It is not at all uncommon for people in long-term therapy to develop romantic feelings toward their therapist. Insecure people are drawn easily to those they regard as authority figures, or even as surrogate parents. Professional counselors have to watch out for this kind of thing all the time.

 A healthy marriage is the joining of a man and a woman as equal partners, both of whom are emotionally mature and secure in their self-image and personal identity.

A healthy marriage is the joining of a man and a woman as equal partners, both of whom are emotionally mature and secure in their self-image and personal identity. If you marry someone who is always looking to you as a counselor, you will never get any rest and they will drain you emotionally. Insecure in his or her own abilities and lacking self-confidence, your spouse will consult you about any and every little thing. Nothing will wear you out faster than a spouse who cannot think for himself or herself, or who will not make any independent decisions. Don't get caught in that trap. No one who needs continual counseling is ready for marriage.

9. Because of having sex.

There is an old teaching that says that a man and a woman who have sex are married in fact if not in law. This is simply not true. We have already seen that sex does not equate to marriage. Sex alone neither makes nor breaks a marriage. According to God's design, sex is appropriate only within the bounds of marriage. It enhances and enriches a marriage that has already been established on other proper foundations. Outside of marriage, sex is inappropriate and psychologically damaging, emotionally dangerous, and sinful. Having sex, therefore, is not a reason to get married; it is a reason to repent. Sexual abstinence is the only appropriate behavior for unmarried people, and especially believers.

Sexual abstinence is the only appropriate behavior for unmarried people, and especially believers.

10. Because of pregnancy.

Becoming pregnant is no more of a reason for getting married than having sex. The age of the "shotgun wedding" is long past. Still, there are some people who feel that even though sex alone is not reason enough for marriage, pregnancy changes things. Without a doubt it raises certain ethical, moral, and legal issues, particularly for the father of the child. Even so, the fact of pregnancy alone is insufficient grounds for marriage. On the surface, a pregnancy is evidence only of sexual activity. It does not necessarily indicate the existence of love or commitment between the man and woman who conceived the child. Compounding the sin and mistake of an out-of-wedlock pregnancy with the mistake of a bad marriage is foolish and unwise. It will lead inevitably to heartache and pain for everyone involved, and especially for the innocent child caught in the middle of it all.

One mistake won't put you out of the race for life. Many people who have conceived and borne children out-of-wedlock later go into happy marriages. Like sex, pregnancy alone is not a reason to get married, but a reason to *repent*. Even if you never marry the person with whom you conceived the child, God can give the two of you the grace and wisdom to behave responsibly for the health and welfare of that child.

Ten Healthy Reasons for Getting Married

Now that we have identified some common unhealthy reasons for marriage, we need to examine some healthy reasons. The ten that follow should not be regarded as separate entities, but as part of a greater whole. While each of these is a good reason for getting married, none of them *alone* are sufficient. A healthy, successful, and godly marriage will embrace most, but not necessarily all, of these reasons.

1. Because it is God's will.

This is perhaps the most important reason of all. God designed marriage, and no one knows it better than He does. As believers, our top priority should be to discern and obey God's will in *all things*. This includes our choice of a mate. For some reason, whether it is due to lack of knowledge or lack of faith, many believers have difficulty trusting God with this area of their lives. A couple who is considering marriage needs to take plenty of time to pray together, seeking God's will in the matter. Just because you are both believers doesn't automatically mean that you are right for each other for marriage. Be patient. Trust God and honestly and humbly seek His will and wisdom. If He is calling you to marry, He wants to join you to someone with whom you can build a strong, godly home filled with love and grace— a home that exalts Jesus Christ as Lord and a harmony in vision and purpose. If you seek His counsel, He will bring the right person into your life, and you will know it when He does.

If God is calling you to marry, He wants to join you to someone with whom you can build a strong, godly home filled with love and grace—a home that exalts Jesus Christ as Lord.

2. Expressing God's love to the other person.

Marriage is a physical picture of the spiritual union and love that exist among the Father, the Son, and the Holy Spirit. It also depicts the love of God for His people and Christ's love for His Church. Divine love, or *agape*, is primal love, the original and highest love from which all other forms of love derive. *Agape* is a *choice*, an act of the will. By His very nature, God *chooses* to love us even though we have nothing within ourselves to commend us in that love. Paul, the great early church leader and missionary, wrote, "But God demonstrates His own love for us in this: While we were still sinners, Christ died for us" (Rom. 5:8). God's love is unconditional love.

Properly expressed, human love in all its forms takes its pattern from the divine agape that issues forth from the Father. Since *agape* is the love that God displays toward all people, a person does not have to be married to experience it. However, marriage does provide a wonderful avenue through which a man and a woman can express this godly love to each other in a uniquely personal way. *Agape* is one of the catalysts for the "fusion" that characterizes true marriage. When a husband and wife *choose* to love each other unconditionally, that choice will carry them through the times when they are unlovable. A successful and healthy marriage always begins with *agape*. Other forms of love grow out of and build upon the firm foundation of God's love.

Properly expressed, human love in all its forms takes its pattern from the divine agape that issues forth from the Father.

3. Expressing personal love for the other person.

Healthy marital love involves the proper blending of the various types and degrees of love. First is *agape*, the unconditional love of God that gives birth to all other forms. Marriage should also be an expression of personal love between the husband and wife, a desire to show a level of esteem and regard toward each other that they show toward no one else. Marital love includes the element of *phileo*, a Greek concept of love best understood as "tender affection." Husbands and wives should be tender and affectionate toward each other. A marriage relationship is also characterized by *eros*, which is physical, or sexual love. These expressions of personal love are healthy reasons for marriage, but they need to be properly founded on the unconditional *agape* love that comes from God.

4. To fulfill sexual needs and desires in a godly way.

Sexual desire is God-given and, in its proper place, healthy and good. By itself, the desire for sex is a poor and shallow reason for getting married. In conjunction with other reasons, however, such as love and the desire for companionship, the desire for sexual fulfillment is a strong and natural motivation. Love that produces in a man and a woman the desire to commit themselves to a lifelong relationship also generates the desire to express that love sexually. Believers who are serious about their commitment to Christ will seek to fulfill their sexual needs and desires in a godly way. Marriage is the God-ordained vehicle for fulfilling God-given sexual desire. Paul's words to the believers in Corinth provide wise and practical counsel on the matter:

> *Now for the matters you wrote about: It is good for a man not to marry. But since there is so much immorality, each man should have his own wife, and each woman her own husband.* **The husband should fulfill his marital duty to his wife, and likewise the wife to her husband.** *The wife's body does not belong to her alone but also to her husband. In the same way, the husband's body does not belong to him alone but also to his wife.* **Do not deprive each other except by mutual consent** *and for a time, so that you may devote yourselves to prayer. Then come together again so that satan will not tempt you because of your lack of self-control.... Now to the unmarried and the widows I say: It is good for them to stay unmarried, as I am.* **But if they cannot control themselves, they should marry, for it is better to marry than to burn with passion** (1 Corinthians 7:1-5, 8-9, emphasis added).

Marriage is the God-ordained vehicle for fulfilling God-given sexual desire.

5. The desire to begin a family.

The desire to have children is a godly desire, but it is neither a primary nor even a necessary reason for marriage. There are many happily married couples who have no children, either by choice or otherwise. Marital happiness and success do not depend on the presence of children. Children are a wonderful blessing and enhance a marriage, and those couples who desire children desire a good thing. Psalm 127:3-5 says, "Sons are a heritage from the Lord, children a reward from Him. Like arrows in the hands of a warrior are sons born in one's youth. Blessed is the man whose quiver is full of them. They will not be put to shame when they contend with their enemies in the gate." There is no better environment in which to raise children than in a Christian home anchored by a strong Christian marriage.

6. Companionship.

The desire for companionship is a worthy reason for getting married. Everyone has a built-in need for a "bosom buddy," an intimate friend or companion. Although such companionship and friendship can be found outside of marriage, the companionship forged between a husband and wife is particularly rich and rewarding. Humans are social beings, created to enjoy and thrive on each other's company. When God created the first man, He found no "suitable helper" for him among all the other creatures.

 A husband should be his wife's best friend and companion, and a wife, her husband's.

So the Lord God caused the man to fall into a deep sleep; and while he was sleeping, He took one of the man's ribs and closed up the place with flesh. Then the Lord God made a woman from the rib He had taken out of the man, and He brought her to the man. The man said, "This is now bone of my bones and flesh of my flesh; she shall be called 'woman,' for she was taken out of man." For this reason a man will leave his father and mother and be united to his wife, and they will become one flesh (Genesis 2:21-24).

A husband should be his wife's best friend and companion, and a wife, her husband's. Marriage is designed for companionship.

7. To share all things together with the other person.

There is a lot of truth in the old saying that when we share our sorrow, our sorrow is halved, and when we share our joy, our joy is doubled. Sorrow and difficult times in our lives are easier to bear when we have a soul mate to share them with. Our joy and laughter multiply when we have a bosom companion who joins in. Godly love that draws a man and a woman together creates in them a desire to share all things with each other, especially the ongoing daily adventure of life itself. Marriage is designed for the man and woman who have decided that they wish to spend the rest of their lives together in a relationship of mutual love, respect, and sharing.

8. To work together to fulfill each other's needs.

Marital love also stirs up in a husband and wife the desire to meet each other's needs. This is a give-and-take process that requires much sensitivity on the part of both. Every person is born with ongoing physical, mental, emotional, and spiritual needs. There is the need for food, water, clothing, and shelter; the need for security and peace of mind; the need to be free from fear; the need for aesthetic enrichment; the need for peace with God and intimate fellowship with Him. Marriage is a tailor-made opportunity for a man and woman to work together to fulfill their legitimate needs. Together, and with steadfast trust in the Lord, they can meet any challenge and overcome any obstacle. "Though one may be overpowered, two can defend themselves. A cord of three strands is not quickly broken" (Eccles. 4:12).

9. To maximize each person's potential.

The key to a successful life is to die empty—to maximize your potential by learning to think and act beyond your self-imposed limitations. In a successful marriage, both partners are committed to helping each other reach their full potential. The desire to help the person you love the most to become all he or she can be is a healthy motivation for marriage. The bounds of the marital union provide an ideal environment in which husbands and wives can strive to express their fullest personal, spiritual, and professional potential. In partnership together they can encourage one another, lift up one another, pray for one another, defend one another, challenge one another, comfort one another, and affirm one another.

 The bounds of the marital union provide an ideal environment in which husbands and wives can strive to express their fullest personal, spiritual, and professional potential.

10. Enhancement of spiritual growth.

Because it comes from God, marriage is designed for believers: men and women who walk by faith and not by sight and live in a daily and growing personal love relationship with Jesus Christ. Both husband and wife together should continually encourage each other to grow in the Lord. They should worship together, pray together, read and discuss the Scriptures together, and hold each other accountable for their spiritual walk with Christ. Structurally, "the husband is the head of the wife as Christ is the head of the church" (Eph. 5:23a). By his leadership and submission to Christ, the husband is to set the tone and direction for the spiritual growth of the family, but both husband and wife bear a mutual responsibility for the spiritual health of their marriage. Any couple who is serious about building a godly marriage will make enhancing each other's spiritual growth a very high priority.

~

One common characteristic of all ten *unhealthy* reasons for marriage is that they are essentially *self-centered*. Selfishness is never a healthy quality on which to try to build a marriage. In contrast, the ten *healthy* reasons are fundamentally *unselfish*. Based as they are on God's nature of unselfish love, they are *self-giving* reasons that focus on the needs and welfare of the other person. This is a critical distinction that can make the difference between success and failure, between happiness and unhappiness, and between a good marriage and a bad marriage.

PRINCIPLES

1. A healthy marriage brings two wholes together, not two halves, forming a union that is greater than the sum of its parts.

2. We all must find our sense of self-worth in our relationship with Christ; in our identity as beloved children of God and heirs to His Kingdom, precious souls created in God's image for whom Jesus died.

3. Ten healthy reasons for marriage:
   - God's will
   - Expressing God's love to the other person
   - Expressing personal love for the other person
   - To fulfill sexual needs and desires in a godly way
   - The desire to begin a family
   - Companionship
   - To share all things together with the other person
   - To work together to fulfill each other's needs
   - To maximize each person's potential
   - Enhancement of spiritual growth

4. Because it comes from God, marriage is designed for believers: men and women who walk by faith and not by sight and live in a daily and growing personal love relationship with Jesus Christ.

CHAPTER FOUR

Everyone Should Have a Garden Wedding

The world's first wedding took place in the Garden of Eden. There God ordained and sanctified the marriage of the man and woman whom He had created. Chapters 1 and 2 of Genesis depict marriage in its ideal state as God designed it, where Adam and Eve enjoyed a relationship characterized by peace, harmony, and equality, along with continual, unbroken fellowship with their Creator. Genesis chapter 3 presents a starkly different picture: Sin has shattered the harmony of the human couple's relationship with each other and destroyed their fellowship with God. Chapters 1 and 2 portray marriage "inside the garden," while chapter 3 shows marriage "outside the garden." The only place to experience God's marriage is "inside the garden." Any marriage "outside the garden" is not God's marriage.

Genesis chapters 1 and 2 picture marriage before the Fall, as God designed it. Chapter 3 reveals what marriage became after the Fall, as the world corrupted it. In practical terms this means that none of the conditions, blessings, or promises that attend the "inside the garden" marriage of chapters 1 and 2 are guaranteed for the "outside the garden" marriage of chapter 3. Inside the garden Adam and Eve enjoy mutual love, respect, and equality; outside the garden they make excuses, blame each other, and lie to God about each other. Inside the garden they share the same spirit, the Spirit of God; outside the garden that Spirit has departed and they are like strangers to each other. Inside the garden they are united in spirit *and* in flesh; outside the garden all they have is flesh.

God's standard of marriage is based on the garden's qualification. No one can truthfully claim that God has joined them who do not come to the marriage altar in the context of the garden. Because it is designed for believers, true marriage is not a union of spirits as much as a union of flesh. In the Garden of Eden, there was no need for Adam and Eve to be married in spirit because they already shared the same spirit. Their spirits were already *fused*. In the flesh, however, they were separate people. Their marriage "inside the garden" was to unite them physically—to *fuse* them into "one flesh," just as they were already "one spirit."

Every day, thousands of couples around the world get married assuming that God has joined them together. In most cases this simply is not true because they have not married within the garden context. They do not share the same spirit because either one or both of them have never been born again of the Spirit of God. Because of this, they have no guarantee of success, no safeguard against the destructive forces that would pull them apart.

God's promises in Scripture apply to all who believe and obey Him—everyone who is called a child of God and who shares His Spirit. No one who is outside the Spirit of God has any guarantee of receiving His promises. Where marriage is concerned, success or failure may depend in large measure on whether or not that marriage exists within the garden context.

 Even though they are born again, many believers have trouble in their marriages because they have unknowingly embraced the world's values and views rather than God's.

Knowledge is a critical key to success in anything, and marriage is no exception. Even Spirit-filled believers may fail in marriage unless they know and understand the fundamental differences between marriage "inside the garden" and marriage "outside the garden." Even though they are born again, many believers have trouble in their marriages because they have unknowingly embraced the world's values and views rather than God's. They need to learn how to look to the Holy Spirit for the wisdom and knowledge to bring their marriage "inside the garden."

Equal Authority, Equal Dominion

The first two chapters of Genesis contain important clues to help us understand what marriage was meant to be and the relationship that should exist between husband and wife. On the sixth and final day of creation, after the heavens and the earth were in place and the earth teemed with plant, animal, and sea life, God put the climax on His creative activity by creating man. Mankind—male and female—was the apex, the crowning glory of God's creativity. He had a special place and plan for these, the greatest of His creations.

*Then God said, "Let Us make man in Our image, in Our likeness, and let **them** rule over the fish of the sea and the birds of the air, over the livestock, over all the earth, and over all the creatures that move along the ground."*

So God created man in His own image, in the image of God He created him; **male and female He created them.** *God blessed* **them** *and said to* **them,** *"Be fruitful and increase in number; fill the earth and subdue it. Rule over the fish of the sea and the birds of the air and over every living creature that moves on the ground"* (Genesis 1:26-28, emphasis added).

Notice that the authority to rule over the created order and to fill and subdue the earth was given to the man and woman *together*. Male and female *both* were created in God's image, each designed to perfectly complete and enhance the other. *Both* were endowed with the capacity and the authority to rule over the physical realm as God's vice-regents. Note also that their authority to rule extended over all of God's lesser creatures—fish, birds, and land animals—but *not* over each other. According to God's original design, man and woman were to exercise *equal* authority and *equal* dominion.

God's command to subdue and rule applied equally to both the man and the woman. In the Garden of Eden, Adam and Eve possessed the same spirit, acted with the same authority, and exercised the same power. They had dominion over "every living creature that moves on the ground." This included the serpent. Genesis chapter 3 makes it clear that satan, that fallen angel, the tempter and accuser, was present in the garden, in the form of a serpent. Because Adam and Eve represented the highest of God's creation, and because satan was in their realm, he was under their jurisdiction. Adam and Eve possessed both the authority and the power to subdue the devil. Their failure to do so led to disaster.

 In the garden Adam and Eve were equal in personhood and authority.

The second chapter of Genesis also reveals that in the garden Adam and Eve were equal in personhood and authority. Genesis 2:18-24 describes how God made Eve from one of Adam's ribs to be a "suitable helper" for him, someone who would be perfectly and completely compatible with him physically. The Hebrew word for "rib" can also be translated as "side." Eve was formed from part of Adam's side. She was of the same "stuff" as Adam: the same spirit, the same mind, the same essence, and the same divine image. She was bone of his bone and flesh of his flesh, in every essential and fundamental way his equal. An ancient Hebrew proverb found in the Talmud, the authoritative collection of Jewish tradition, says, "God did not create woman from man's head, that he should command her, nor from his feet, that she should be his slave, but rather from his side, that she should be near his heart."

One in spirit and one in flesh, the man and woman in the garden exercised equal power and authority, ruling together the physical, earthly domain that God had given them.

One in spirit and one in flesh, the man and woman in the garden exercised equal power and authority, ruling together the physical, earthly domain that God had given them.

Male Headship Is Based on Knowledge

Equality of personhood, power, and authority does not mean that there was no priority of leadership in the garden between Adam and Eve. One thing that Genesis chapter 2 makes clear is that God positioned the man as head of the family unit. In God's design, headship in marriage is the man's responsibility. As soon as God placed Adam in the Garden of Eden, He established the parameters under which the man would live and work.

The Lord God took the man and put him in the Garden of Eden to work it and take care of it. And the Lord God commanded the man, "You are free to eat from any tree in the garden; but you must not eat from the tree of the knowledge of good and evil, for when you eat of it you will surely die" (Genesis 2:15-17).

Being responsible for caring for the garden gave Adam fruitful and productive work to do. At the same time, God gave him free reign throughout his environment. The only restriction on Adam's freedom was God's prohibition against eating from the tree of the knowledge of good and evil.

It is important to note that Adam received these instructions before Eve came on the scene. Because he was created first, Adam was privy to information from God that Eve did not have. It was Adam's responsibility to pass along this information to his wife. As "head" of the unit, Adam was the covering for his family. That covering was based on his responsibility.

Why was Adam made the head of the family? Was it because he was physically stronger? No. Today it is commonly known that men and women are essentially equal in physical strength, but in different ways. Generally, men are stronger from the waist up while women are stronger from the waist down. A woman's body is specifically designed for bearing the physical stress and pressure of childbirth. Very few men could handle that kind of pain. Adam's position of headship was not due to physical strength.

Was it his physical appearance? I don't think so. Physically, women in general are more attractive than men. Someone once said tongue-in-cheek that because the man was made first, he was the "rough copy" while the woman was the more refined end product.

Was Adam smarter? No. Men and women have the same intellectual capacity. Was Adam more spiritual? No. Adam and Eve shared the same spirit.

It appears that Adam's headship was as much a matter of timing as anything else. Adam was head because he was created first and possessed information that Eve did not have. Adam's headship was based on *knowledge*. This fact has serious implications for understanding what headship means. The husband is the head of his wife (see Eph. 5:23) but this does *not* mean that he rules over her as her boss. *Headship is not rulership; it is **leadership***. As head, the man is to provide spiritual leadership and direction to the family. He is supposed to chart the course. His spiritual temperature should set the climate for his entire house.

 Headship is not rulership; it is leadership.

Many marriages today, including Christian marriages, suffer because the husbands do not properly understand or carry out their responsibilities as the head of their families. Too often their headship degenerates into an authoritarian rule that dominates both wife and children. Sometimes they abdicate their leadership entirely so that the headship falls to their wives, at least in practice if not in name.

When both husband and wife are clear on the issue of headship, that understanding will promote marital harmony and success. The husband decides where the family is going, while the wife decides how they are going to get there. The husband provides direction; the wife, maintenance. Where a husband goes has a lot to do with what his wife does, and what a wife does has a lot to do with where her husband goes. Both are necessary and both work together. Direction is the first step, and action is the second step.

In his headship, Adam had vital information from God upon which Eve's security and welfare depended. He bore the responsibility for instructing her on God's command regarding the tree of the knowledge of good and evil. The man's headship, therefore, is based on *knowledge* and primarily involves teaching and instructing his family in the ways of God and all spiritual matters in general.

Leaving the Garden

In the beauty of the Garden of Eden Adam and Eve exercised dominion over the created order, enjoyed full marital bliss and harmony, and engaged in unbroken fellowship with their Creator. These idyllic conditions were shattered by the subtle and crafty schemes of the adversary. Appearing in the guise of a serpent, this archenemy of God set his sights on destroying the purity, innocence, and order of life in the garden. The woman was his target, and doubt was his weapon.

> *Now the serpent was more crafty than any of the wild animals the Lord God had made. He said to the woman, "Did God really say, 'You must not eat from any tree in the garden'?" The woman said to the serpent, "We may eat fruit from the trees in the garden, but God did say, 'You must not eat fruit from the tree that is in the middle of the garden, and you must not touch it, or you will die.'" "You will not surely die," the serpent said to the woman. "For God knows that when you eat of it your eyes will be opened, and you will be like God, knowing good and evil." When the woman saw that the fruit of the tree was good for food and pleasing to the eye, and also desirable for gaining wisdom, she took some and ate it. She also gave some to her husband, who was with her, and he ate it. Then the eyes of both of them were opened, and they realized they were naked; so they sewed fig leaves together and made coverings for themselves* (Genesis 3:1-7).

Because Eve expressed no surprise when the serpent spoke to her, it is reasonable to conclude that this probably was not their first conversation. In her innocence regarding the knowledge of good and evil, Eve had no reason to distrust the serpent's words or to suspect him of trickery. His question was very subtle, skillfully sowing in her mind a seed of doubt regarding God's integrity: "Did God *really* say, 'You must not eat from any tree in the garden'?" (emphasis added). This is the way the adversary operates. God's archenemy, identified in the Judeo-Christian Scriptures as the devil, or satan, seeks to undermine God's character in people's minds through innuendo and doubt and by twisting the truth.

 One of the adversary's primary tactics is to make us doubt who we are.

Eve's response to the serpent's question reveals that Adam had fulfilled his responsibility to inform her of God's command regarding the tree of the knowledge of good and evil. When she said that to eat from the tree or touch it meant death, the serpent flatly contradicted God: "You will not surely die, [but] your eyes will be opened, and you will be like God, knowing good and evil." One of the adversary's primary tactics is to make us doubt who we are. In whose image and likeness were Adam and Eve created? *God's*. They did not need to eat the fruit of the tree of the knowledge of good and evil in order to become like God; *they were already like Him!*

The seed of doubt grew in Eve's mind until she was confused about who she was and about what God had said. In her confusion, and because the fruit of the tree looked appealing, she decided to eat it. Where was Adam while all of this was going on? According to verse 6 he was *with her*, at least at the time she ate the fruit, because she gave some to him and he ate also. The passage does not tell us where he was during Eve's conversation with the serpent. Although there is no break in the narrative, Eve's decision to eat the fruit did not necessarily occur immediately afterward. Some time may have passed while her doubt grew and the temptation got stronger.

It appears that Adam was not around when Eve and the serpent talked. By his absence, Adam failed in his responsibility to protect and cover his wife. Although they both possessed the authority to rule over the serpent, they surrendered that authority by listening to him, and he gained control over them. Eve was deceived, but Adam sinned with his eyes wide open. The "knowledge" they received for all their trouble was awareness that they had sinned and that God's Spirit had departed from them. Suddenly, they were estranged from each other as well as from God. The "honeymoon" was over. By their disobedience to God, their marriage moved "outside the garden."

Adam, Where Are You?

After Adam and Eve disobeyed God in the garden, He confronted them with their sin, and the way He did it reveals an important truth about His design for marriage.

> Then the man and his wife heard the sound of the Lord God as He was walking in the garden in the cool of the day, and they hid from the Lord God among the trees of the garden. But the Lord God called to the man, "Where are you?" He answered, "I heard You in the garden, and I was afraid because I was naked; so I hid." And He said, "Who told you that you were naked? Have you eaten from the tree that I commanded you not to eat from?" The man said, "The woman You put here with me—she gave me some fruit from the tree, and I ate it." Then the Lord God said to the woman, "What is this you have done?" The woman said, "The serpent deceived me, and I ate" (Genesis 3:8-13).

Notice that although it was Eve who listened to the serpent, who was deceived by him, and who first took the forbidden fruit and ate it, when God confronted them He sought out *Adam*. "But the Lord God called to *the man*, 'Where are you?' " This was not a question of location but of disposition. God already knew where Adam was and what he had done. The intent of His question was to get Adam to acknowledge his sin and take responsibility for his actions. The Lord was saying to Adam, "How did you get in the state you are in? You have fallen and My Spirit has left you. There is no longer any fellowship between you and Me. How did you get into this position?"

If Eve was the instigator, the first to disobey by eating the forbidden fruit, why then did God seek out Adam? There are at least two reasons. For one thing, even though Eve sinned first, Adam was just as guilty because he also ate the fruit. He could have refused, but he did not. More importantly, however, God came to Adam because, as head of the family, Adam was responsible. Adam bore the responsibility not only for telling his wife what God said, which he apparently had done, but also for watching over her and guarding her. He was supposed to be her covering. Where was he during his wife's encounter with the adversary? Because he was not where he was supposed to be, or doing what he was supposed to be doing, Adam bore direct responsibility for their failure.

 Fear and separation are not part of God's plan or desire for us.

Adam's response to the Lord's question makes it clear that some fundamental changes had occurred in their relationship. "I heard You in the garden, and I was afraid because I was naked; so I hid." When a person loses fellowship with God, several significant things happen. First, their sense of separation from God causes them to run from Him. Adam hid himself. Second, they become fearful. Adam was afraid. Until he disobeyed God he had never known fear. Now fear dogged his every step.

 Love and fear cannot coexist. Where love abounds, fear is banished; where fear rises, love diminishes.

Fear and separation are not part of God's plan or desire for us. He created us to love Him and to enjoy permanent fellowship with Him. Fear is a foreign element in that relationship. It interferes with the free expression of love. In his second letter to Timothy, his young protégé, Paul, the great missionary and teacher of the first century wrote, "For God did not give us a spirit of timidity, but a spirit of power, of love and of self-discipline" (2 Tim. 1:7). Another word for timidity is *fear*. John, a writer of the New Testament and one of Jesus' special disciples, wrote, "God is love. Whoever lives in love lives in God, and God in him....There is no fear in love. But perfect love drives out fear, because fear has to do with punishment. The one who fears is not made perfect in love" (1 Jn. 4:16b, 18).

Love and fear cannot coexist. Where love abounds, fear is banished; where fear rises, love diminishes. Because of their sin, Adam and Eve forfeited the love, peace, harmony, and fellowship they had enjoyed with the Lord and with each other, and found that guilt and fear had replaced them. This change affected every area of their lives, including their marriage. A marriage without love is a slave to fear and division. Such are the common characteristics of marriage "outside the garden."

    A marriage without love is a slave to fear and division.

Playing the Blame Game

Another sign of the fundamental change that sin brought to their relationship is that Adam and Eve began playing the blame game. Blame flourishes where love is absent. Adam blamed Eve, Eve blamed the serpent, and neither was willing to accept personal responsibility for their actions. People often say and do ridiculous things when they try to avoid taking responsibility. Consider what Adam said: "The woman You put here with me—she gave me some fruit from the tree, and I ate it." He makes it sound as though he was completely helpless. In effect, Adam is telling God, "It's her fault, this woman that *You* gave me. She body-slammed me, got me in a headlock, tore my mouth open, stuffed the fruit in, and moved my jaws up and down saying, 'Come on, chew it.' "

    Blame flourishes where love is absent.

Simply stated, Adam did not want to take responsibility for what happened to his family. Neither did Eve. When God asked, "What is this you have done?" she tried to pass the buck. "The serpent deceived me, and I ate." On the surface, what she said is true; the serpent *did* deceive her. That did not excuse her from responsibility, however. She knew what God had said and chose to disobey.

Reluctance to assume responsibility is a very common problem in our modern society, a symptom of the sinfulness of a human race in rebellion against our Creator. "Pop" psychology tells us that we are all "victims." If we're messed up it is because of our environment, or because we were abused as children, or we were socially or economically deprived, or any number of other excuses. We bear no responsibility for our actions or for how we turned out. No matter what happens, it is always someone else's fault—our husband, our wife, our children, our boss—anyone except ourselves.

This same attitude characterizes marriage "outside the garden." When no one is willing to accept responsibility, everybody suffers. People can become downright illogical when they want to avoid responsibility. In an effort to justify irresponsible behavior they start using excuses that don't make any sense and state them as if they are irrefutable law. The world's design for marriage is the opposite of God's design. Marriage "outside the garden" is the marriage of blame, irresponsible activity, transferring and passing the buck, and men failing to take their rightful and responsible place as head of the home. In the world's system, marriage can be jettisoned when the going gets rough.

One additional characteristic of marriage "outside the garden" is husbands exercising authoritarian rule over their wives. This is a consequence of Eve's sin. God said to her, "I will greatly increase your pains in childbearing; with pain you will give birth to children. Your desire will be for your husband, and *he will rule over you*" (Gen. 3:16, emphasis added). It is important to note that this is not part of God's original design for the husband and wife relationship, but a description of the situation that now exists because of sin.

 The husband bears overall responsibility for the health and welfare of his wife and family, but he is not the "boss."

In God's kind of marriage, the husband does not *rule* his wife but exercises *headship*. He gives leadership and direction and they rule together. The husband bears overall responsibility for the health and welfare of his wife and family, but he is not the "boss." As head of the family he leads the family, not as a tyrant or dictator, but with love, grace, wisdom, and knowledge under the lordship of Christ.

PRINCIPLES

1. According to God's original design, man and woman were to exercise *equal* authority and *equal* dominion.

2. In God's design, headship in marriage is the man's responsibility.

3. Headship is not rulership; it is *leadership.*

4. The man's headship is based on *knowledge* and primarily involves teaching and instructing his family in the ways of God and all spiritual matters in general.

5. Marriage "outside the garden" is the marriage of blame, irresponsible activity, transferring and passing the buck, and men failing to take their rightful and responsible place as head of the home.

6. As head of the family, the husband leads the family, not as a tyrant or dictator, but with love, grace, wisdom, and knowledge under the lordship of Christ.

~ CHAPTER FIVE ~

A Happy Marriage Is No Accident

$\mathcal{A}$ happy marriage is no accident. As with every other area of life, success in marriage does not happen automatically. The secret to success in any endeavor is *planning*, and successful planning depends on *knowledge*. It is only when we have accurate and adequate information that we can plan for success.

Many of us are willing to spend years in school receiving an education that we believe will prepare us for success in our chosen career or profession. We pursue education because education makes us versatile, and versatility increases our marketability. Increased marketability enhances the likelihood of our success. Rather than leave our success to chance, we plan carefully for it.

There was a time when a person entering the labor force at age 18 or 21 spent his or her entire working life with the same employer. Today it is not at all uncommon for workers to change jobs or employers four or five times or more during their careers. The fact that frequent career changes have become the norm in modern society makes education and knowledge even more important to success.

If we are so careful about planning for career success, why aren't we just as careful about planning for success in marriage? After all, we spend years preparing for a career that may change at any time, yet devote very little time preparing for a relationship that is supposed to last a lifetime. If we are not careful we can end up spending too much time preparing for the wrong things. There is nothing wrong with going to school and getting an education or deliberately planning for success in meeting career goals. The problem is that there are many people who have successful careers but failed marriages because they spent much time learning how to get along with their boss and no time learning how to get along with their spouse. We invest more in preparation to make a living than to live life effectively.

As with any other endeavor in life, success in marriage depends on information and planning. Marriage is an investment, and success is directly proportional to the amount of knowledge and time invested in it. Success is not a gift, but the result of careful and deliberate preparation. Success is directly related to investment: when you invest in time and passion, you will more-likely succeed.

No one who hopes to build a new house approaches the project haphazardly. Success in such a venture means buying the right piece of property, securing the services of a qualified architect, and making certain that sufficient financing is available to bring the whole project to completion. It is important to plan for the *end* before beginning, to count the cost up front, and try to anticipate the pitfalls and difficulties that will occur along the way.

Jesus emphasized the importance of this kind of advance planning when He said, "Suppose one of you wants to build a tower. Will he not first sit down and estimate the cost to see if he has enough money to complete it? For if he lays the foundation and is not able to finish it, everyone who sees it will ridicule him, saying, 'This fellow began to build and was not able to finish' " (Lk. 14:28-30). Although Jesus was speaking here specifically of counting the cost of following Him as a disciple, His words provide wise counsel for us with regard to any endeavor we undertake. We must *plan* for success. We must give the same attention to building a home as we do to building the house. Many beautiful houses are not homes.

Knowledge and Revelation

Marriage is no different. The same principle applies. A happy marriage cannot be left to chance. Just like building a house, a successful marriage is the product of careful planning and deliberate design, the right material, good advice, and qualified contractors.

Many believers make the mistake of assuming that because they know the Lord and have the Holy Spirit they are guaranteed success in marriage. Proverbs 1:7 says, "The fear of the Lord is the beginning of knowledge, but fools despise wisdom and discipline." Fear of the Lord is the *starting place* of knowledge. No matter how smart we are or how educated, until we know the Lord we have no true knowledge. That is where we must begin.

 We must become students of the Word of God, fluent in the spiritual principles that govern life.

One of the ministries of the Holy Spirit in our lives is to bring us into the knowledge of the truth. Jesus said, "But the Counselor, the Holy Spirit, whom the Father will send in My name, will *teach you* all things and will *remind you* of everything I have said to you" (Jn. 14:26, emphasis added). The Holy Spirit cannot teach us if we will not sit down to learn, and He cannot remind us of something we never learned to begin with. We must become students of the Word of God, fluent in the spiritual principles that govern life. Only then can the Holy Spirit teach us and remind us.

When it comes to marriage, we have no guarantee of success if we do not know the principles of success. We cannot expect the Spirit of God to "remind" us of principles or truths we never learned in the first place. If we never learn how to communicate with our spouse, if we never learn how to relate properly or how to deal with conflict, the Holy Spirit has nothing of which to "remind" us. That is why knowledge is so important. At the same time, knowledge by itself is not enough. Knowledge alone can lead us to wrong conclusions. When illuminated by the Holy Spirit, knowledge becomes revelation. We need the wisdom of the Spirit to enable us to properly understand and apply our knowledge.

Knowledge Overcomes Marital Illiteracy

One of the biggest challenges facing couples today, whether married or unmarried, is marital illiteracy. Many marriages fail or otherwise fall short of reaching their full potential because the couples never learn what marriage is really all about. What understanding they do have is either very shallow, or shaped by the philosophy of the world rather than by the principles of God, or both. Likelihood of success increases greatly when the misconceptions of ignorance are dispelled by the light of truth and knowledge.

The marriage relationship is a school, a learning environment in which both partners can grow and develop over time. Marriage does not demand perfection but it must be given priority. It is an institution peopled exclusively by sinners, and finds its greatest glory when those sinners see it as God's way of leading them through His ultimate curriculum of love and righteousness.

 Marriage is a learning environment in which both partners can grow and develop over time.

Marriage has the potential of expressing God's love to its fullest possible degree on earth. The will of the couple is the critical factor. A marriage relationship will express God's love only as far as both partners are willing to allow the Lord to really work in and through them. This is a totally unselfish love where the husband and wife "submit to one another out of reverence for Christ" (Eph. 5:21); where the wife respects her husband (v. 33) and submits to him "as to the Lord" (v. 22); and where the husband loves his wife as himself (v. 33), "just as Christ loved the church and gave Himself up for her" (v. 25). When two totally different people come together and live and work as one, giving unselfishly of themselves and loving, forgiving, understanding, and bearing with each other, outside observers will see at least a little bit of what the love of God is all about.

 Marriage is one of the refining processes by which God shapes men and women into the people He wants them to be.

A Christian marriage is the total commitment of a husband and wife to each other and individually to the person of Jesus Christ, a commitment that holds nothing back in either the natural or the spiritual realm. It is a pledge of mutual fidelity, a partnership of mutual subordination. Marriage is one of the refining processes by which God shapes men and women into the people He wants them to be.

Building on a Firm Foundation

Anything of a lasting nature is built on a firm and solid foundation, and marriage is no different. The only sure foundation for life is the Word of God. In one of His most famous teachings, Jesus vividly illustrated the danger of trying to build a life on an inadequate foundation.

> *Therefore everyone who hears these words of Mine and puts them into practice is like a wise man who built his house on the rock. The rain came down, the streams rose, and the winds blew and beat against that house; yet it did not fall, because it had its foundation on the rock. But everyone who hears these words of Mine and does not put them into practice is like a foolish man who built his house on sand. The rain came down, the streams rose, and the winds blew and beat against that house, and it fell with a great crash* (Matthew 7:24-27).

Just as a house built on a poor foundation will be blown away in a storm, so a marriage is unlikely to survive the tempests of life unless it is firmly established on bedrock spiritual principles. Let's consider ten foundation stones upon which to build a happy and successful marriage.

1. Love.

Love can be described in many different ways, but we are concerned here with agape, the love that defines the very nature of God. Agape is self-denying and self-giving, sacrificial love of the type that Paul, one of the writers of the New Testament, spoke of when he wrote:

> *Love is patient, love is kind. It does not envy, it does not boast, it is not proud. It is not rude, it is not self-seeking, it is not easily angered, it keeps no record of wrongs. Love does not delight in evil but rejoices with the truth. It always protects, always trusts, always hopes, always perseveres. Love never fails* (1 Corinthians 13:4-8a).

Love in marriage is more than just a feeling or an emotion; it is a *choice*. Love is a decision you make anew every day with regard to your spouse. Whenever you rise up in the morning or lie down at night or go through the affairs of the day, you are choosing continually to love that man or that woman you married.

Love in marriage is more than just a feeling or an emotion; it is a **CHOICE.**

Understanding that love is a choice will help keep you out of trouble when temptation comes (and it will). Knowing you have made a decision to love your husband or your wife will carry you through those times when he or she has made you angry, or when you see that handsome or attractive coworker at the office. You could have married someone else, but that's not the point. The point is, you made a decision. When you married your spouse, you chose to love and cherish him or her for the rest of your life. That love must be freshened daily.

One of the most important foundation stones for a happy marriage is a sacrificial love for your spouse that you choose to renew daily.

2. Truth.

Truth is fundamental in marriage. A marriage that is not based on truth is headed for trouble right away. The greatest and most reliable source of truth is the Bible, which is the Word of God, who is Himself truth and the one who designed and instituted marriage. Every conscientious husband and wife should measure their marriage by the unchanging standard of the principles found in God's Word. The Bible is a truthful and reliable guide for every area of life.

Every conscientious husband and wife should measure their marriage by the unchanging standard of the principles found in God's Word.

Truthfulness between husband and wife is an indispensable part of a successful marriage. No one's interests are served if spouses are not honest with each other. Honesty, tempered and seasoned with love, fosters an environment of trust.

3. Trust.

Trust is closely related to truth. If a husband and wife want their marriage to be happy and successful, they must be able to trust each other implicitly. Nothing damages a marriage more than broken trust. It's hard to grow and prosper in an atmosphere of bitterness, resentment, and suspicion.

That is why both partners should take great care to ensure that they do not say or do anything to give each other any reason to doubt or distrust them. Trust enables a husband and wife to enjoy a relationship characterized by openness and transparency, with no secrets or "locked rooms" that are kept off limits to each other. Trust is also an essential element of commitment.

 Nothing damages a marriage more than broken trust.

4. Commitment.

Commitment is a frightening word to many people in our society today. They are afraid of being locked in or tied down to any kind of a long-term arrangement. That is one reason why many marriages do not last. A man and a woman approach the marriage altar and exchange their vows but are just going through the motions, giving only lip service to commitment. Their idea of marriage is to hang together until the going gets rough, and then they can split. If their marriage "works," okay, and if it doesn't, oh well. Few people who marry *plan* for their marriages to fail, but neither do they specifically *plan* for success. Those who do not plan for success are virtually guaranteed to fail.

Commitment is the lifeblood of marriage. Part of our problem is that we do not understand the nature of a covenant. Marriage is a "blood covenant" of sorts and, like the blood covenants of old, it lasts a lifetime. A blood covenant was neither entered into nor broken lightly. Violation of a blood covenant brought serious consequences. Marriage involves just as serious a commitment. It is first of all a commitment to the institution of marriage and, second, an exclusive commitment to that person we have chosen to love and cherish for life.

 Commitment is the lifeblood of marriage.

5. Respect.

Any healthy relationship, marriage included, must be built on mutual respect. To respect someone means to esteem that person, to consider him or her worthy of high regard. Wives should respect their husbands and husbands should respect their wives. One reason why so many marriages are in trouble is because the husband has never learned to regard his wife with proper respect. Many men grow up to regard women as little more than sex objects to be possessed and used at will. Never learning any different, they carry this same ignorant viewpoint into marriage.

*Whoever **desires** respect must **show** respect to others and live in a manner worthy of respect.*

God created man—male and female—in His own image. He created them equal in every significant way. Husbands and wives who see each other as made in God's image will never have any problems with respect. Whoever *desires* respect must *show* respect to others and live in a manner worthy of respect. Anyone who would be respected must be respectable.

6. Submission.

Healthy marriages are built not only on mutual respect but also on mutual submission. We hear so often that wives are supposed to submit to their husbands that we forget that submission goes both ways. "Submit to one another out of reverence for Christ. Wives, submit to your husbands as to the Lord....Husbands, love your wives, just as Christ loved the church and gave Himself up for her" (Eph. 5:21-22,25). Jesus' giving Himself up in death out of love for His Church was the ultimate act of submission. Ephesians 5:25 says that husbands are supposed to love their wives in that same way, a love characterized by sacrificial, self-giving submission.

Submission is the willingness to give up our right to ourselves, to freely surrender our insistence on having our own way all the time.

Properly understood, there is nothing demeaning about submission. It is chosen freely, not imposed from without. Essentially, submission is the willingness to give up our right to ourselves, to freely surrender our insistence on having our own way all the time. Submission means putting the needs, rights, and welfare of another person ahead of our own. A marriage built on this kind of submission will grow healthy, strong, and fulfilling.

7. Knowledge.

It would be almost impossible to over-emphasize the importance of knowledge as a firm foundation for marriage. Many marriages struggle or fail because of lack of knowledge. Couples enter married life with no clue as to what marriage is or is not. They carry unrealistic and unreasonable expectations of themselves, their spouses, and their relationship as a whole.

With all the resources that are currently available, and because so much is at stake, there is no excuse today for marital ignorance or illiteracy.

This is why a period of courtship and engagement is so important and why premarital counseling is indispensable. Couples considering marriage need time to get to know one another. They need time to talk about their dreams, their desires, and their expectations. They need time to study and learn the spiritual foundations and principles for marriage that God has given in His Word. With all the resources that are currently available, and because so much is at stake, there is no excuse today for marital ignorance or illiteracy.

8. Faithfulness.

Faithfulness is closely related to commitment and also has a lot to do with trust. When we speak of faithfulness in marriage, we most often have sexual relations in mind. Faithful partners will be true, reserving sexual expression exclusively for each other. This is why many married couples who were sexually active before marriage often have trouble in their relationships. The basic element of faithfulness is missing. Even if they have pledged to be faithful to each other, there is always that shadow of doubt. It doesn't take much for that shadow to become a dark storm cloud looming over everything.

 Marital fidelity means that your spouse's health, happiness, security, and welfare take a higher place in your life than anything else except your own relationship with the Lord.

Marital faithfulness involves more than just sexual fidelity. Being faithful to your wife also means defending her and affirming her beauty, intelligence, and integrity at all times, particularly before other people. Faithfulness to your husband means sticking up for him, always building him up and never tearing him down. Marital fidelity means that your spouse's health, happiness, security, and welfare take a higher place in your life than anything else except your own relationship with the Lord.

9. Patience.

Patience is another essential foundation stone for building a successful and happy marriage. Why? Marriage brings together two totally different people with different experiences, different backgrounds, different temperaments, different likes and dislikes, and sometimes even different cultures. Because of these differences, both partners will have to make major adjustments in their lives and attitudes if their marriage is to succeed. Some bumps and bruises along the way are inevitable. She may wear her hair in a way he doesn't like. He may drive her up the wall with his habit of leaving his dirty clothes lying around everywhere. They may have conflict regarding expectations, money management, use of leisure time, sex, parenting—

any number of things. The critical key in dealing with conflict and adjusting to differences is patience. Both partners will need truckloads of it!

The critical key in dealing with conflict and adjusting to differences is patience.

10. Financial stability.

Financial stability is one of the most often overlooked foundation stones of marriage. Many young couples who are planning to marry give little thought to the importance of entering marriage with a well-established financial base. I cannot count the number of times I have seen this for myself. A young couple comes to me and says, "We would like to get married."

"Are either of you working?"

"No."

"Then how do you expect to make it?"

"We're in love. We'll make it. Love will find a way."

Love is certainly important, even critical, but let's be practical. Love won't pay the rent or put food on the table. Adjusting to married life is difficult and challenging enough on its own. The last thing a couple needs is to go into the marriage with a lot of minuses. Financial instability is one of the biggest minuses of all. If you're having money problems *before* you are married, what makes you think they will go away *after* you are married?

The time to think about finances is *before* the wedding—long before. A couple should discuss the matter frankly and honestly and have a clear financial plan in place before they take their vows. There should be a steady and dependable source of income. At the very least, the man should have steady employment. No woman, even if she has her own career and plans to continue working, should marry a man who does not have a job. If she does, she will most likely end up supporting him, rather than the other way around.

Financial difficulty is one of the main causes of marital failure. *Never* underestimate the importance of financial stability to a successful marriage.

Financial difficulty is one of the main causes of marital failure.

Checking Your "Marriage Ability" Traits

In addition to these foundation stones, there are several "marriage ability" traits we should consider—qualities of personality and character that will enhance the building of a strong marriage. Check these out and see where you stand. I have listed eight.

1. Adaptability. This is simply the ability to adapt to changing conditions. No matter how carefully we prepare for marriage, we cannot predict everything. Unexpected situations will pop up with annoying frequency, forcing us to change our plans. Just the fact of two completely different people coming together as one will inevitably call for flexibility. Be adaptable. Expect the unexpected. Consider it as an opportunity to grow, to move in a direction you might never have thought of otherwise.

2. Empathy. This is sensitivity to the needs, hurts, and desires of others—the ability to feel with them and experience the world from their perspective. A lot of conflict and misunderstanding between spouses could be avoided if they would simply try to increase their ability to empathize with each other, to walk in each other's shoes for awhile.

3. Ability to work through problems. This is not the same as *solving* problems. Some problems cannot be solved, but married couples need the ability to identify and analyze problems, propose and choose a possible solution, and follow it through. They will be able to solve *most* problems this way, and will learn to work around the ones they can't solve. The important thing is being committed to deal with problems, not walk away from them.

4. Ability to give and receive love. This is not as easy as it sounds, particularly for most men. Giving and receiving love comes more naturally for women. Men, on the other hand, have been taught in society that being manly or "macho" means not showing their sensitive side openly. As a result, many men have trouble expressing their true feelings. Marriage is a constant give-and-take, and this includes expression of love.

5. Emotional stability. This means being able to control our emotions and not let them run away from us. It means bridling our temper and not making excuses for immature emotional outbursts. Occasional loss of control is human but a pattern of it reveals a deeper problem. Anyone who constantly flies off the handle then says, "I can't help myself," is not being honest. If that is *truly* the case, then that person needs professional help. Usually, however, it is not a matter of being unable, but of being unwilling. Emotional stability means being willing and able to accept responsibility for our feelings, words, and actions.

6. Ability to communicate. True communication is not easy and happens rarely. Communication is the ability to ensure that people understand not only what you say but also what you mean. It is also the ability to listen to and understand others. Developing both of these aspects of communication takes a lot of time, patience, and hard work.

7. Similarities between the couples themselves. Any marriage involves the joining of two totally different people, but there should be some distinct similarities as well: common interests, common hobbies, a common faith, or similar political views for example. There needs to be some common meeting ground between the two.

8. Similar family background. Although this is not a highly critical factor—people of distinctly different backgrounds build successful marriages every day—similar family background is always helpful. A couple should enter marriage with all the advantages or "pluses" that they can, and similarity of family background is definitely a "plus."

~

As important as they are, foundation stones alone are incomplete. They merely form the base upon which the completed structure must be built. The foundation stones of love, truth, trust, commitment, respect, submission, knowledge, faithfulness, patience, and financial stability are not ends in themselves. Rather they are bases upon which to build and display the beautiful jewel that we call marriage—a fusion of two distinct persons into one flesh, soul, and spirit. Success and happiness are no accident, but the result and reward of deliberate planning, diligent pursuit, and patient growth.

PRINCIPLES

1. Marriage is an investment, and success is directly proportional to the amount of knowledge and time invested in it.

2. A successful marriage is the product of careful planning and deliberate design.

3. Ten firm foundation stones for building a successful marriage:
    - Love
    - Truth
    - Trust
    - Commitment
    - Respect
    - Submission
    - Knowledge
    - Faithfulness
    - Patience
    - Financial stability

4. Eight important "marriage ability" traits:
    - Adaptability
    - Empathy
    - Ability to work through problems
    - Ability to give and receive love
    - Emotional stability
    - Ability to communicate
    - Similarities between the couples themselves
    - Similar family background

~ CHAPTER SIX ~

Loosing the Ties That Bind

$\mathcal{A}$ny experienced counselor will tell you that marital problems outnumber all other life and relationship problems combined. More problems arise in marriage than arise from drugs, crime, financial issues, or emotional or psychological disorders. It is a sobering sign of our times that an institution as critical to our culture and civilization as marriage should be in such crisis.

One of the toughest challenges newlywed couples face in adjusting to married life is learning how to relate to their parents and families of origin in light of their new circumstances. Marriage brings about fundamental changes in the relationships that exist between a couple and the families in which they grew up. Many newlyweds have trouble loosing the ties that bind them to their parents and to the lifestyle they knew as single adults. They often feel torn between their responsibility to their new spouse and their perceived responsibility to their parents. This tension creates conflict in the marriage, particularly when one partner finds it harder to let go than the other.

Adjustments to married life can be just as difficult for the parents of newlyweds as for the couple themselves. Sometimes parents compound the problem by trying to hold onto their married children, at least emotionally. Whether consciously or subconsciously, many parents try to make their children feel guilty for trying to break away on their own. They struggle with the idea of their "baby" leaving the nest. If they have become emotionally or financially dependent on that child, they fear the changes that may come in that relationship because of the new person in their child's life.

Regardless of the direction from which it comes, confusion over how a newlywed couple should relate to their parents and families will cause stress in their marriage. Unless they learn how to deal with it, the "ties that bind" may become a noose that chokes the life out of their relationship.

Marriage Is the Primary Human Relationship

According to the Bible, the highest and most important relationship of all is that between an individual human being and God. This is the fundamental and essential spiritual relationship. In the natural realm, and second only to the divine/human relationship, is the marriage relationship between a man and a woman. The husband/wife relationship is the primary human relationship. Problems always result when either of these relationships is removed from its position of priority. Most of the root causes of problems in life stem from people placing some other person or thing higher in their priority than either God or their spouse.

The relationship between husband and wife is primary because God established it first as the most basic human relationship.

So the Lord God caused the man to fall into a deep sleep; and while he was sleeping, He took one of the man's ribs and closed up the place with flesh. Then the Lord God made a woman from the rib He had taken out of the man, and He brought her to the man. The man said, "This is now bone of my bones and flesh of my flesh; she shall be called 'woman,' for she was taken out of man." For this reason a man will leave his father and mother and be united to his wife, and they will become one flesh (Genesis 2:21-24).

Notice that when God created the human race He began with a husband and wife, not a parent and child. By God's design, the husband/wife relationship precedes and takes priority over the parent/child relationship. Verse 24 says that a man is to leave his father and mother and be united to his wife. The word "leave" suggests a temporary state while the word "united" indicates a permanent condition. In marriage a husband's and wife's primary responsibility is to each other, not to their parents or their siblings.

The husband and wife relationship is foundational and the key to every other relationship in life. Adam and Eve were husband and wife before they were parents. One reason the marriage relationship takes priority over the parent/child relationship is because a husband and wife make a covenant promise to meet each other's companionship needs for life. No such covenant exists between parents and their children. Parents have a responsibility to love and care for their children and to meet their physical, emotional, and spiritual needs, but this is fundamentally different from the "oneness" that they share as husband and wife.

 The parent/child relationship is temporary and must be broken, while the husband/wife relationship is permanent and must not be broken.

Essentially, the parent/child relationship is temporary and must be broken, while the husband/wife relationship is permanent and must not be broken. Parents should raise their children with the deliberate objective of seeing them grow into mature, *independent* adults. Once children are grown and on their own, a fundamental change occurs in their relationship with their parents. This change is even more pronounced once the children marry. Although parents should always be loved, honored, and respected, they no longer have the predominant place in the lives or priorities of their children. These married children have a new priority that takes precedence over their parents—their spouse. This is as it should be. The temporary relationship of parent/child gives way to the permanent relationship of husband/wife.

Marriage Means Leaving Home

In some cultures it is customary to think of marriage as joining two families into one. The husband represents his family of origin, the wife represents hers, and together they and all their relatives become part of one big happy family. As common as this mentality may be in places, it is incorrect and unscriptural. *Marriage does not combine two families into one, but creates a third family*. When a husband and wife come together they form a distinct, separate, complete, and individual family unit that is independent of their respective families of origin. That is why Genesis 2:24 says, "For this reason a man will *leave his father and mother* and be united to his wife, and they will become one flesh" (emphasis added). In marriage, a man and a woman from two separate families join together to form a third family that is separate from the other two.

Although this verse speaks specifically of the husband leaving, it also includes the wife. How can a man be united to his wife unless she leaves home as well? It is only when they both leave their parents that they can successfully establish their own home. This verse emphasizes the man because he is the one who will become the head of the new family, the new decision-making unit established by this marriage.

One of the quickest roads to conflict in a marriage is when a husband has to compete with his wife's parents for priority of relationship. The same is true for a wife whose husband has trouble cutting the ties. This is why the instruction of the Scripture is so strong and so specific when it says that they are to *leave* their father and mother and be united to each other.

Leaving home is a fundamental principle of marriage. The first marriage-related instruction found in the Bible is the command to "leave." Although the main thought is that of leaving home, there is more to the idea than just physical departure. When a man and a woman marry they are to leave their families of origin not only physically, but also mentally, financially, and emotionally. This does not mean they must sever all future connections with their families, but it does mean that their families should not play a significant role in the decisions they make as a couple or in the way they build their home and marriage. Leaving means that a married couple is neither burdened by nor a burden to their parents.

 When a man and a woman marry they are to leave their families of origin not only physically, but also mentally, financially, and emotionally.

The word *leave* implies that the family of origin may or may not want them to go. Many parents struggle with this very thing, finding it hard to let go of their children and allow them to live their own lives as mature and independent adults. That is why God in His wisdom does not leave the option to the parents. When an adult child gets married and leaves the nest, he or she is saying, "I'm ready to live my own life now. I have chosen this person to spend the rest of my life with. I love you, but I have to make my own decisions. No matter how you feel, I'm leaving. Your opinion matters to me, but I can't let it be the determining factor in what I do. I have to choose what is right for me."

Many young people would rather not leave home until they get their parents' consent. While this is not a scriptural requirement, there is certainly nothing wrong with it. Leaving home with your parents' blessing is always nice, but it is also okay to leave home without it. The primary consideration is doing God's will. It is more important to obey God than to obey your parents' wishes. Staying home to satisfy their desires after God has told you to leave is to disobey God.

Cultivating Companionship

There are many reasons why it is essential for young married couples to leave home physically and emotionally. One of the most important is to give them the opportunity from the very beginning of their marriage to cultivate companionship with each other. Companionship is the basis for all successful marriage. The parent/child relationship is established by birth or adoption, but the husband/wife relationship is established by covenant, and there is a difference. Because marriage is a covenant established by God and sealed by the Holy Spirit, it supercedes blood ties. Blood may be thicker than water, but it is not thicker than promise.

 The parent/child relationship is established by birth or adoption, but the husband/wife relationship is established by covenant.

In marriage, our spouse is more important than any other person on earth. Other than the Lord, no one, and I mean *no one*, should take precedence over our husband or our wife either in our attention or our affection. We should give deference to each other ahead of parents, siblings, or any other ties of blood or family. The opinions, desires, or demands of family members no longer hold sway. Spouses must give each other first place. They need to take time to be alone together, to get to know each other not only as spouses and lovers but also as friends and lifelong companions. Companionship in marriage is more important than circumstances of blood or birth.

 Companionship in marriage is more important than circumstances of blood or birth.

Like any other worthwhile endeavor, building companionship requires patience, time, and hard work. Companionship must be cultivated. Anyone who desires to have a beautiful garden must be willing to take the time to turn and prepare the soil, add fertilizer, plant the seeds, irrigate carefully, pull up weeds diligently, and give patient, daily attention to the new plants. Companionship in marriage must be nurtured with the same degree of care. It will not develop overnight or accidentally. Any "weeds" that would choke out the developing flower of companionship must be rooted out.

One of those "weeds" that troubles far too many marriages is the well-intentioned but inappropriate interference of family members into the daily affairs of the couple's life and relationship. Once a man and woman have married, the only thing they should receive from their parents is advice and counsel, and then *only* when they ask for it. Parents should not offer opinions or advice without being asked. To do so undermines the development of the leadership and self-determination of the couple. When they married, the leadership and decision-making responsibilities transferred from their former homes to the new home they are building together. All leadership now devolves on them. They are responsible for making their own decisions. Part of cultivating companionship is learning how to exercise these responsibilities effectively together.

How critical is this principle of independence for the success of a new marriage? It is so vital that the couple, even at the risk of sounding rude or hurting feelings, must do whatever is necessary to prevent their parents or other family members from imposing their opinions or advice uninvited. It may not be easy, but it is necessary in order to be obedient to God's Word.

Should Children Support Their Parents?

Many young couples just starting out in married life struggle with understanding what responsibilities they now have toward their parents. A common attitude in the Bahamas, where I live, is for parents to expect their grown children, even those who are married, to support them financially and in other ways on an ongoing basis. After all, it is only right for children to "repay" their parents in this way for raising and taking care of them. This attitude is not unique to the Bahamas, or even to the third world. To a greater or lesser degree it is found in every culture, particularly in families and ethnic groups where traditional generational ties are very strong.

Is this attitude correct? Are married children responsible for support-ing their parents? To find the answer we need to look to the Bible, the Word of the God who originally designed marriage and the family. Con-sider what Paul, the first-century Christian missionary, theologian, and writer had to say:

> *Now I am ready to visit you for the third time, and I will not be a burden to you, because what I want is not your possessions but you. After all, children should not have to save up for their parents, but parents for their children* (2 Corinthians 12:14).

 True independence works both ways: Children are not dependent on their parents, and parents are not dependent on their children.

Although in context Paul was referring to the believers in the church in Corinth as his spiritual "children," the principle applies also in the realm of human family relations: "Children should not have to save up for their par-ents, but parents for their children." Paul pledged to the Corinthian church that he would not be a burden to them when he visited. In the same manner, parents should not be a burden to their children, either financially or in any other way. On the contrary, this verse says that parents should "save up" for their children. Parents have the responsibility to support their children and do everything they can to prepare the way for their children to become mature, productive, and independent adults. True independence works both ways: Children are not dependent on their parents, and parents are not dependent on their children.

Adjusting to married life is challenging enough without the couple feel-ing the pressure of guilt or custom to support their parents. They need the freedom to establish their own home, set up their own budget, and determine their own priorities. This does not mean that they should have no concern for their parents' welfare. If their parents are truly in need, and if the couple genuinely has the means to help, fine. The decision to help should be a choice freely made by the couple together, however, and not imposed on them from outside as a custom or expectation.

At the same time, the Bible clearly indicates that children do bear some responsibility for the welfare of their parents, particularly those who are widowed or who have no legitimate means of caring for themselves. Jesus Himself, even while hanging on the Cross, made a point as the eldest son of His earthly family to commit His mother into the care of John, His disciple and close friend (see Jn. 19:26-27). James speaks of believers' responsibility to "look after orphans and widows in their distress" (Jas. 1:27b). Orphans and widows represented the lowest and most powerless classes of society in that day—people who had no one to speak for them. Although James' instructions are to the Church as a whole, undoubtedly some of these orphans and widows had children or other relatives in the Church.

In the fifth chapter of First Timothy, Paul provides practical counsel for dealing with a specific situation involving widows.

> *Give proper recognition to those widows who are really in need. But if a widow has children or grandchildren, these should learn first of all to put their religion into practice by caring for their own family and so repaying their parents and grandparents, for this is pleasing to God....If anyone does not provide for his relatives, and especially for his immediate family, he has denied the faith and is worse than an unbeliever* (1 Timothy 5:3-4,8).

The Church in this case had a responsibility and ministry to care for widows who were "really in need." These were women who without their husbands had no one else to care for them. Many of these men may have died as martyrs for their faith. Persecution could have so greatly swollen the ranks of widows who needed help that the resources of the church were severely taxed. Paul said that the Church's primary responsibility was to those widows who had no one—not even children or grandchildren—to take care of them. Widows who had children or grandchildren in the Church were the responsibility of those children or grandchildren.

In other words, children or grandchildren are responsible under God for caring for parents or grandparents who, because of health, destitution, or other reasons, *cannot care for themselves.* Parents who are healthy and possess the means of supporting themselves should not become burdens to their children. Children, on the other hand, have the responsibility to provide for the welfare of parents who can no longer provide for themselves.

Establish Relationship Parameters up Front

Much conflict and confusion between a married couple and their respective families could be avoided by simply taking the time at the beginning to establish clear parameters for how these families will relate to each other, and making sure that everyone involved understands those parameters. This is one important purpose of the engagement period. Engagement is not only to provide time for the couple to get to know each other and to plan their wedding, but to allow members of the two families involved to get acquainted as well.

A married couple should take time at the beginning of their marriage to establish clear parameters for how their families will relate to each other, and make sure that everyone involved understands those parameters.

During the engagement the couple should thoroughly discuss their philosophies of life and agree on the principles that will guide their marriage. They should share their dreams, identify their goals, and plan their strategy for realizing those dreams and goals. They should come to a mutual understanding regarding financial planning, including investments, savings, and an ongoing household budget. Everything the couple does during this planning period should be for the purpose of establishing safeguards to protect both them and their marriage.

It is important for the members of both families to understand that this marriage will create a new, separate family, resulting in certain fundamental changes in the way the couple relates to them. Let's consider a couple of common scenarios that can cause great problems for everyone if not handled correctly.

Suppose that prior to getting married a young man (let's call him John) has had a good job and has helped his parents out with their bills and other expenses. There is nothing particularly unusual about this arrangement, particularly if he was living at home. If his parents have come to rely on his financial assistance, his upcoming marriage may create a crisis for them. What will they do? How will they make it if their son no longer helps out?

One day not long after the wedding John receives a phone call from his mother. "John," she says, "you've always been so good to help out when we needed it. Our light bill is coming due and we're a little short of money. Can you help out?" At this point John has three choices. He can say no, he can say yes, or he can say, "Let me talk it over with Sarah" (his wife). "We'll have to see if it will fit in with our budget."

If John values his relationship with his mother, he probably will not give her a flat "no." If he values peace and harmony in his marriage he will not give her an immediate "yes." If he is smart, he will discuss her request with Sarah before making a final decision. Since John and Sarah worked out their financial plan together and established their budget together, they need to decide together on any changes to their plan. Their first priority is the strength and stability of their own home and circumstances. If their budget allows them to assist with his mother's light bill, and they both agree to it, fine. Then, the help is coming from both of them, and not just from "mama's little boy." If not, then they need to tell her gently but clearly, "I'm sorry, but we cannot help this time."

When John and Sarah married, they became each other's number one priority. If they have established this understanding up front with each other and with their parents, they will avoid a lot of heartache and hurt feelings.

Another common problem newlyweds sometimes face is when parents or other family just "drop in" uninvited and make themselves at home, or offer unsolicited opinions or advice. There are times when married couples simply want to be alone together, and during such times nothing cranks up the tension level as much as the unexpected arrival of family.

Suppose John's mother and sister drop in uninvited. Sister goes immediately to the refrigerator and helps herself to some leftovers. John's mother looks at the new rug on the floor and says, "I don't like that rug. I think you ought to get another one." At this point, John is in a dilemma. He doesn't want to hurt his mother or his sister, yet Sarah is standing quietly at one side of the room fuming. John's sister has invaded her house unannounced and raided her refrigerator uninvited. What's even worse, John's mother has just criticized the new rug that Sarah picked out herself, thereby criticizing Sarah and her sense of taste. A potential explosion is brewing.

The situation may not blow up while John's mother and sister are there, but it will after they leave. If Sarah complains, John may become defensive and make matters worse. After all, this is *his* family she is criticizing. Unless John deals with the problem, Sarah's resentment may grow until the next time she sees his mother and sister, when she "tells them off." This is guaranteed to poison Sarah's relationship with John's family.

In this kind of disagreement the worst thing to do is to let the opposite partner confront the family. The right thing is for *John* to go to his mother and sister and say, "I don't appreciate your coming over unannounced. Mom, your comment about the rug was uncalled for and it hurt Sarah's feelings. Sis, you have no right to just help yourself to our food when you come over." They may get angry and pout for awhile, but at least John is *family*, and by confronting the issue with them himself he has protected Sarah and removed her as the focus of their anger and resentment.

These are only two examples of common problems involving a married couple's relationship to their families, but the principle should be clear.

A husband's top priority is to protect his wife and a wife's, her husband. Together they are committed to protecting each other, preserving their marriage, and cultivating their companionship. Loosing the ties that bind a husband and wife to their families is not always easy but it is necessary. Establishing parameters in advance for the loosening of those ties will make the process easier for everyone and give a new marriage one of those "pluses" that is so important for success.

PRINCIPLES

1. The husband/wife relationship is the primary human relationship.

2. The husband and wife relationship is foundational and the key to every other relationship in life.

3. Leaving home is a fundamental principle of marriage.

4. Companionship is the basis for all successful marriage.

5. Companionship in marriage is more important than circumstances of blood or birth.

6. Parents who are healthy and possess the means of supporting themselves should not become burdens to their children. Children, on the other hand, have the responsibility to provide for the welfare of parents who can no longer provide for themselves.

7. At the beginning of a marriage, the couple should establish clear parameters for how their families will relate to each other.

8. A husband's top priority is to protect his wife and a wife's, her husband. Together they are committed to protecting each other, preserving their marriage, and cultivating their companionship.

CHAPTER SEVEN

Vive la Difference!

Let's face it, men and women are different. There is no doubt about it. Although the obvious physical differences have been noted and appreciated from the very beginning, it is only in the last generation or so that the essential psychological and emotional differences between men and women have been identified and confirmed scientifically.

The male and female of the human species are "wired" differently. They do not think, speak, or act the same way in response to the same stimuli. Men and women send, receive, and process information differently. Because they view the world through different mental and emotional "filters," men and women can look at the same thing and see completely different aspects. They can be exposed to the same information and draw totally dissimilar conclusions. They can examine the same data and yet be poles apart in how they interpret that data.

Needless to say, this fundamental difference in the way men and women think and act lies at the heart of much of the conflict, confusion, and misunderstanding that has occurred between the sexes for centuries. Communication problems between men and women are so commonplace as to be proverbial. Does this sound familiar? "I just don't understand him (or her). Whenever we try to talk, it's as though we are on different wavelengths." Have you ever heard anyone say, "Isn't that just like a woman!" or "He's acting just like a man!"

As with anything else, knowledge can banish confusion where male/female relations are concerned. Understanding not only that men and women *are* different but also *how* they are different is vital to improving male/female communication and relationships at every level. This knowledge is particularly critical for young couples who want to ensure that their marriage has the greatest chances of success and happiness.

In the beginning, God created man as a spirit and placed that spirit in two flesh and blood "houses"—male and female. This "joining" of the male and female "houses" is the *only* God-ordained method for producing *new* "houses." The basic purpose of male and female "houses" is to produce new houses.

A spirit has no gender. Whether man or woman, all members of the human race have the same spirit, the same essence. Males and females, however, have biological and psychological differences according to God's design. He made the male house different from the female house because they have different functions.

 The male is "wired" for logic. The female, on the other hand, is "wired" for emotional response.

Males and females have different chemical and hormonal balances which cause them to think and behave differently. Because God intended for the male to be the head of the family unit, He endowed him chemically and hormonally for logical thinking. The male is "wired" for logic. The female, on the other hand, is "wired" for emotional response. Her body's chemical and hormonal balance sets her up to operate from a feelings-based center. Because both genders have both male and female hormones, "logical" males have an "emotional" side and "emotional" females have a "logical" side. In general, however, males and females view the world according to how they are wired—males from a logical center and females from an emotional center.

Fifteen Essential Differences Between Men and Women

Many husbands and wives suffer needlessly from confusion, misunderstanding, and hurt feelings simply because they do not understand each other's fundamental differences. Let's consider fifteen specific ways that men and women differ, all of which can have a profound effect on how they relate to each other, particularly in the context of marriage. These fifteen statements are not intended to lump all men and women indiscriminately into one group or the other—there are always exceptions to every rule—but they are *generally* true of most men and women with regard to their psychological and emotional makeup.

1. A man is a logical thinker while a woman is an emotional feeler.

To be logical means to think in a reasoned, organized, and orderly manner. A logical thinker has an analytical mind that works like a computer, processing and evaluating information in a precise and predictable pattern. If one plus one equals two, then two cut in half is two ones; that's logic. In general, that's the way men think. They look for the facts and act accordingly.

Women are emotional. They approach issues more from feelings than from reason. This is not a bad thing. Being emotionally centered is neither better nor worse than being logical; it is just different. Another way of looking at it is to say that a man leads with his mind while a woman leads with her heart.

While logic and emotion might seem incompatible on the surface, in reality they complement each other very well. What kind of world would this be if everyone was exclusively logical? Life would be rather empty, with no spirit, no passion, no fire, and little or no art. At the same time, emotion without logic would result in life without order. Both logic and emotion are necessary, not only for fulfillment but for survival. This reveals the brilliance of God's design.

 A man leads with his mind while a woman leads with her heart.

Here's an example. John and Sarah are standing in their living room and John notices that an armchair is blocking easy access to the air conditioner. He says, "That chair is in the way. We need to move it." He is thinking logically. At the same time, Sarah is thinking how nicely the chair offsets the couch and the curtains and how beautiful a vase of flowers would look on the end table next to it. She is thinking emotionally. Neither viewpoint is right or wrong, or better or worse than the other one. They are just different. If John and Sarah understand that they view the same situation in two different ways, they can reach a common consensus.

In general, men are logical and women are emotional.

2. For a woman, language spoken is an expression of what she is feeling. For a man, language spoken is an expression of what he is thinking.

A woman says what is on her heart while a man says what is on his mind. This is another expression of the emotion/logic dichotomy between the ways women and men think. Women are emotional feelers and their spoken words need to be understood from that frame of reference. Men are logical, and their words often do not adequately express their true feelings. Both may have similar thoughts or feelings but will express them in different ways. Unless they understand this difference, a married couple will experience communication problems.

 A woman says what is on her heart while a man says what is on his mind.

Let's suppose that John has promised to pick up Sarah at 5:00, right after work. John is running late and the later he gets the more steamed Sarah becomes. She is pacing and sweating and fuming and rehearsing in her mind the speech she will give John when she sees him.

John finally pulls up at 6:00. Giving Sarah a sheepish grin he says, "Hi. I'm sorry I'm late." John really means it; he *is* sorry he's late. He's telling Sarah what he's thinking. He may have trouble showing how sorry he is, but at least he thought enough to apologize. Ignoring John's words, Sarah slides into the passenger seat, slams the door and sits right up next to it, as far away from John as possible. She says nothing as John drives off.

After several minutes of complete silence, John asks, "What's wrong?" As far as he is concerned the matter is finished. He was late, he apologized, end of story. Everybody has a right to be late once in awhile. That's his logical thinking at work.

"Nothing's wrong," Sarah snaps.

After several more minutes of silence, John tries again. "Why don't we go out for dinner? I'll take you to a really nice place."

"No. I don't want to go out."

Pulling up to a florist, John makes another attempt. "I just want to run in here and get some flowers."

"For who? If you loved me that much you'd have been there at 5:00 like you said you would."

Through all of this, John should not listen to what Sarah is saying as much as listen to how she is feeling. Sometimes when a person tries to tell how he or she feels, the words don't come out right. Logical John needs to understand emotional Sarah. At the same time, Sarah needs to realize that John has already said what was on his mind. They both have a responsibility to understand what lies beyond spoken words and minister to each other.

3. Language that is heard by a woman is an emotional experience. Language that is heard by a man is the receiving of information.

When a woman speaks, although she may be expressing what she feels, a man will usually hear it as information, often on an impersonal level. When a man speaks, even if he is simply saying what's on his mind, a woman will usually receive his words at a much deeper personal and emotional level.

It is easy to see how conflict could develop because of this. John offers to take Sarah out for dinner, but she says, "No. I don't want to go out." John hears that as information: "Okay, she doesn't want to go out." The problem is that Sarah is saying what she is feeling, not what she is thinking. Sarah is thinking, "I'm so mad at you. You kept me waiting for an hour and now you have the nerve to suggest we go to dinner as though nothing happened? Not so fast, mister."

 Hearing is not the same as understanding. What one person says may not be what the other person hears.

Because John receives spoken language as information, he has completely missed the deeper level of where Sarah is emotionally. She, on the other hand, interprets his words as shallow, uncaring, and inadequate. Both are sincerely trying to communicate but are not connecting because they do not understand each other's frame of reference.

Hearing is not the same as understanding. What one person says may not be what the other person hears. That is why communication is such an art. Husbands need to remember that every word they say will be received by their wives as an emotional experience. Wives need to keep in mind that every word they say will be received by their husbands as information. In order to understand each other better, husbands and wives both should learn to think in terms of how the other receives and interprets their words, and speak accordingly.

4. Women tend to take everything personally. Men tend to take everything impersonally.

This difference is directly related to the way men and women are "wired": Men are logical thinkers and women are emotional feelers. A woman interprets everything from an emotional perspective while a man is looking for information. John may remark to Sarah, "Honey, I don't like the way your hair looks today." He is imparting information and even though he includes the qualifier "today," Sarah doesn't hear that. All she hears is "I don't like the way your hair looks." What John offered as information Sarah interprets emotionally, and becomes angry and hurt. As a result, she may rush off to the hairdresser and get a new cut or a new style, and all the while John is wondering why she is making such a big deal of the whole thing. It is because she took it personally.

Sarah may say to John, "Those pants don't look good on you. They are not hanging right." John's response may be, "Okay, no big deal. I'll change it tomorrow when I change clothes." He has received her criticism as information, and has filed it away in his mind like a computer. He may take action in response to her comment but he doesn't take it personally.

Because women tend to take everything personally, men need to learn to be careful what they say to women and how they say it. A woman will remember an irritating action or an offhand comment for years. On the other hand, because men take things impersonally, women must be careful in how they interpret men's responses to what they say. Just because a man does not react emotionally in the same way as a woman does not mean that he has no feelings or that he does not care. He is looking for information and trying to determine an appropriate way to respond.

5. Women are interested in the details—the "nitty-gritty." Men are interested in the principle—the abstract or the philosophy.

Sarah asks John, "How was your day?" and he answers, "Fine." That's not the kind of answer Sarah was looking for. She wants to hear the step-by-step, moment-by-moment details of John's day. She isn't trying to pry; that's just the way she thinks. John's simple response reflects the way he thinks: "I had a good day, it was great. Now, let's move on to something else." He is focusing on the principle (he had a good day) not on the nitty-gritty details (I did this and that and thus and so).

Suppose John invites another couple to come over for dinner. He is focusing on the principle that he wants to be hospitable to his friends. As soon as he tells Sarah, she immediately looks at all the details. What will we fix for dinner? What dishes should we use? How should we set the table? What about that ragged carpet in the living room? The drapes are dirty; can we get them cleaned? What about that spot on the wall?

All John is thinking about is hosting their friends for a fun evening. He isn't worrying about the drapes or the dirty wall or the ragged carpet or the dishes. A simple principle for him may be an ordeal of details for Sarah.

Leaders need to think in principles and concepts, not the nitty-gritty details. Managers and company presidents don't have time to focus on the details. Their responsibility is to consider the principles, the philosophy of where the company is going, and to determine goals. A leader sets the vision and direction, and those under the leader work out the details to accomplish the vision. Under God's design for the home, the husband sets the vision and direction—the principles. That is his gift and role. The wife is gifted to know how to bring the vision to fruition—the details. Together it is a powerful combination.

6. In material things, women tend to look at goals only. Men want to know the details of how to get there.

Sarah dreams of all the different things she would like to have for herself and her family: some new jewelry, a new refrigerator, a new car, a new house. While John may have the same dreams and desires, he may not voice them as plainly because, in his logical and analytical way of thinking, he focuses on the practical aspects and challenges of those dreams. How are we going to do this? Where are we going to get the money? Will our budget allow for a new refrigerator right now? Do we have the means to buy a new car?

It's easy to see how this could create conflict and misunderstanding in a marriage. Sarah gets upset and angry because John does not seem to share her dream with the same level of enthusiasm as she. In her opinion he is dragging his feet as if he does not really care whether or not they realize their dreams. At the same time, John is frustrated with Sarah because she does not seem to understand the financial realities. "What is it with this woman? Does she think money grows on trees?" It's not that John doesn't share what Sarah's dreams; he is concerned with the practical nuts-and-bolts details of how to make those dreams come true.

 In material things, women focus on the what and men focus on the how.

In material things women are concerned with goals and men are concerned with getting there. To state it another way, women focus on the what and men focus on the how.

7. In spiritual or intangible things, men look at goals. Women want to know how to get there.

In the spiritual realm, men focus on the goal while women want to know the details. Once again, this difference between men and women is part of God's design. Spiritually, the husband is supposed to be the head of the home, and therefore needs to know the direction, the goals, and the objectives for the spiritual growth and development of the family. The wife is interested in the details, the specifics of how they are going to reach their spiritual goals. This is the exact opposite of the material realm. In this case, men focus on the what and women focus on the how.

John tells Sarah that their goal as a family is to grow close to the Lord. That is the vision, the principle. When Sarah asks "How?" John proposes, "Let's have prayer with each other and with the children every morning before work, and an hour of Bible study together every evening." That is a good plan and bears fruit as long as they follow it. If John reaches a point where he does not follow through, Sarah will become frustrated.

 In spiritual things, men focus on the what and women focus on the how.

Failure of men to take and maintain the spiritual lead in their homes and marriages is one of the biggest problems in the family today. Countless wives have been forced by default to assume the spiritual leadership in their homes because their husbands either will not or cannot carry out that role. This is not as it should be. Wives can be of great value in helping plan the specifics for reaching marriage and family spiritual goals, but the husband should be the visionary, the one who determines the direction and sets the pace.

8. A man's mind is like a filing cabinet. A woman's mind is like a computer.

Show a man a problem or a task that needs to be done and he will take the information, file it away in his mind, close the drawer, and deal with it when he can. In the meantime, he continues with other things. A woman will identify a problem or a task and, like a computer that is running all the time, not relax until the problem is dealt with or the task completed.

Sarah comes to John and says, "The bathroom walls need to be painted." John answers, "Okay," and files the information away. He doesn't forget about it, but is waiting until a better or more appropriate time to do it. As far as John is concerned, the matter is at rest. Sarah identified the task, passed it on to John, and he has processed the information. He *will* do it.

Two days go by. Sarah says, "The bathroom walls still haven't been painted." Her mind will not rest on this subject until the job is done. John, however, is a little annoyed by her reminder. "I know. I haven't forgotten. I'll do it. Just give me some time." A wife should be sensitive to her husband's "filing cabinet" approach to thinking, and give him room to do the things he has said he will do. A husband, on the other hand, should be sensitive to the way his wife's mind works, and try to respond in as timely a manner as possible. This involves a fair amount of give-and-take on both sides.

9. A woman's home is an extension of her personality. A man's job is an extension of his personality.

It's easy for a woman to get wrapped up in her home and her husband not understand why, and for a man to get caught up in his work and his wife be just as puzzled. A woman can work for years and never become attached to her job. It is different with a man. His job becomes a part of him, a part of his self-identity. A man's career is an extension of his personality. A woman can detach herself from her job and immerse herself in her home. A man will often bring his job home with him, at least in his mind and attitude, if not physically. John's job is to him a symbol of his manhood, his self-worth, and his ability to provide for Sarah and their children. Sarah should be sensitive to this and careful never to berate or belittle John with regard to his work. If she criticizes his job or career choice, she is criticizing him.

In the same way, a woman's home is an extension of her personality. Anything that touches a woman's home touches her, because her home represents who she is and how she sees herself. That's why a woman normally is very sensitive about the condition and appearance of her home. Quite often, husbands do not adequately understand this. They do not fully appreciate how important the physical aspects of their residence are to their wives' sense of pride and self-esteem. When a woman talks about her house, she is talking about herself. If Sarah tells John they need new living room curtains, he needs to be sensitive to what she is really saying. The curtains may look fine to him, but Sarah may see things that he misses. For her sake John needs to learn to see their house through her eyes and not just his own.

10. Men can be nomadic. Women need security and roots.

A woman needs to be constantly reassured that she is grounded and secure in her marriage relationship. She needs to be continually affirmed that she is the most important person in her husband's life. He needs to tell her regularly and often that he loves her. It's not enough for him to assume that she knows this; she needs to hear it. It's not that she does not believe or trust her husband, it's just the way she is made. A man does not need the same kind of emotional stroking as a woman.

 Constant reassurance brings security.

A man is like a camel, in that he can take one "drink" and go for a long time. A woman is like the deer of Psalm 42:1 that "pants for streams of water." She needs a "drink" more often. Because of their nomadic nature, men usually find it easier to be by themselves than women do. Wives often have trouble understanding that there are times when their husbands simply want to be alone for awhile. If a wife is in the least bit insecure in her relationship with her husband, she may read this as rejection or as a sign that she no longer satisfies him. That's why he needs to be sensitive and careful to reassure her of his love through both his words and his actions. Constant reassurance brings security.

Most men can pull up stakes and move around easily, but women need roots. They want to be settled. It's easy for a guy to just pick up and change, but it's not as easy for a woman, because she is an emotional feeler and becomes more attached to places and things than a man does. With this in mind, a husband needs to be aware that he cannot simply get up and move without considering his wife's need for the security of "settled-ness."

11. Women tend to be guilt prone. Men tend to be resentful.

Because of her emotion-centered base a woman is prone to blame herself and take responsibility for anything that goes wrong in a relationship, even if it is not really her fault. Sometimes she will even rehearse over and over in her head a list of reasons why she is to blame. Many women walk around every day under a cloud of guilt that quite often they have placed there themselves and which is usually unjustified. When problems arise in their relationships women tend to second-guess themselves. "What did I say to make him mad? What could I have done to keep us from fighting?" Many times it is not the woman's fault at all, but she still has trouble accepting that.

A man is different. When something goes wrong in a relationship he will resent the woman or even another man before he will acknowledge his own responsibility. Many men will do almost anything to avoid carrying around a sense of personal guilt. They would rather lash out in anger than accept blame.

These two responses are opposites and feed off of each other. A man will refuse to accept his guilt while a woman will take upon herself even guilt that is not her own. She then becomes an object of the man's resentment and anger, an easy target for his spite as he acts out against the guilt that he refuses to bear. Married couples need to be very watchful and wary of these tendencies because they can destroy a relationship more quickly than almost anything else.

12. Men are stable and level off. Women are always changing.

Once again, this difference between men and women is due to the specific chemical and hormonal balances in their bodies and the particular frame of reference—logical or emotional—from which they operate. Many men would say that few things aggravate them as much as a woman who is always changing her mind. Women, on the other hand, would argue that men often seem to be unfazed—even cold or callous—no matter what happens. This is primarily a difference in perspective.

In general, a man can make a decision and stick with it, even to the point of stubbornness. A woman may tell him one thing and then a few minutes later say, "I've changed my mind." Neither trait is better or worse than the other; they merely reveal the different ways that men's and women's mental processes work.

Suppose that John and Sarah are preparing to go to a banquet. John chooses his gray suit and puts it on. Now he waits as Sarah tries first her blue dress, then her red dress, then her lavender dress…and finally settles on the blue dress she tried on first. Like her home, Sarah's clothes make a personal statement. Everything has to be perfect; she has to look just right.

All the while John is fidgeting and thinking, *Choose something, for Pete's sake, and let's go!* As long as his suit is clean and his tie is straight he's fine.

 Stability and spontaneity—both are important for a healthy and fulfilling relationship.

Another way to look at this difference is to say that men are more stable or stolid while women are more spontaneous. Stability and spontaneity—both are important for a healthy and fulfilling relationship. Stability provides necessary grounding while spontaneity injects a healthy dose of adventure.

13. Women tend to become involved more easily and more quickly than men do. Men tend to stand back and evaluate before they get involved.

Because they are emotionally centered, women are more apt than men to involve themselves quickly in a cause or movement or project. Women tend to lead with their hearts. They see a need or recognize a noble or worthy cause that touches their hearts, and off they go. Logic-driven men, however, lead with their minds, and tend to hold themselves aloof and apart, carefully observing and evaluating before they commit themselves. Because of their logical focus men tend to be skeptical and must analyze something from every direction before joining themselves to it. Although it may take a man longer to come around, once he makes a decision he is every bit as committed as a woman. Men and women may travel by different roads but eventually they arrive at the same destination.

 Reason and emotion complement each other.

Here again the genius of God's design is revealed. Reason and emotion complement each other. Together they bring completeness to life and faith. Logic without passion is dry, austere, and lifeless. Passion without logic lacks order and stability. Married couples who understand and appreciate the inter-connectedness of logic and emotion have a much higher probability of building a stable marriage characterized by strength, love, and a passionate zest for life.

14. Men need to be told again and again. Women never forget.

A man's mind is like a filing cabinet; anything spoken to him he files away for later retrieval. Just because he doesn't act on it immediately does not mean he has forgotten or ignored what he was told. He has simply filed it away. That's why it so often seems as though a man needs to be told or reminded again and again. A woman's mind is like a computer that never forgets anything, but keeps it ready for immediate recall on demand. Women never forget anything they say to a man or anything that a man says to them, and they also make sure that he doesn't forget.

Either of these qualities may be negative or positive depending on the situation. Because they tend to receive things impersonally, men are more apt to overlook or forget disparaging comments made by them or to them. Generally, men are less prone to hold a grudge. However, on the negative side, this "forgetfulness" can cause men to become terribly insensitive and unresponsive to the needs of their wives and children.

Because a woman receives everything emotionally and holds words and feelings close to her heart, she is naturally more sensitive and responsive to the needs she sees around her. On the down side, a woman's tendency to remember everything and take everything personally can cause her to allow a hurt or an insult or an offense to fester and grow for weeks, months, and even years, creating continual stress, anger, and heartache.

How can husbands and wives deal with these differences effectively in their relationships? Husbands must be careful what they say and how they say it, remembering the wise counsel of the Book of Proverbs: "A gentle answer turns away wrath, but a harsh word stirs up anger" (Prov. 15:1). Wives should temper their remembering with grace, in accordance with the words of Paul: "[Love] is not easily angered, it keeps no record of wrongs" (1 Cor. 13:5b).

15. Men tend to remember the gist of things rather than the details. Women tend to remember the details and sometimes distort the gist.

This is akin to the old "he said, she said" controversy. Men tend to remember conversations or events in general overview, while women recall specific details with laser-like precision. Women sometimes accuse men of hedging on what they said they would do when in reality the men simply cannot recall the specifics of the conversation. Men are clear on the gist of what was said, but the details are less important. Women are sharp on the details but sometimes not as clear in remembering the gist.

Both tendencies can distort the truth. Recalling the gist without the details is like trying to describe an elephant seen dimly in a fog: "All I know is, it was big." Fixating on the details is like four blindfolded people in a room trying to describe that same elephant from touch alone. One touches the leg, another the trunk, the third the tail, and the fourth an ear. Their descriptions will be quite different from each other.

This difference in the manner of recall between men and women is one of the most basic causes for communication problems between them. Sarah reminds John of a previous conversation and he admits, "Yes, I think I did say something like that."

"No," Sarah replies, "that is *exactly* what you said."

"Well, that's not what I meant."

"Maybe not, but that's what you said."

John remembers the gist of the conversation and Sarah remembers the specifics. This kind of communication confusion is summed up pretty well in the statement: "I know you think you understand what you thought I said, but I'm not sure you realize that what you heard is not what I meant."

As always, patience and understanding go a long way in relieving the tension and stress created by the natural differences that distinguish men and women and the way they think.

~

A common complaint in male/female relationship problems is "You just don't understand me" or, in other words, "You want me to be just like you." That is simply not the way things are, and we should not wish it otherwise. Men and women are different, and thank God that they are.

A husband should not expect or desire his wife to start thinking in the logical and analytically centered way he does. Likewise, a wife should not look to her husband to see things through her emotional framework. Both should learn to value and celebrate the vital differences that God has built into each gender of the creature called *man*.

Look how those differences complement each other. A world of logic without feelings would be a world populated by mindless and heartless computers. God did not create computers. He created man—male and female—and endowed them with all the varied and complementary qualities that are necessary for rich and full living.

Men and women are not the same, and for good reason. Celebrate the difference!

PRINCIPLES

1. A man is a logical thinker while a woman is an emotional feeler.

2. For a woman, language spoken is an expression of what she is feeling. For a man, language spoken is an expression of what he is thinking.

3. Language that is heard by a woman is an emotional experience. Language that is heard by a man is the receiving of information.

4. Women tend to take everything personally. Men tend to take everything impersonally.

5. Women are interested in the details—the "nitty-gritty." Men are interested in the principle—the abstract or the philosophy.

6. In material things, women tend to look at goals only. Men want to know the details of how to get there.

7. In spiritual or intangible things, men look at goals. Women want to know how to get there.

8. A man's mind is like a filing cabinet. A woman's mind is like a computer.

9. A woman's home is an extension of her personality. A man's job is an extension of his personality.

10. Men can be nomadic. Women need security and roots.

11. Women tend to be guilt prone. Men tend to be resentful.

12. Men are stable and level off. Women are always changing.

13. Women tend to become involved more easily and more quickly than men do. Men tend to stand back and evaluate before they get involved.

14. Men need to be told again and again. Women never forget.

15. Men tend to remember the gist of things rather than the details. Women tend to remember the details and sometimes distort the gist.

CHAPTER EIGHT

Friendship: The Highest Relationship of All

The husband/wife relationship is the oldest and most preeminent of all human relationships. It predates and goes ahead of any other relationship, including parent/child, mother/daughter, father/son, and sister/brother. No relationship should be closer, more personal, or more intimate than that which exists between a husband and wife. Such intimacy involves not only love but also knowledge. A husband and wife should know each other better than they know anyone else in the world. They should know each other's likes and dislikes, their quirks and pet peeves, their strengths and weaknesses, their good and bad qualities, their gifts and talents, their prejudices and blind spots, their graces and their character flaws. In short, a husband and wife should know everything about each other, even those undesirable traits that they hide from everyone else.

 Relationship does not guarantee knowledge.

This kind of knowledge is not automatic. It does not happen simply because two people get married. Relationship does not guarantee knowledge. One of the greatest problems in marriage or any other human relationship involves the labels we use. Words like "husband" and "wife," "mother" and "daughter," "sister" and "brother," or "father" and "son" describe various relational connections within a family. They also imply a knowledge or intimacy that may or may not exist.

For example, a mother and daughter may assume that they really know each other simply because their "labels" imply a close relationship. Certainly a mother knows her daughter and a daughter, her mother. This is not necessarily so. The same thing could be said of other relational connections. If I call you my brother or my sister I am implying that I already know you. I assume that because we are related there is no need for us to spend time together getting to know each other.

Marriage is a lifelong journey into intimacy, but also into friendship.

Labels that imply closeness and intimate knowledge may in reality hinder true relationship building. A husband and wife may assume that they know each other simply because they are married. As a result, they may do nothing more than scratch the surface, never plumbing the depths of each other's personalities to gain true knowledge and build a deep and intimate relationship.

Marriage is a lifelong journey into intimacy, but also into friendship. A husband and wife should be each other's best friend. There is no higher relationship. After all, who knows us better than our friends? Most of us will share with our friends things about ourselves that we never even tell our own families. Husbands and wives should have no secrets from each other. As their relationship develops they should grow into true friends, who know everything there is to know about each other, good and bad, and yet who love and accept each other anyway.

No Longer Servants, but Friends

From the biblical standpoint, the highest relationship of all is that of "friend." No greater testimony could be given to the life of a biblical personality than to say that he or she was a "friend of God." Abraham fit that description: " 'Abraham believed God, and it was credited to him as righteousness,' and he was called God's friend" (Jas. 2:23b). Moses was another who knew God as a friend: "The Lord would speak to Moses face to face, as a man speaks with his friend" (Ex. 33:11a). David, the second king of Israel, was known as a man after God's own heart (see 1 Sam. 13:14). This is another way of saying that David was God's friend.

In the Bible, the highest relationship of all is that of "friend."

Jesus made clear in His teaching the exalted place of friendship. In the 15th chapter of the Gospel of John, after telling His followers that their intimacy with Him was like that of branches to the vine, Jesus linked that intimacy to friendship.

My command is this: Love each other as I have loved you. Greater love has no one than this, that he lay down his life for his friends. You are My friends if you do what I command. I no longer call you servants, because a servant does not know his master's business. Instead, I have called you friends, for everything that I learned from My Father I have made known to you (John 15:12-15).

In these verses Jesus announces that His relationship to His followers is entering a new dimension, rising to a higher level. A fundamental change is occurring in the way they will now relate to one another. Beginning with the command to "Love each other," Jesus then describes that love, declaring that the greatest love of all is where a person is willing to "lay down his life for his friends." Jesus would demonstrate that kind of love the very next day when He went to the cross. It is significant that Jesus said "friends" here and not "family." There is a quality to true friendship that transcends and rises above even the ties of family relationships. In the Old Testament, David, the future king of Israel, and Jonathan, son of Saul, the current king, enjoyed a friendship that was deeper than family. Even as Saul sought David's life, Jonathan protected David because he was "one in spirit with David, and he loved him as himself" (1 Sam. 18:1b).

Jesus next states the new and deeper nature of the relationship: "You are My friends if you do what I command." Obedience is the test of friendship with Jesus; it is also the test of love. Jesus is not looking for obedience based on obligation such as a servant would render, but obedience based on love which grows out of the context of friendship. The first kind of obedience is imposed from without while the second kind is freely chosen from within. There is a world of difference between the two.

 Obedience is the test of friendship with Jesus; it is also the test of love.

In the rest of the passage Jesus draws a clear and sharp contrast between the old and new ways He and His followers will relate to each other. "I no longer call you servants, because a servant does not know his master's business. Instead, I have called you friends, for everything that I learned from my Father I have made known to you." Servants had no freedom of choice. They could not exercise their own will but were bound to do the will of their master. Rarely if ever were they privy to knowledge of the deep and intimate aspects of the life of their master or his family. Although they might live, work, eat, and sleep in their master's house, they knew nothing of his business. It was different with family and friends. They were privileged to walk in his inner circle and share in the most personal dimensions of his life.

Jesus said, "I no longer call you servants...Instead, I have called you friends..." He was telling His followers, "I do not want the kind of relationship where you are committed to Me by obligation. No more slave mentality. You are My friends, and I share everything with My friends—everything I have learned from My Father."

What was Jesus alluding to when He said, "Everything that I learned from My Father I have made known to you"? What did Jesus tell His disciples—His closest friends and followers—that He did not reveal to anyone else? He opened His heart and soul to them. He held nothing back. Jesus spoke to the multitudes in parables but later, in private with His friends, He explained everything clearly and in greater detail (see Mk. 4:33-34). He lived and worked intimately with them for three years, training and preparing them to carry on after He was no longer with them.

 Friends share everything with each other, good or bad, happy or sad.

One important characteristic of friends is that they share everything with each other, good or bad, happy or sad. This quality is what sets friends apart from mere acquaintances and, often, even from family members. From their earliest days together, Jesus shared with His friends all the bad or unpleasant things that would come because of their friendship. He told them that He would be betrayed, arrested, beaten, scourged, and have His beard plucked out. He would be crucified, would die and be buried, and on the third day would rise from the dead. Jesus informed His disciples that because of their friendship with Him they would be hated, despised, persecuted, and even killed. He also assured them that He would be present with them always and that they would live and walk in His power and authority. Jesus hid nothing from them. He pulled no punches and did not hedge His words. This kind of openness and transparency is the mark of true friendship.

Friends Are Open and Honest With Each Other

Jesus wanted His friends to know all of this in advance so that when these things took place they would be prepared. "All this I have told you so that you will not go astray....I have told you this, so that when the time comes you will remember that I warned you" (Jn. 16:1,4a). He did not want them to be taken by surprise.

This illustrates an important truth: Friends are open and honest with each other. Nowhere is this principle more important than in a marriage relationship. One of the big problems in many marriages is that the husband and wife have trouble relating to each other as friends. They are more like "servants" than friends, more like brother and sister than husband and wife. Opening up to each other is just as difficult as opening up to family or to casual acquaintances. Most people do not share their inmost selves with their parents or siblings. They do not speak candidly about their highest dreams or their deepest fears, their greatest virtues or their worst flaws. They will, however, reveal these things to their friends. Friendship between a husband and wife, with its characteristic honesty and openness, is absolutely essential for a happy, successful, and thriving marriage.

Most couples enter married life without having told each other everything about themselves. In some ways this is to be expected. It is impossible at the beginning to be completely open and candid because some things will come out only as the relationship grows over time. Nevertheless, a couple should know as much as possible about each other—good and bad—before they stand together at the marriage altar.

The period of courtship and engagement is very valuable for this purpose. Too often, however, the man and woman will focus all their attention on always being on their best behavior for the other, careful to reveal only their good side. Out of fear of jeopardizing the budding relationship they will tiptoe around problems and avoid any mention of annoying habits or idiosyncrasies they may observe in each other. Unless they learn to be honest with each other at this stage of their relationship, they are in for a rude awakening later when, after they get married, these things inevitably come to light.

 A couple should know as much as possible about each other—good and bad—before they stand together at the marriage altar.

For example, if John has a problem with his temper, he should be honest with Sarah about it, and sooner rather than later. "I really struggle with my temper. I fly off the handle easily. The Lord is working with me about it, but I still have a long way to go. I just wanted to tell you so that whenever my temper flares up you will forgive me and not take it personally." This way, Sarah will not be caught completely off guard the first time John spouts off.

Sarah may struggle with feelings of jealousy or tend to be hypercritical of other people. If she is up-front and aboveboard with John about this they can waylay any misunderstanding before it starts. Together they can work on their problems and help each other grow through them and beyond them.

Obviously, any couple must feel comfortable together if this kind of honesty is to develop. Creating such a relaxed atmosphere depends a great deal on mutual respect and trust. While both of these qualities grow out of love, they also feed and nourish it. In the Bible, friendship and love are closely linked. "A friend loves at all times, and a brother is born for adversity" (Prov. 17:17). "A man of many companions may come to ruin, but there is a friend who sticks closer than a brother" (Prov. 18:24). "His mouth is sweetness itself; he is altogether lovely. This is my lover, this my friend, O daughters of Jerusalem" (Song 5:16).

Marriage is the highest of all human relationships and friendship is the highest level of that relationship. Every married couple should set their sights on rising to that level and never rest until they attain it. Even then they should not stop growing. True friendship has a breadth and a depth that no amount of time or growth can ever exhaust.

 Marriage is the highest of all human relationships and friendship is the highest level of that relationship.

Friendship is the catalyst that ultimately will fuse a husband and wife into one like a precious gem. Marriage is an earthly, fleshly picture of the relationship in the spiritual realm between not only God the Father, God the Son—who is Jesus Christ—and God the Holy Spirit, but also between God and the race of mankind whom He created. Friendship characterizes the perfect unity and intimacy that exists among Father, Son, and Holy Spirit, and was also the nature of the relationship that Adam and Eve enjoyed with God and with each other in the Garden of Eden.

God's desire is to restore the friendship relationship between Himself and humanity that sin destroyed. The modern world desperately needs to see a clear and honest picture of what friendship with God is like. No earthly relationship comes as close to that picture as marriage, and a marriage where the husband and wife are truly friends comes closest of all.

Despite the attacks and challenges of modern society, the institution of marriage will last as long as human life on earth remains. God ordained and established marriage and it will endure until He brings all things in the physical realm to their close. No matter how much social and moral attitudes may change, marriage will remain, rock-solid as always, the best idea in human relationships ever to come down the pike, because it is God's idea.

Marriage is *still* a *great* idea!

PRINCIPLES

1. A husband and wife should be each other's best friend. There is no higher relationship.

2. True friendship transcends and rises above even the ties of family relationships.

3. Openness and transparency are marks of true friendship.

4. Friends are open and honest with each other.

5. Friendship between a husband and wife, with its characteristic honesty and openness, is absolutely essential for a happy, successful, and thriving marriage.

6. Friendship is the catalyst that ultimately will fuse a husband and wife into one like a precious gem.

~PART TWO~

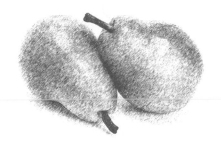

Understanding Love™
and the Secrets of the Heart

~ CHAPTER ONE ~

This Thing Called Love

A poet once wrote, "To love is to live, and to live is to love." That may be true, but what does it mean? The poet never defined his terms. What is this thing called "love"?

Probably no other dimension of human experience has been pondered, discussed, debated, analyzed, and dreamed about more than the nature of true love. Love is everywhere—in our songs and in our books, on our televisions and on our movie screens. Talk of love is always on the tips of our tongues, never far from our thoughts or our conversation.

Yet, for all our thinking and talking, for all our discussing and debating, how many of us truly understand love? Do we really know what true love is? Francois, Duc de La Rochefoucauld, a 17th-century French author and moralist, made an astute observation when he wrote, "True love is like ghosts, which everybody talks about and few have seen."

Where can we turn for genuine knowledge in matters of true love? The world offers many different concepts of love, but are they reliable? Western popular culture tends to equate love with warm feelings, physical attraction, and sexual activity. This view of love is hammered into our brains every day through the books and magazines we read, the songs we listen to, and the movies and television shows we watch. The epidemic of broken relationships, failed marriages, and sundered families that characterize so much of our modern society should tell us that something is terribly wrong with the way we look at love.

The best way to learn anything is to consult an expert. If we wish to improve our golf game, we go to a golf pro; if we desire to play the piano, we study under a qualified teacher. Who is the expert on love? No one understands love better than God. Not only did God *create* love and establish it as a central foundation stone of human experience, but according to the Bible, God Himself *is* love (see 1 Jn. 4:8,16). Love defines God's very nature.

 Love defines God's very nature.

What then does God say about love? Contrary to the common assumption of the world in general, love as presented in the Bible is not primarily an emotion, but an attitude of the heart. Emotions are not subject to command; no one can be ordered how to feel about a certain person or thing. Yet, throughout the Bible the Lord *commands* His people to love. Biblical love is a command. Consider these examples:

Love the Lord your God with all your heart and with all your soul and with all your strength (Deuteronomy 6:5).

Do not seek revenge or bear a grudge against one of your people, but love your neighbor as yourself. I am the Lord (Leviticus 19:18).

But I tell you: Love your enemies and pray for those who persecute you (Matthew 5:44).

A new command I give you: Love one another. As I have loved you, so you must love one another (John 13:34).

My command is this: Love each other as I have loved you (John 15:12).

Let no debt remain outstanding, except the continuing debt to love one another, for he who loves his fellowman has fulfilled the law (Romans 13:8).

The entire law is summed up in a single command: "Love your neighbor as yourself" (Galatians 5:14).

Jesus replied: " 'Love the Lord your God with all your heart and with all your soul and with all your mind.' This is the first and greatest commandment. And the second is like it: 'Love your neighbor as yourself.' All the Law and the Prophets hang on these two commandments" (Matthew 22:37-40).

If we are commanded to love, how do we carry it out? What does it mean to love God? What does it mean to love another person? These are very important questions that cut right to the heart of meaningful relationships. So many relationships today fail because of an inadequate concept and understanding of love.

Love is not primarily an emotion, but an attitude of the heart.

Part of the problem, at least in the English-speaking world, is the limitations of our language. In English we have only one basic word for love, and we therefore use it to describe our feelings or attitude toward a wide range of objects. We say, "I love cheesecake," or "I love my dog," but we also say, "I love my children," and "I love my wife," or "I love my husband." We "love" to go to the beach or to the park or somewhere else. In all of these cases we use the same word "love" to describe feelings and attitudes that are vastly different in scope and degree. Hopefully, our "love" for cheesecake is not on the same par as our love for our children or spouse!

Many other languages are not as restrictive as English in their words for love, particularly Hebrew and Greek, the original languages of the Bible. The ancient Greeks used four different words for love—*phileo, storge, eros,* and *agape*—with each word identifying a separate and distinct type or degree of love. Only two of these words—*phileo* and *agape*—are actually found in the New Testament, but examining all four "loves" will help us better understand what true love *is* as well as what it is *not*.

Phileo: THE LOVE OF FRIENDSHIP

Taking its root meaning from the related word *philos,* which means "friend," *phileo* is the most general term in Greek for love. It refers to the love that one has for a friend or acquaintance. *Phileo* is love on the level of casual friendship, the affection we have for someone we are familiar with.

Because of its general and casual nature, *phileo* is not the kind of love you need to get married. Marriage requires a deeper, more focused love than *phileo* provides. If a married couple feel the same toward each other as they do toward their casual friends, their marriage is headed for trouble.

Phileo is a common experience for all of us because we are social creatures by nature. We are naturally attracted to other people who share similar interests with us or in whom we find a kindred spirit. True friendship is a spice of life. A friend is someone with whom we can share our deepest thoughts and our inmost selves, often more so than we can with family members. We all need the nourishment of meaningful relationships with a few really good friends. *Phileo* describes that kind of relationship.

 True friendship is a spice of life.

As positive and beneficial to our lives as this friendship love is, however, *phileo* does not qualify as the highest and deepest form of love. As a matter of fact, *phileo* often develops certain characteristics that can create problems in the relationship if we are not careful. One of these is a sense of obligation. Because it is based so frequently on mutual attraction and similarities, *phileo* can easily become a relationship of "you scratch my back and I'll scratch yours." We feel obligated to respond to each other because of the relationship.

Another common characteristic of *phileo* is that it tends to focus on personalities and physical attraction. This is natural and there is nothing wrong with it as long as we don't confuse it with "true love." Personality traits and physical characteristics change over time, so they alone are not reliable factors upon which to base a permanent, long-term relationship.

This emphasis on personality and physical attraction often results in a *phileo* relationship that is based on mutual compatibility. One reason friendships develop is because the people involved feel that they are compatible with each other to some degree or another. This is fine for a casual friendship, but many people look at "compatibility" as a criterion for a potential spouse. The main problem with that idea is that two people in a long-term relationship who are "compatible," or very much alike, may feel that they are competing with each other, which can lead to contention. In my experience, the most successful relationships usually involve two people who are either opposites or at least very different from each other. Because of their differences they balance each other out, complementing and adding to each other. With relationships as with magnets, it is true that opposites attract.

With these kinds of criteria, *phileo* tends to be a "conditional" love: As long as certain conditions exist, the relationship exists. If those conditions change, so does the relationship. Conditions in a relationship create expectations, and expectations inevitably result in disappointment. This is why a conditional relationship is insufficient for building a long-term commitment such as marriage. Spouses should certainly be each other's best friend—they should have a *phileo* characterized by tender affection—but more than that is needed to sustain their relationship over the long term.

Storge: THE LOVE OF FAMILY

Closely related to *phileo*, but more close-knit, *storge* is the word the Greeks used to refer to the love of family relationships. *Storge* describes the tender affection of parents toward their children and that of children toward their parents. It also takes in the affectionate or close feelings that normally exist between siblings and toward members of one's extended family: grandparents, cousins, aunts, uncles, nieces, and nephews.

Storge is more close-knit than *phileo* because *storge* has to do with family, and family implies relationship. That is precisely where the key danger lies with this kind of love. Because of the family relationship, we *assume* that we love our parents and our siblings and that they love us. We take that love for granted; after all, we're family, aren't we? Although most of the time that love is genuine, it is still a dangerous assumption. The problem is that being family does not guarantee relationship. Being related by blood does not automatically lead to friendship.

Consider your own relationships, both inside and outside your family. Who are you closest to? Who do you share your most intimate and personal thoughts and feelings with? Who knows you—the *real* you— better than anyone else? Is it a family member, or a friend? If we are honest, most of us will admit that we are closer to a friend than we are to members of our own family.

Where parents or siblings are concerned, we assume relationship and love because we're family. If someone were to ask you, "Do you love your parents?" you would probably respond automatically with, "Of course I do." If your questioner then asked, "Why?" you might answer, "Well...because they are my parents." That's the whole point. Even though our love for our parents and our siblings is real, there is still an underlying sense that we love them because we are *supposed* to. Whenever an unloving feeling arises in us toward any family member, a feeling of guilt usually arises with it. We don't *feel* loving, yet at the same time we feel that we *should*.

From this perspective, then, *storge* is similar to *phileo* in that it can easily foster a sense of obligation. We love, not because we want to but because we have to. Obligation produces pressure, pressure produces stress, and sustained stress endangers any relationship. If we are involved in such a conditional relationship we feel guilty every time we fail to live up to our obligation, and angry, bitter, or resentful when other people fail to live up to theirs. Once again, as with *phileo*, we are back to expectations and conditions.

The love of family represented by *storge* is not limited to blood relations. It is quite common for people in the Church—those who believe in and follow Christ as Savior and Lord—to refer to themselves collectively as members of the "family" of God and to regard each other as brothers and sisters in the Lord. This view is entirely consistent with the teaching of God's Word. In Galatians 6:10 Paul speaks of "the family of believers." Hebrews 2:11 says that all who are "made holy" by Jesus are His brothers and members of His family. In First Peter 4:17 Peter refers to believers as "the family of God."

Because of this sense of family, communities of believers face the same temptations as "blood" families do—assuming relationship, allowing familiarity to cause them to take each other for granted, and developing a mind-set of obligation. In this regard it would be helpful for believers to think of each other not only as family, but also as friends, thus opening the way for greater intimacy and deeper relationships.

Despite the risk of developing a mind-set motivated by a sense of obligation, *storge* is nonetheless an important and beneficial dynamic in human experience, both in "blood" families and the family of believers. Love of family is fundamental to the peace and stability of any society. The family is the basic building block of society, and if families fall apart, society will soon follow.

 Love of family is fundamental to the peace and stability of any society.

Eros: Sexual Love

Referring to *eros* as "sexual love" is really not very accurate because, strictly speaking, sex has nothing to do with true love. Sex can occur without love; it happens all the time. Love can exist without sex; the two are not dependent upon each other. Within the sacred and monogamous bounds of marriage as established and ordained by the Creator, sex is a warm, intimate, and beautiful *expression* of love, but by itself it is not love. This is where the world's viewpoint has become so completely turned around.

The ancient Greeks delighted in, and in a way, even worshiped the beauty of the human body and sexuality. *Eros* was their word for sexual activity in all its forms, which they regarded as a type of love. *Eros* was also the name the Greeks gave to their god of love. Worship of *Eros* involved, among other things, ritual sex acts and prostitution.

The "god" *Eros* still reigns today in virtually every segment of society. Millions of people worship daily at the altar of *Eros* and call it love.

 Within the sacred and monogamous bounds of marriage as established and ordained by the Creator, sex is a warm, intimate, and beautiful expression of love, but by itself it is not love.

In its fullest and most literal sense, the word *eros* embraces sexual longing, craving, and desire with no respect for sanctity; sensual ecstasy that leaves moderation and proportion far behind. Another word to describe *eros* would be *lust*. Utterly selfish at its core, *eros* seeks to fulfill its lust at the expense of another.

Unlike true love, *eros* is completely sensual. It centers on the physical stimulation of the five senses—sight, smell, hearing, taste, and touch— and the desires and cravings aroused by those senses. Because it is physical in nature, *eros* is controlled by chemical reactions and interactions within the body. As such, it is driven completely by the flesh; whatever the flesh desires, *eros* seeks to gratify. Erotic love is emotional love, fueled by feelings, and therefore rises and falls as feelings do. True love, in contrast, is constant, neither motivated nor controlled by emotions.

A person who is driven by *eros* alone sees his or her potential partner as nothing more than a sex object, a target to conquer. It is a sad state of affairs indeed that our modern society so often encourages the view that members of the opposite sex are challenges to win or "scores" to be "made," and then calls it "love." Relationships built around *eros* last only as long as the physical attraction and desire that drew the people together in the first place.

In its selfishness, *eros* has no regard for the feelings or desires of the other person, being interested only in the personal gratification it can get from that person. *Eros* knows little and cares less of human dignity or respect. It is desire out of control, unleashed and unrestrained passion in the spirit of the modern philosophy that says, "If it feels good, do it."

Agape: The Divine Love

In many ways *agape*, the fourth and highest kind of love, is in a class by itself. Because of its unique nature, this love needed a unique word to describe it. No ordinary word for love such as *phileo, storge,* or *eros* was sufficient to plumb the depths of meaning represented in this highest degree of love, so, under the inspiration of the Holy Spirit, New Testament writers coined the word *agape* to fill the need. Outside of the New Testament, *agape* is found in only one instance in ancient Greek texts, in a passage describing parents' love for their only child. Essentially, *agape* is a uniquely biblical word for a uniquely biblical concept, which is in keeping with its uniquely spiritual nature.

Agape refers to *divine* love, the love God has for His people as well as the love His people give back to Him. It is also the kind of love that the people of God are supposed to have toward one another. Unlike *phileo* and *storge*, *agape* carries no obligation, holds no expectations, and lays down no conditions. *Agape* is unconditional love. Unlike *eros*, which is the epitome of selfishness, *agape* acts first and foremost for the good and welfare of another. Rather than self-serving, *agape* is self-giving, a sacrificial love that pours itself out for the sake of someone else.

 Unlike **EROS**, *which is the epitome of selfishness,* **AGAPE** *acts first and foremost for the good and welfare of another.*

The greatest example of *agape* in action was when Jesus Christ, the sinless Son of God, poured out His life on the cross for the sake of sinners (which includes all of us) that they might become children of God. This truth is encapsulated in one of the most well-known verses in the Bible: "For God so loved [*agape*] the world that He gave His one and only Son, that whoever believes in Him shall not perish but have eternal life" (Jn. 3:16).

God alone is the source of *agape*. Apart from Him it cannot be known. He has revealed it through Jesus Christ, and gives it freely to all who become His children by faith—who believe in and trust in Jesus Christ as Savior and Lord—who then pass it on to others. God loves all people in the world with divine *agape*, but only those who are of the community of believers know that love by personal experience. To the world at large, *agape* is an unknown quantity.

One of the best illustrations of the *agape* relationship between God and His people is found in the New Testament Book of First John:

How great is the love the Father has lavished on us, that we should be called children of God! And that is what we are! The reason the world does not know us is that it did not know Him....This is the message you heard from the beginning: We should love one another....We know that we have passed from death to life, because we love our brothers. Anyone who does not love remains in death....This is how we know what love is: Jesus Christ laid down His life for us. And we ought to lay down our lives for our brothers. If anyone has material possessions and sees his brother in need but has no pity on him, how can the love of God be in him? Dear children, let us not love with words or tongue but with actions and in truth (1 John 3:1,11,14,16-18).

Dear friends, let us love one another, for love comes from God. Everyone who loves has been born of God and knows God. Whoever does not love does not know God, because God is love. This is how God showed His love among us: He sent His one and only Son into the world that we might live through Him. This is love: not that we loved God, but that He loved us and sent His Son as an atoning sacrifice for our sins. Dear friends, since God so loved us, we also ought to love one another. No one has ever seen God; but if we love one another, God lives in us and His love is made complete in us (1 John 4:7-12).

These verses help us understand several important truths about *agape*. First, *agape* is not physical or chemical, nor is it an emotion or a philosophy. *Agape* is a *Person*. First John 4:8b says, "God is love." When we know *agape*, we know the Person who embodies it. As the Son of the God who is love, Jesus Christ was *agape* in human flesh.

Second, *agape* is oneness. All those who know *agape* are one with God and one with each other in heart and spirit. Literally speaking, *agape* means that God became one with us. In Christ He took on our low estate, becoming like us so that He could make us like Him.

Literally speaking, AGAPE means that God became one with us.

Third, *agape* is others-conscious, not self-conscious. *Agape* is constantly watching out first for the welfare of others, looking continually for opportunities to give. True love is not complete until it gives itself.

Fourth, *agape* is self-initiating. *Agape* takes responsibility. It does not wait for others to act first. Romans 5:8 says, "But God demonstrates His own love for us in this: While we were still sinners, Christ died for us." *Agape* is proactive. It acts whether or not anyone else responds or reciprocates. Jesus said, "Do to others as you would have them do to you" (Lk. 6:31). That's just what *agape* does. *Agape* takes the initiative.

Finally, *agape* is a choice. It is based not on emotion but on deliberate decision. The Bible plainly states that God loves us but it never tells us *why* He loves us. There is no "why." God loves us because He is love and it is His nature to love. God loves us because He has chosen to do so. His love is without discrimination. *Agape* does not choose *who* to love, it chooses simply to love. It does not matter who the object is.

Because it is a decision—a deliberate choice—*agape* is constant. Unlike emotion-based "love," *agape* never changes.

 AGAPE *does not choose* WHO *to love, it chooses simply to love.*

Agape is the only "true love" in the world, and the foundation for everything else we sometimes call love. Correctly understood and exercised in the proper environment, *phileo, storge,* and *eros* can all be legitimate and beautiful expressions of *agape,* but not one of them by itself is a sufficient base upon which to build a meaningful and lasting long-term relationship. Only *agape* is sufficient for that.

Understanding *agape* is the key to understanding the secrets of the human heart. To do so we need to consider several facets of this glittering jewel that is *agape*: God's love for us, our love for God, our love for ourselves, and our love for others, particularly as it relates to our spouse or potential spouse.

PRINCIPLES

1. *Phileo* is love on the level of casual friendship, the affection we have for someone we are familiar with.

2. *Storge* describes the tender affection of parents toward their children and that of children toward their parents.

3. *Eros* embraces sexual longing, craving, and desire with no respect for sanctity; sensual ecstasy that leaves moderation and proportion far behind.

4. *Agape* refers to *divine* love, the love God has for His people as well as the love His people give back to Him.

5. *Agape* is unconditional love.

6. *Agape* is self-giving.

7. *Agape* is a *Person*.

8. *Agape* is oneness.

9. *Agape* is others-conscious.

10. *Agape* is self-initiating.

11. *Agape* takes responsibility.

12. *Agape* is proactive.

13. *Agape* is a choice.

14. *Agape* never changes.

~ CHAPTER TWO ~

God Loves You

*I*f we hope to gain any understanding at all of true love, we must start at the source. The poet who wrote, "To love is to live, and to live is to love," was not far from the mark because life and love have their source in the same Person: God the Creator. He is the one in whom "we live and move and have our being" (Acts 17:28a). To know love (*agape*) is to know God because God *is* love: "Dear friends, let us love one another, for love comes from God. *Everyone who loves* has been born of God and *knows God*. Whoever does not love does not know God, *because God is love*" (1 Jn. 4:7-8, emphasis added).

One of the greatest truths ever revealed to mankind is the truth that God loves us. Love lies at the core of everything God does and has done for humanity. God's love for us is one of the central themes of the Bible, permeating its pages throughout both the Old and New Testaments. No other sacred text in the world contains such a message. In its proclamation that God deliberately, consciously, and unconditionally loves all people, the Bible is utterly unique.

Here are just a few examples:

Know therefore that the Lord your God is God; He is the faithful God, keeping His covenant of love to a thousand generations of those who love Him and keep His commands (Deuteronomy 7:9).

I have loved you with an everlasting love; I have drawn you with loving-kindness (Jeremiah 31:3b).

For God so loved the world that He gave His one and only Son, that whoever believes in Him shall not perish but have eternal life (John 3:16).

But God demonstrates His own love for us in this: While we were still sinners, Christ died for us (Romans 5:8).

But because of His great love for us, God, who is rich in mercy, made us alive with Christ even when we were dead in transgressions—it is by grace you have been saved (Ephesians 2:4-5).

How great is the love the Father has lavished on us, that we should be called children of God! (1 John 3:1a)

This is love: not that we loved God, but that He loved us and sent His Son as an atoning sacrifice for our sins (1 John 4:10).

If the Bible clearly reveals God's love for us, one thing it does *not* reveal is *why* He loves us. There is no "why." Love with a "why" is love with conditions. God's love is unconditional; He loves us because He loves us and because it His nature to love us. To search out the "why" of God's love would be an exercise in futility.

In its proclamation that God deliberately, consciously, and unconditionally loves all people, the Bible is utterly unique.

Nevertheless, there is much we can learn from the Scriptures about the character and quality of God's love. That is where any honest inquiry into the nature of true love must begin. Until we understand something of the love of God we cannot truly understand love in any of its other dimensions, and particularly how it affects the most significant relationships of our lives, whether friends or family.

Our quest takes us back to creation itself.

Created and Made

The first three chapters of the Book of Genesis lay the foundation for everything that follows in the rest of the Bible. Genesis chapters 1 and 2 reveal God's original design in creation; chapter 3 describes how that design was corrupted; and the remaining chapters and Books of the Bible show how God sets things right once more. Stated simply, the Bible tells the story of paradise established, paradise lost, and paradise restored. Everything that happens in the Bible is for the purpose of restoring mankind and all of creation to their original state and condition as described in the first two chapters of Genesis.

One key to understanding Genesis chapters 1 and 2 is to clarify the distinction between two important words: *create* and *make*. Three verses in chapter 1 illustrate this difference:

In the beginning God created the heavens and the earth (Genesis 1:1).

*Then God said, "Let Us make man in Our image, in Our likeness, and
let them rule over the fish of the sea and the birds of the air, over the
livestock, over all the earth, and over all the creatures that move along
the ground." So God created man in His own image, in the image of God
He created him; male and female He created them* (Genesis 1:26-27).

In verses 1 and 27, the Hebrew word for "created" is *bara*, while in
verse 26 the word for "make" is *asah*. Throughout the first two chapters
of Genesis, *bara* appears seven times, while *asah* occurs ten times.
Although the two words appear to be used interchangeably to a certain
degree, there is essentially a distinct difference in their basic meanings.
Bara means to fashion something out of nothing. It refers to creation in
the absolute sense, and is used in the Bible only in connection with God
because He alone can create from nothing. In the very beginning, God
was alone; nothing else was. From that nothingness God created the
heavens and the earth simply by willing them to be and speaking them
into existence. That is what *bara* means.

Asah, on the other hand, means to fashion something out of preexist-
ing material. In addition to its occurrence in verse 26, *asah* is used in reference to God "making" the expanse of the heavens (1:7), the sun and
moon (1:16), the wild animals (1:25), the earth and heavens (2:4), and the
woman, man's "helper" (2:18).

With these two words, *bara* and *asah*, we can see two specific aspects
of God's creative activity: the creation of some things out of nothing,
and the making of other things out of material He had already created.
Whichever the case, the principle is the same: God creates by *speaking*.

Throughout Genesis chapter 1 runs the phrase, "And God *said*...,"
each time preceding a specific creative act. God is a "said-ing" God; He
does things by speaking. Words are exposed thoughts, thoughts that
have been unwrapped. A thought, therefore, is a silent word.

God's words express His thoughts. He thinks before He speaks.
Whenever God says something, He has thought about it first. Before He
does anything, God has a picture in His mind of everything that He is
going to do. In the beginning, God created all things by expressing His
thoughts about them. Everything that exists originated first in the mind
of God.

In the beginning, God created all things by expressing His thoughts about them.

The first chapter of Genesis reveals that whenever God prepared to "make" (*asah*) something, He "spoke" to what He had already "created" (*bara*), and that to which He spoke brought forth what He desired. For example, when God wanted vegetation to cover the earth, He spoke to the earth:

Then God said, "Let the land produce vegetation: seed-bearing plants and trees on the land that bear fruit with seed in it, according to their various kinds." And it was so. The land produced vegetation: plants bearing seed according to their kinds and trees bearing fruit with seed in it according to their kinds. And God saw that it was good (Genesis 1:11-12).

When the Lord wanted stars in the sky, He spoke to the heavens: "Let there be lights in the expanse of the sky..." (Gen. 1:14); when He wanted fish in the sea He spoke to the waters: "Let the water teem with living creatures..." (Gen. 1:20), and when He wanted land animals He again spoke to the earth: "Let the land produce living creatures according to their kinds..." (Gen. 1:24).

One of the basic principles of creation is that all created things are sustained by that from which they came. Plants and animals depend on the earth for life because they came from the earth. Fish depend on water for life because that is where they came from.

It is a different story, however, with the appearance of the human species. As the first chapter of Genesis makes clear, the creation of mankind stands apart from the rest of creation for at least three reasons. First, both *bara* and *asah* are used in different places to describe the creation of man. This may be due partly to using the two words interchangeably, but I believe there is more involved. In a very real sense, man was both created and made. God created (*bara*) spiritual beings which He called "man" and then made (*asah*) from the dust of the earth physical "houses"—male and female bodies—for them to dwell in.

This brings us to the second point. When God got ready to create mankind He did not speak to the earth, as He did for the plants and animals, or to the sky, as He did for the stars. When God was ready to create man, He spoke to Himself: "Then God said, 'Let us make man in Our image, in Our likeness....' So God created man in His own image..."

(Gen. 1:26-27). Because God is Spirit, that which came forth from Him when He spoke to Himself also was spirit. As human beings, we are spiritual beings, and that is what sets us apart from the rest of God's creation. Of course, the angels are also spiritual beings, but they are not like we are, which leads us to the third point.

As human beings, we are spiritual beings, and that is what sets us apart from the rest of God's creation.

God created us in His image. Nowhere does the Bible make that statement about angels or any other created thing. Humans are the only beings in all of God's creation that are fashioned in His image and likeness. As spiritual beings created in God's image, we are unique. God created us to be like Him.

Created to Receive God's Love

A natural question to ask at this point is, "Why did God create man?" If God is all-sufficient and complete within Himself, what motivated Him to create spiritual beings in His image and likeness? The answer, in a word, is *love*. Let me explain.

God reveals Himself to us in many ways, but mainly through His Word, the Bible. Its pages describe numerous qualities and attributes of God. He is holy, righteous, and just. He is mighty, powerful, and strong. God is omnipresent, omnipotent, and omniscient. He is faithful. God is all of these and more, self-contained and self-sufficient, needing nothing and no one else to make Him complete. In His self-sufficiency God is "all one," which is another way of saying that He is "alone." This is not the same as saying that God is lonely. It simply means that He is unique; there is no one else like Him.

The Bible also says that God is love, and herein is the problem, if we want to call it that. God is alone and God is love, yet love cannot exist and be complete alone. In order to be complete and fulfilled, love must have an object. Love by nature must express itself, and therefore must have someone or something to express itself to. In expressing itself, love must give itself. Therefore, love must have a receiver.

In the beginning God was all one—alone. He was love and, as love, needed to give, yet there was no one to give to. The Bible reveals God as a trinity—one God who nevertheless manifests Himself in three distinct persons: Father, Son, and Holy Spirit. Within this triune Godhead perfect love exists and continually expresses itself. Even so, God's eternal love always needs to give itself. Because He was alone and there was no one else, God had to provide for Himself someone to receive His love.

God is love, love needs to give, and giving needs a receiver. In order for giving to be complete, the receiver must be just like the giver. God could not give in this way to the plants or the animals because they were not like Him. Nothing else was like God; He was alone. Since God was alone, but needed someone like Himself to give His love to, He had to call forth that someone from out of Himself.

God, who is Spirit, but who is also love and has to give, needs a receiver who is like Himself. He speaks to Himself to bring that receiver into being: "Let us make man in Our image, in Our likeness....So God created man in His own image, in the image of God He created him; male and female He created them" (Gen. 1:26-27).

Being created in God's image means, among other things, that each of us is a spirit being just as God Himself is Spirit. In our spirit we are genderless because spirits have no gender. God created us as spirit beings like Himself in order that we might receive His love. Then He fashioned physical bodies with gender distinctiveness—male and female—so that we could rule over the earth and all of its creatures. As spirit we were created for the purpose of receiving God's love. As male and female we were created to exercise dominion together over the created order as co-regents with God.

 As spirit we were created for the purpose of receiving God's love. As male and female we were created to exercise dominion together over the created order as co-regents with God.

God loves us because He is love and must express Himself. God loves us because He created us for that very purpose. God loves us because there is no one else—neither the angels nor any other creature—who is like Him and therefore able to receive His love. The receiver must be like the giver. We alone are created in the image and likeness of God. We alone are like God—the giver—and we alone are able to be receivers of His great love.

God has no one else to love but us. That's why the Bible never tells us why God loves us. There is no why. God loves us because He created us for that purpose. There is nothing we can do to make God love us, nor is there any need to; He already loves us thoroughly. In his New Testament letter to the believers in Rome, Paul wrote, "But God demonstrates His own love for us in this: While we were still sinners, Christ died for us" (Rom. 5:8). If God loved us that much even in our sin, how could we do anything to make Him love us more? God has us clearly in His sights and He has targeted us with arrows of love.

    God loves us because He created us for that purpose.

Like spiritual satellite dishes, we are designed and hardwired to receive God's love. That is why He created us. God is very jealous of those He loves, and will do whatever is necessary to preserve that relationship. Romans 5:8 is proof. When sin disrupted our "reception," and broke the connection, God sent His Son to repair and restore it.

God Needed a Seed

God created man to receive His love. Love expresses itself through giving. Motivated by His love, God gave man—male and female—a gift: Dominion over the earth. His plan was for everything on earth to be subjected to the rule of man. Earth was to be man's domain, his "kingdom" under the overall sovereignty of God.

Things didn't work out that way. Seduced by satan, that fallen angel, that tempter and adversary of both God and man, Adam and Eve traded their "birthright" of dominion over the earth for the fleeting and deceptive pleasures of the "forbidden fruit" of self-rule. By their acquiescence, their rightful place was usurped by satan who gained illegal access to the throne of earth's dominion.

This development did not catch God by surprise. He knew it was coming. Immediately He set into action the plan He had prepared even before time began, a plan to send His Son to earth as a human being to restore the race of men to their rightful place of dominion as well as bring them back into the fellowship of His love. Why did the Son of God have to become a man in order to accomplish this? Why didn't God simply intervene directly and set things right immediately? The answer to these questions goes right back to this whole issue of dominion.

Because God gave mankind dominion over the earth, He will not arbitrarily usurp that dominion as satan did. The gifts of God are irrevocable. God is bound by His Word; whatever He says, He does. God's Word stands, regardless of the actions of men. The Bible affirms this over and over.

For God's gifts and His call are irrevocable (Romans 11:29).

What God gives He never revokes.

But the plans of the Lord stand firm forever, the purposes of His heart through all generations (Psalm 33:11).

Once God has a plan, that plan is forever. God will never change His original plan, which is for mankind to dominate the earth.

The grass withers and the flowers fall, but the word of our God stands forever (Isaiah 40:8).

Once God speaks, that's it.

So is My word that goes out from My mouth: It will not return to Me empty, but will accomplish what I desire and achieve the purpose for which I sent it (Isaiah 55:11).

Every word that God speaks will be accomplished.

By giving man dominion over the earth, God essentially gave up His right to interfere in the affairs of this planet. This in no way diminishes His sovereignty as Creator or His place as Lord of the universe. It simply means that He has chosen to limit Himself to acting in the earth only after obtaining "legal" access to do so. Gaining this access requires the willing participation of humans. God honors His Word. In order to win back His lost love—mankind—and rescue us from our sin, God needed a human seed.

 God has chosen to limit Himself to acting in the earth only after obtaining "legal" access to do so.

That is why God called Abraham and promised to bless him with a son even though he and his wife, Sarah, had no children and were beyond childbearing age. God needed humans through whom He could freely work to bring His seed into the world at the appropriate time.

The miracle child born to Abraham and Sarah, their son of promise, was Isaac, who had twin sons of his own, Jacob and Esau. Jacob fathered twelve sons, whose families grew into the twelve tribes of the nation of

Israel. Judah, one of Jacob's sons, was an ancestor of King David. Mary and Joseph, Jesus' earthly parents, were both descendants of David. This line of descent from Abraham to Mary provided God the human bloodline He needed in order for His Son's entry into the world to be legitimate.

One of the great truths of the Bible is that whenever God gets ready to do anything in the earth, He always works through a person or a group of people whom He has called and who have willingly responded to Him. The human factor is key for God's activity on the earth. When God prepared to deliver the Israelites from Egypt, He called Moses. When He got ready to rescue His people from the Midianites, He called Gideon. When God wanted to warn His disobedient people of His judgment and call them back to Him, He called Elijah, Isaiah, Jeremiah, Amos, and the other prophets. When God was ready to send His Son into the world, He chose Mary, a humble peasant girl, to be His mother. When Jesus Christ prepared to send His message of salvation throughout the world, He called and anointed men and women—His Church—and commissioned them for the mission.

This illustrates an incredible principle under which God operates: Without God we *cannot*, and without us God *will not*. For everything that God desires to do in the earth, He enters into partnership with those to whom He has already given dominion.

No Greater Love

How great is God's love for us? It is great enough that while we were still sinners, while we were still in a state of rebellion against God, He sent His Son, Jesus Christ, who was without sin, to die for our sins so that we could be brought back into a love relationship with Him. Because of His great love for us, God did for us what we could never have done for ourselves. He was willing to pay any price—and did—in order to win back His lost love.

Consider these words of Paul from his New Testament letter to the believers in Ephesus: "As for you, you were dead in your transgressions and sins....But because of His great love for us, God, who is rich in mercy, made us alive with Christ even when we were dead in transgressions—it is by grace you have been saved" (Eph. 2:1,4-5).

How did Christ accomplish this? The only way was for Him who was the Son of God to become the son of man by taking on human flesh.

He became like us so that we could become like Him. This is how the writer of the New Testament Book of Hebrews described what Jesus did:

> *But we see Jesus, who was made a little lower than the angels, now crowned with glory and honor because He suffered death, so that by the grace of God He might taste death for everyone....Since the children have flesh and blood, He too shared in their humanity so that by His death He might destroy him who holds the power of death—that is, the devil—and free those who all their lives were held in slavery by their fear of death. For surely it is not angels He helps, but Abraham's descendants. For this reason He had to be made like His brothers in every way, in order that He might become a merciful and faithful high priest in service to God, and that He might make atonement for the sins of the people* (Hebrews 2:9,14-17).

There is no greater demonstration of love than this. In fact, Jesus Himself said, "Greater love has no one than this, that he lay down his life for his friends" (Jn. 15:13). God sent His Son to save us because He loves us. Jesus Christ willingly died for us because He loves us. The love of God is an everlasting love; it will never quit or fade away. Indeed, it cannot because love is the very nature of God Himself.

God is love and love has to give, so He created us to receive His love. For love to be complete, the receiver must be like the giver. We are created in the image and likeness of God. As He is Spirit, we too are spirit. As God is love, we too are love. We were made to receive God's love, but also to love Him in return and to love others as well.

PRINCIPLES

1. God creates by *speaking*.

2. When God was ready to create man, He spoke to Himself.

3. God created mankind in His image.

4. God is love.

5. To be complete, love must give; therefore, love needs a receiver.

6. For love to be fulfilled, the receiver must be like the giver.

7. God created man to receive His love.

8. By giving man dominion over the earth, God essentially gave up His right to interfere in the affairs of this planet.

9. In order to win back His lost love—mankind—and rescue us from our sin, God needed a human seed.

10. Without God we *cannot*, and without us God *will not*.

~ CHAPTER THREE ~

Loving God

God is love, and love needs to give, so God created man—a spiritual being like Himself—so He would have someone to love and to give to. Please understand that I am referring to man in the generic sense, "man" as the name for the human species. "Man" in this sense is neither male nor female, but spirit, because God is Spirit.

The first thing that God gave to this spirit man He had created was dominion over the earth, a physical realm. Spiritual beings cannot apprehend or appreciate physical realities because the spiritual and the physical are on two entirely different planes. So God took "the dust of the ground"—part of that physical realm—and fashioned a physical body as a "house" for the spirit man to dwell in. He endowed that body with a heart, lungs, nervous system, and the five senses of sight, smell, taste, touch, and hearing so that His spirit man could have legal access to and fully appreciate the physical world over which he was to exercise dominion.

As it happened, the first body God fashioned for man was male in gender. When Adam, the male "man" proved to be just as alone in his realm as God had been in His before creation, God took a part of Adam's body and formed a female body, which also housed a spirit "man." Male and female then enjoyed completeness with each other as well as uninterrupted fellowship with God. In their spirits, Adam and Eve needed no one else except God for complete fulfillment. In their maleness and femaleness, however, they needed each other in order to be complete. It is the same with each of us.

God's fundamental purpose for creating us was to love us; dominion over the earth was His first gift to us. He created us to love us, and to prove His love He gave us dominion. So then, what is man's purpose on the earth? Are we here simply to exercise dominion over the created order? Adam and Eve ruled over their physical environment—but they also enjoyed continual fellowship with God.

We are receivers of God's love because that is how He created us. He also created us with the capacity to give love in return. Whatever comes forth from God is like God. Because God is love, we also are love in our spirit because we came forth from God. Our purpose on earth is not primarily to dominate, but to receive God's love and to love Him in return. The Westminster Shorter Catechism, a classic statement of the foundational truths of the Christian faith, says that the chief end of man is "to glorify God and enjoy Him forever." That is a beautiful and apt description of love received and returned between God and man.

 Our purpose on earth is not primarily to dominate, but to receive God's love and to love Him in return.

Our chief and primary purpose is to love God. Sometimes we get so caught up in taking over the earth that we forget that God has said, "Your first allegiance is to love and worship Me." Jesus made this clear when He was asked which commandment was the most important:

One of them, an expert in the law, tested Him with this question: "Teacher, which is the greatest commandment in the Law?" Jesus replied: "'Love the Lord your God with all your heart and with all your soul and with all your mind.' This is the first and greatest commandment. And the second is like it: 'Love your neighbor as yourself.' All the Law and the Prophets hang on these two commandments" (Matthew 22:35-40).

Our first priority as humans—our "chief end"—is to love God with everything we've got. Only then can we truly fulfill the second commandment to love our neighbors as ourselves. Success and genuine happiness in all of our relationships hinge on how well we love God. God loves us and we are to love Him in return. How do we do that? What does it mean to love God?

God's will and desire—His pleasure—is that we love Him. We cannot please God unless we love Him. We cannot love Him unless we know Him, and we cannot know Him unless we have faith in Him. "And without faith it is impossible to please God, because anyone who comes to Him must believe that He exists and that He rewards those who earnestly seek Him" (Heb. 11:6).

The first prerequisite, then, for loving God is to know Him by faith. Without knowing God, it is impossible to love Him. We come to know God through His Son, Jesus Christ, whose death on the cross paid the penalty for our sin and opened the way for us to be restored to a right relationship with our heavenly Father. As Paul writes in the Book of Romans, "For all have sinned and fall short of the glory of God, and are justified freely by His grace through the redemption that came by Christ Jesus" (Rom. 3:23-24).

Sin broke our relationship with God, but Jesus sealed the breach with His blood. When in faith we turn from our sin and trust Jesus Christ as our personal Savior and Lord, "He is faithful and just and will forgive us our sins and purify us from all unrighteousness" (1 Jn. 1:9b). He also fills us with the Holy Spirit, who enables us to walk in continual fellowship with our Father. It is then and only then that we are truly able to love God.

Worship

As believers, there are many ways we can practice and demonstrate our love for God. One of the most important of these is through worship. At this point it is important to understand that much of what we often call worship is really something else. True worship occurs on a spiritual rather than a physical plane. So much of our so-called worship takes place on the physical level: Singing, praying, lifting hands, dancing, speaking in tongues, etc. While these activities engage the body and the mind, they do not necessarily or automatically engage the spirit. We can do all those things with great fervor and energy, and yet never enter into genuine worship.

 True worship occurs on a spiritual rather than a physical plane.

What most believers call worship is in reality praise: Acknowledging God for His greatness and His goodness, thanking Him for His miracles and His blessings, and celebrating His presence and power. To praise God means to lift Him up, to speak well of Him, to hold Him in highest esteem, to ascribe to Him glory and majesty and honor. All of these things are good and proper and appropriate—but they are not true worship.

Praise prepares the way for worship, but that's as far as many believers ever go.

Genuine worship lies beyond praise. It lies beyond the songs and the prayers and all the other physical activities that we tend to think of as worship. Praise is more for our benefit than for God's. It prepares our spirit for worship by helping us bring our bodies under subjection so that true worship can take place. In a sense, praise helps us to get out of our bodies, out of the restrictions of our flesh so that our spirit can worship in complete freedom. For this same reason it can also distract us if we are not careful.

True worship always occurs spirit to Spirit—our spirit mingling with the Spirit of God. More often than not, it takes place without words. Worship is when we lose ourselves in God. If we get too caught up in praising and carrying out other activities that cause us to focus on the flesh—on the physical—we will not be able to enter wholeheartedly into worship. The time must come when we leave the physical behind and commune with God on a purely spiritual level. Praise is the "booster rocket" that gets us off the launching pad, but only our spirit can enter "orbit."

The word *worship* means to intercourse, to bow down, to kiss. In short, worship means *intimacy.* That is what sets worship apart from praise. There is no such thing as long-distance intimacy. We can praise God from a distance, but we cannot *worship* Him from a distance. Praise is physical; worship is spiritual. Worship is an exchange of selves.

 We can praise God from a distance, but we cannot WORSHIP Him from a distance.

God is love and He created us to receive His love. Because we came from a loving God who is also a giver, we have the capacity not only to receive love, but also to give it back. Worship takes place when God gives His love, and we receive His love and give it back to Him. Our spirit interacts with God's Spirit, and love is exchanged. God loves and gives; we receive and respond, giving back to God the love He has already poured out on us.

Abiding in Christ

Such an intimate interchange of love as this requires that we stay close to God. Intimacy is impossible at a distance. Part of loving God, then, is maintaining our "connection" to Him. He is the source for everything we have and are and ever hope to be. The answers to all of our questions lie within God. The solutions to all of our problems are deposited in God. In Him resides peace for our confusion. God holds the key to every mystery and to all that is unknown. Wisdom, knowledge, and life itself are found in Him.

This is the point Jesus was making when He compared the relationship between His followers and Himself with branches on a vine.

> *I am the true vine, and My Father is the gardener....Remain in Me, and I will remain in you. No branch can bear fruit by itself; it must remain in the vine. Neither can you bear fruit unless you remain in Me. I am the vine; you are the branches. If a man remains in Me and I in him, he will bear much fruit; apart from Me you can do nothing. If anyone does not remain in Me, he is like a branch that is thrown away and withers; such branches are picked up, thrown into the fire and burned. If you remain in Me and My words remain in you, ask whatever you wish, and it will be given you....As the Father has loved Me, so have I loved you. Now remain in My love. If you obey My commands, you will remain in My love, just as I have obeyed My Father's commands and remain in His love* (John 15:1,4-7,9-10).

Branches of a vine have no life in themselves; their life is in the vine. Any branch that is separated from the vine will die because it cannot sustain itself. Although it is the branches that bear the leaves and the fruit, they can do so only as long as they remain connected to the vine. The life that is in the vine flows through the branches and causes them to bear fruit. No branch can produce or bear fruit by itself.

In the same way, Jesus said that we can do nothing apart from Him. We are branches, but He is the vine, our source of life and fruit. Everything we need, everything we can ever have or be is in Him. In order to be fruitful and fulfill our purpose for being we must stay in vital, constant connection to Jesus, our vine.

Jesus commands His followers to "Remain in Me, and I will remain in you" (Jn. 15:4a), and then follows up His command with a promise: "If you obey My commands, you will remain in My love" (Jn. 15:10a). Remaining or abiding in Christ, then, is essential for the interchange of love between the Lord and us. The reason is simple: We must stay in one position—close to Him—so that we can fully receive His love.

In order to be fruitful and fulfill our purpose for being we must stay in vital, constant connection to Jesus, our vine.

All love has its source in God. Our ability to love anyone—God, ourselves, or others—is dependent on the love of God. We can love only because God first loved us. John explained it this way in his first New Testament letter:

Dear friends, let us love one another, for love comes from God. Everyone who loves has been born of God and knows God. Whoever does not love does not know God, because God is love. This is how God showed His love among us: He sent His one and only Son into the world that we might live through Him. This is love: not that we loved God, but that He loved us and sent His Son as an atoning sacrifice for our sins (1 John 4:7-10).

The key to love is "not that we loved God, but that He loved us and sent His Son." How do we love God? We love God by staying in one place—close to Him—so that we can receive His love. His love received into our hearts enables us to respond in love to Him. How do we stay close to God? We do so through worship, through prayer, by spending time reading, meditating, and studying His Word, the Bible, by walking in the Spirit of God, and by maintaining regular fellowship with other believers. Anyone we love we want to spend a lot of time with. We love God by spending time with Him, and by staying close to Him so that He can love us and teach us His ways in order that we can become like Him.

We love God by staying in one place—close to Him—so that we can receive His love.

Intimacy With God

One of the clear principles of life is that we become most like the people we spend the most time with. The only way to really get to know someone is to be with that person a lot. One of the ways we love God is by getting to know Him. Another word for knowing God is *intimacy*. As a matter of fact, in the Bible the concepts of knowledge and intimacy are very closely related. In the Old Testament, the Hebrew word *yada* is used to refer both to "knowing" God and to having sexual relations. For example, Moses "knew" God "face to face" (see Deut. 34:10), and "Adam knew

Eve his wife" (Gen. 4:1a KJV). Both instances imply closeness and intimate familiarity.

 One of the ways we love God is by getting to know Him.

Proverbs 1:7 says, "The fear of the Lord is the beginning of knowledge, but fools despise wisdom and discipline." Knowing God is the starting place for all true knowledge. It is the difference between success or failure, in love as well as in life. The opposite of knowledge is ignorance. Ignorance stifles creativity and potential and holds its victims in intellectual and spiritual bondage. Knowledge, on the other hand, liberates. Jesus said, "If you hold to My teaching, you are really My disciples. Then you will know the truth, and the truth will set you free" (Jn. 8:31b-32).

It is not simply the truth that sets us free, but *knowledge* of the truth. That's what makes the difference. Truth that we do not know is of no use to us. Jesus said that we would know the truth by holding onto His teaching. Everything that Jesus said and did—the whole example of His life—was for the purpose of revealing His Father. The aim of Jesus' teaching is for us to know God. When we know God we know love, for God is love. When we know God we know life, for God is life.

If we hope even to begin to understand God and know how to love Him, we must get to know Him. Is it possible for us to understand God? On the one hand, no; there is no way that we with our finite minds can ever fully understand or comprehend an infinite God. On the other hand, however, God does not want us to be ignorant of Him. He wants us to know Him and relate to Him on an intimate basis. That is why He has done everything necessary to reveal Himself to us through His Word, through His Son, and through His Spirit.

 When we know God we know love, for God is love. When we know God we know life, for God is life.

Many believers are under the mistaken notion that it is impossible to understand God, that He is supposed to remain a mystery forever. This is simply not so. The Bible is a trustworthy record of God's ongoing and progressive self-revelation to mankind. Psalm 98:2 says, "The Lord has made His salvation known and revealed His righteousness to the nations." One verse that some believers use to support their claim that God is an unknowable mystery is First Corinthians 2:9: "However, as it is written: 'No eye has seen, no ear has heard, no mind has conceived what God has prepared for those who love him,' " but they often overlook the very next verse: "but God has revealed it to us by His Spirit" (1 Cor. 2:10).

God is knowable and He wants us to know Him. He has revealed Himself in many ways so that we *can* know Him. One way to love God is by taking the time and making the effort to know Him—to get on intimate terms with Him. He stands waiting for us to respond to His invitation: "Come near to God and He will come near to you" (Jas. 4:8a).

Knowing God's Ways

God wants us to know Him and to love Him. This involves more than just knowing a lot of facts about God; more than mere head knowledge. To know means to understand the nature and the properties of a thing or a person. If you are a good automobile mechanic, you know more about cars than just their physical dimensions. You understand the principles under which they operate. You know the engine inside and out, you know the transmission and the exhaust system and the electrical system. Whenever something is not functioning properly, you can locate it and repair it because you understand the nature and properties of automobiles. You can truly say that you *know* cars.

To know a person means to understand his or her nature and personality. It means knowing that person's beliefs, passions, likes, dislikes, strengths, weaknesses; it means knowing what makes that person "tick." This kind of "knowing" reaches far beneath the surface—far beyond superficial words or actions—to touch the inner core of another person's being. Intimate knowledge of another involves a meeting not just of minds but also of hearts. It means knowing not only a person's *acts* but also his or her *ways*.

Loving God means learning to know His ways. This is far different from simply knowing His works and deeds. In Psalm 95:10 the Lord says, "For forty years I was angry with that generation; I said, 'They are a people whose hearts go astray, and they have not known My ways.' " He is talking about the people of Israel, His chosen people, who nevertheless did not know His ways. These are the people who had witnessed God's plagues against Egypt that had brought them out of slavery. They had seen God part the waters of the Red Sea and deliver them from the pharaoh's army. They had followed God's pillar of smoke by day and pillar of fire by night. He had provided water from the rock for them to drink. They had enjoyed His miraculous provision of manna for their food every day for forty years in the wilderness. During all that time, their clothes and shoes had never worn out. The Israelites had seen all of God's mighty works. They knew His acts, but they never came to know His ways.

 Intimate knowledge of another involves a meeting not just of minds but also of hearts.

Moses, on the other hand, enjoyed a different, more intimate relationship with God. David alludes to this in Psalm 103:7 when he writes of the Lord, "He made known His ways to Moses, His deeds to the people of Israel." Two relationships are implied here. Moses knew God's ways, but the people knew only His performance. Moses was in touch with God's heart and mind, but the people were acquainted only with His deeds. That's why the people never really got into the presence of God.

The same problem exists today. There are many believers who can testify to the miracles of God, and the blessings of God, and who can tell how God provided for a specific need, and yet still do not know His ways. They can appreciate the things of God and the power of God, but they have never known His presence. They have never tuned their hearts to His heart or their minds to His mind.

Knowing God's ways brings another element into the picture of loving God that is probably the most important of all: obedience. Jesus said,

If you love Me, you will obey what I command....Whoever has My commands and obeys them, he is the one who loves Me. He who loves Me will be loved by My Father, and I too will love him and show Myself to him....If anyone loves Me, he will obey My teaching. My Father will love him, and We will come to him and make Our home with him (John 14:15,21,23).

Obedience to God is the greatest demonstration—the greatest *proof*—of our love for Him. We love God by obeying Him. Without obedience, any professions of love and devotion we make are empty, meaningless, and hypocritical. Isaiah 29:13a clearly reveals God's attitude toward this: "The Lord says: 'These people come near to Me with their mouth and honor Me with their lips, but their hearts are far from Me.' "

Obedience to God is the greatest demonstration—the greatest PROOF—of our love for Him.

What is your desire? Are you simply after a blessing, or do you want to know God? Are you content merely to receive from Him, or do you yearn for an intimate relationship with Him? Are you satisfied being an acquaintance of God, or do you long to be His friend?

Love must give itself away in order to be fulfilled; therefore, love needs a receiver. For love to be complete, the receiver must return it to the giver. That's the relationship God has designed each of us for, and to which He invites all of us. We were created to receive God's love and give it back to Him. His desire is for us to enter into a deep and intimate love relationship with Him that goes beyond outward appearances and connects us to Him heart to heart and spirit to Spirit. God calls us to love Him with all our heart, soul, and mind. This is the kind of love that will enable us to fulfill our chief end: "to glorify God and enjoy Him forever."

Are you satisfied being an acquaintance of God, or do you long to be His friend?

PRINCIPLES

1. Our chief and primary purpose is to love God.

2. The first prerequisite for loving God is to know Him by faith.

3. True worship always occurs spirit to Spirit—our spirit mingling with the Spirit of God.

4. Worship is an exchange of selves.

5. Part of loving God is maintaining our "connection" to Him.

6. Abiding in Christ is essential for the interchange of love between the Lord and us.

7. Knowing God is the starting place for all true knowledge.

8. One way to love God is by taking the time and making the effort to know Him—to get on intimate terms with Him.

9. Loving God means learning to know His ways.

10. God's desire is for us to enter into a deep and intimate love relationship with Him that goes beyond outward appearances and connects us to Him heart to heart and spirit to Spirit.

11. We love God by obeying Him.

~ CHAPTER FOUR ~

Loving Yourself

*L*ove lies at the very center of God's design for all human relationships, whether natural or spiritual. Jesus told us that the two greatest commandments are, first, to "Love the Lord your God with all your heart and with all your soul and with all your mind" (Mt. 22:37), and second, to "Love your neighbor as yourself" (Mt. 22:39b). The two are inseparably linked. God created us not only to receive His love, but also to give love back to Him as well as extending it to others. By severing our relationship with God, sin broke the essential "connection" in our ability to give and receive love. Without a vital love relationship with God it is impossible for us to love either our neighbor or ourselves as we should. When we are confident of God's love for us, however, we can return that love to Him, and that free interchange of love enables us to love ourselves and, in turn, to love others.

Self-hatred is probably the greatest single problem in human society, regardless of culture. Decades of research, study, and experience in the fields of human psychology and behavior have revealed that self-hatred lies at the heart of the vast majority of mental, emotional, and psychological problems. Many people have trouble living with others because they have trouble living with themselves. They find it hard either to give love or to receive love from others because they cannot love themselves.

Unfortunately, the problem of self-hatred is not limited to secular culture or the world of the mentally ill or emotionally unstable. The same plague afflicts many followers of Christ as well. Many of us who are believers have an inferiority complex under which we are constantly putting ourselves down, saying negative things about ourselves, and denying our gifts, talents, and abilities. This sense of inferiority is the product of centuries of teaching in the Church that says it is wrong for us to love ourselves. Such teaching equates self-deprecation with humility, when in reality the two are not the same at all. Self-deprecation says, "I am noth-ing. I am worthless, useless, with nothing of value to give to anyone." Humility, on the other hand, is simply believing and accepting what God says about us, and God says that we are anything but worthless.

When Jesus said, "Love your neighbor as yourself," He meant that we are to love our neighbor as much as or to the same degree as we love ourselves. Stated another way, we can love our neighbor only to the same extent that we love ourselves. People who do not love themselves cannot truly love anybody else.

 Humility is simply believing and accepting what God says about us, and God says that we are anything but worthless.

Please understand that I am not referring to a narcissistic and egotis-tical self-love that struts around with an inflated opinion of itself while looking down its nose at everybody else. By "loving ourselves" I mean having a positive self-image and a healthy sense of self-worth based on a proper understanding of our place in the love of God and in relation-ship to God and others.

Why should we love ourselves? What reason do we have? The answer lies in the heart and purpose of God. God created us in His image and likeness, the greatest act and crowning glory of all His cre-ative work, and He pronounced it "good." Sin marred and distorted that image in us. Nevertheless, we were still so important to God and of such great worth to Him that He sent His Son to pay for our sin on the cross so we could be restored to Him. Through Christ, God recreated us in His image—He remade us, as it were—and again pronounced it "good." We should love ourselves, not in a conceited manner, but simply by accept-ing for ourselves the value that God Himself places on us.

We Are Accepted by God

One of the first steps in developing a healthy self-love is to realize and believe that we are completely and absolutely accepted by God. Paul put it this way in his New Testament letter to the believers in Ephesus:

For He chose us in Him before the creation of the world to be holy and blameless in His sight. In love He predestined us to be adopted as His sons through Jesus Christ, in accordance with His pleasure and will—to the praise of His glorious grace, which He has freely given us in the

One He loves. In Him we have redemption through His blood, the for-giveness of sins, in accordance with the riches of God's grace that He lavished on us with all wisdom and understanding (Ephesians 1:4-8).

Verse 6 in the King James Version reads, "To the praise of the glory of His grace, wherein *He hath made us accepted* in the Beloved" (emphasis added). Paul is talking here about a *present* reality, not a *past* experience. In the past we were unacceptable. Because of our sin, God could not accept us. We were outcasts, separated from Him with no hope on our own of returning to Him. Then Jesus came to earth and died on the cross, taking with Him all the things that made us unacceptable. He bore them in His own body, endured the stain of our sin, was obedient to the point of death, and on the third day rose from the dead. With His blood He washed us clean of our sin, making us pure and holy again. Then He brought us before His Father and the Father said, "Accepted!"

If God has accepted us, we should be able to accept ourselves. God is not concerned about outward appearances; those don't matter to Him. Regardless of the flaws or defects we may see or imagine in our-selves, God looks at us and says, "I love you. You are accepted. You are beautiful to Me."

God accepts us even with all of our imperfections. Why then do we have such problems with self-acceptance? One reason is the way we per-ceive our worth, both to ourselves and to others. Many of us may walk around *saying*, "I'm worthy. God has made me worthy," yet deep inside still feel that we are worthless. We look at our education (or lack of it), our physical appearance, our job skills (or lack of them), our gifts, talents, and abilities (or lack of them) and conclude that we are not worth much.

We will always end up with a false picture of ourselves whenever we evaluate our worth according to criteria that God ignores. Our self-worth has nothing to do with physical tangibles, the standards we usu-ally use to judge our value. God does not look at those things.

The true value of anything is the worth that is placed on it by another. For example, gold is simply a shiny yellow metal, a product of the earth and worthless in itself except for the value that humans place on it. Many people have lusted, fought, killed, and died because of the value they put on gold. In the same way, we need to look not to our own standards to measure our value, but to the value placed on us by another—God, our Creator.

We will always end up with a false picture of ourselves whenever we evaluate our worth according to criteria that God ignores.

How much are we worth to God? Looking back at Ephesians 1:4-8 we see that God "chose us...before...creation...to be holy and blameless in His sight" (v. 4). "He predestined us to be adopted as His sons through Jesus Christ, in accordance with His pleasure and will" (v. 5). He "freely" poured out His grace—His unmerited favor—on us (v. 6). He regarded us as valuable enough to send His precious Son, through whose shed blood we have received "redemption" and "the forgiveness of sins" (v. 7). He did all of this deliberately, out of His own "wisdom and understanding" (v. 8) simply because He wanted to.

We are valuable to God; priceless, in fact. We should be careful never to confuse our self-worth, which is given by God, with our appearance, assets, or behavior, or with the behavior or attitudes that others take toward us.

If we make a dumb mistake, we should say, "I made a mistake," not, "I *am* a mistake." Whenever we fail at something, we should acknowledge, "I failed," but never say, "I *am* a failure." We should always keep our behavior or performance separate from our sense of self-worth. No matter what happens, no matter how badly we mess up, or how often, we are still worthy and acceptable to God. He has already declared it to be so, and His Word never changes.

We Are New Creatures in Christ

The past is the past. Who or what we used to be doesn't matter anymore. What matters is who and what we are now and who and what we can become in the future. In his second letter to the believers in Corinth, Paul describes who we are as children of God and reveals the way God sees us: "Therefore, if anyone is in Christ, he is a new creation; the old has gone, the new has come!" (2 Cor. 5:17)

In Christ, everything is new. All the old things have passed away. That means we can forget all the negative, cutting, and hope-destroying things that people have said about us in the past. They're gone! Now we can take hold of the new things. We can dress differently, walk differently, talk differently, and respond to life differently based on the new creation that we are in Christ. No longer do we have to live like poverty-stricken beggars, weak and wallowing in the mud of negative circumstances and depression, bowed low with discouragement and despair.

The picture that we have of ourselves—our self-concept—will always determine how we respond to life. We should not have to look to others to tell us who we are. God has already told us, and shown us in His Word. We are new creations, loved, accepted, and precious in His sight.

 The picture that we have of ourselves—our self-concept— will always determine how we respond to life.

If you have trouble seeing yourself this way, try making a list of everything you can find in the Bible that tells how God feels about you. Tape it to your mirror or somewhere else where you will see it regularly as a reminder to think and act like a beloved child of God, the King and Lord of the universe. Your list might say something like this:

I'm washed, I'm forgiven, I'm whole, and I'm healed. I'm cleansed and I'm glory bound. I am only a sojourner on the earth. I am but a pilgrim on this planet, on my way to perfection, and I don't need anybody to tell me who I am, because I know who I am. I am a child of the King, a son (or daughter) of God, born again through Jesus Christ, bought with the price of His blood. I am a new creation, totally new, thoroughly loved and completely accepted as a child of my Father, precious in His sight.

The people most successful at both giving and receiving love are not the ones who walk around degrading and bad-mouthing themselves all the time, but those who are fully in love with themselves and fully aware that they are loved by God. Because they are at peace within themselves about themselves, they are free both to give love and to allow others to love them.

People who are full of self-hatred have trouble receiving love. They tend to think, *I'm unlovable; how could anyone possibly love me?* This negative self-image and mind-set cause them to reject expressions of love from others as being false or misdirected. At the same time, they cannot give love effectively because their own "love bank" is overdrawn. They have insufficient "deposits" of love from which to draw in loving others.

Any time we base our self-image on how we *feel*, we will run into problems because our feelings change. As long as we feel good, our self-image is good. When we begin to feel bad, however, our self-image plummets. We need to anchor our self-image on something that does not change. Where do we find it?

When we become believers, we become new creations in Christ, recreated in His image. The image of Christ in us will never change. Although our outward appearance will change over time, Christ's image in us will stay the same. Like His image, Christ's attitude toward us also will never change. No matter how good or bad we may feel, no matter how up or down we may be, Christ loves us, accepts us, and thinks the world of us. His opinion of us is the only opinion that matters. We should base our self-image on what He thinks about us, not on what others think, or even on what we think about ourselves.

It is time for us as believers to stop walking around with a second-class opinion of ourselves. We must stop apologizing for being children of God. God takes no pleasure in our dying below our privilege. We are new creations in Christ, and once we start acting and living that way before the world, more and more people will come to Christ as they see us living in victory and joy and at peace with ourselves and with others.

 It is time for us as believers to stop walking around with a second-class opinion of ourselves.

Specific Evidences of Self-Rejection

Another term for self-hatred is self-rejection. People who hate themselves cannot accept themselves as they are. Self-rejection shows up in many different ways. I want to list twelve of the most common symptoms of self-rejection, along with Scripture verses that are useful for countering those symptoms. We need always to measure our attitudes and beliefs against the standard of the Word of God, and adjust them accordingly.

1. Overattention to clothes. People who show undue concern for clothing or fashion may be attempting to compensate for a perceived defect or undesired but unchangeable physical feature. There is nothing wrong with dressing nicely, but we should never let our clothes define who we are. Jesus said, "So do not worry, saying, 'What shall we eat?' or 'What shall we drink?' or 'What shall we wear?' For the pagans run after all these things, and your heavenly Father knows that you need them.

But seek first His kingdom and His righteousness, and all these things will be given to you as well" (Mt. 6:31-33).

2. Inability to trust God. People caught up in self-rejection often have trouble trusting God. If they feel dissatisfied with the way God made them, how can they trust Him with other areas of their lives? Our adversary, satan, by causing us to feel discontent and mistrustful of God, seeks to steal our joy and our hope. Speaking of this, Jesus said, "The thief comes only to steal and kill and destroy; I have come that they may have life, and have it to the full" (Jn. 10:10). Have no fear; we can trust the Lord—completely.

3. Excessive shyness. Shyness stems from the fear of what others think. People who are excessively shy feel that they have nothing worth giving, no useful contribution to make. Not wanting to be hurt, they shut themselves off into their own little world. Being shy is different from being quiet; some people are simply quiet by nature. Shyness, however, is based on fear. This is what the Lord says: "So do not fear, for I am with you; do not be dismayed, for I am your God. I will strengthen you and help you; I will uphold you with My righteous right hand" (Is. 41:10).

4. Difficulty in loving others. This, of course, stems from one's inability to love oneself, which most often is due to one's lack of confidence in the love of God. There is no reason to be unsure of God's love; He declares it in His Word: "I have loved you with an everlasting love; I have drawn you with loving-kindness" (Jer. 31:3b).

5. Self-criticism. This involves complaining about unchangeable aspects of one's person, such as abilities, parentage, social heritage, or undesirable physical features. Isaiah 45:9 contains a warning against this kind of attitude: "Woe to him who quarrels with his Maker, to him who is but a potsherd among the potsherds on the ground. Does the clay say to the potter, 'What are you making?' Does your work say, 'He has no hands'?" Don't fret over what cannot be changed. God made you and loves you just the way you are, and He can use you to do things no one else can do. Let Him bring you into becoming the person that only you can be.

6. Wishful comparison with others. This is related to self-criticism in that it involves one's desire to be different in areas that cannot be changed. The distinction, however, lies at the point of desiring not just change, but to have specific characteristics observed in other people. We should desire not to be like others, but to become like Christ. As Paul wrote to the believers in Rome, "Do not conform any longer to the pattern of this world, but be transformed by the renewing of your mind" (Rom. 12:2a).

7. Floating bitterness. Some people never have anything positive to say. No matter how upbeat a conversation may begin, almost immediately they start gossiping or complaining or badmouthing or expressing anger and bitterness of any other kind. People who walk around with bitterness in their hearts suffer from low self-esteem. In his letter to the believers in Ephesus, Paul had this to say about our speech: "Do not let any unwholesome talk come out of your mouths, but only what is helpful for building others up according to their needs, that it may benefit those who listen" (Eph. 4:29).

8. Perfectionism. There is nothing wrong with desiring to do a good job or to continually improve. Both are healthy attitudes. The problem comes when the time expended outweighs the value of the accomplishment. A perfectionist cannot tell the difference. Often, perfectionism is an effort to compensate for a low self-image. Perfectionists tend to be very legalistic, intolerant of the slightest deviation from the "norm." If that is your problem, lighten up! Again writing to the Romans, Paul said, "Through Christ Jesus the law of the Spirit of life set me free from the law of sin and death" (Rom. 8:2).

9. An attitude of superiority. People who are in self-rejection often overcompensate by affecting a posture of superiority toward others. Boasting of one's achievements, using "highfalutin" vocabulary, and refusing to associate with certain classes of people are all signs of both pride and an inner sense of insecurity and inferiority. A superior attitude is just a cover. The counsel of God's Word is, "Do nothing out of selfish ambition or vain conceit, but in humility consider others better than yourselves" (Phil. 2:3).

10. Awkward attempts to hide unchangeable defects. Self-conscious actions or statements that people use to cover up unchangeable defects may indicate self-rejection. If we have a defect that we cannot change, and God has not yet changed it through prayer, we can claim His promise in Second Corinthians 12:9a, "My grace is sufficient for you, for My power is made perfect in weakness."

11. Extravagance. People who are always trying to overdo it with lavish spending for expensive items in the hopes of eliciting admiration and envy from others may be trying to cover up their self-rejection and sense of personal inadequacy. Life is much more than a preoccupation with things. Jesus said, "Watch out! Be on your guard against all kinds of greed; a man's life does not consist in the abundance of his possessions" (Lk. 12:15).

12. Wrong priorities. Neglecting God-given responsibilities in order to spend great amounts of time in pursuits that will bring acclaim from others may be a sign of self-rejection. Anyone is headed for trouble who concentrates on secondary matters while giving short shrift to the primary issues of life. It would be wise to heed Jesus' warning: "What good is it for a man to gain the whole world, yet forfeit his soul?" (Mk. 8:36)

We Do Not Need Man's Approval—Only God's

Kith and kin to self-rejection is a craving for approval. Everyone needs to feel approved and accepted. Those who cannot approve of themselves seek approval from others. The real danger here is that the approval that the world gives is empty and unfulfilling. Only that approval which comes from God nourishes and satisfies. It is God's approval we need, not man's.

In Second Corinthians 10:17-18, Paul writes, "But, 'Let him who boasts boast in the Lord.' For it is not the one who commends himself who is approved, but the one whom the Lord commends." All who are believers, God has already approved; we do not need anyone else's approval. God has already commended us. To commend means to speak highly of. God speaks highly of His people, even if others speak low of them. Next to salvation itself, the truth that we are approved by God is probably the greatest revelation in the Bible.

Ultimately, seeking approval from the world is a vain pursuit, especially for believers. God's Word actually promises that the opposite will occur. All who bear the name of Jesus and seek to live in obedience to Him are guaranteed to experience persecution from a world that is hostile to His name. As Paul wrote to Timothy, his young protégé in the ministry, "In fact, everyone who wants to live a godly life in Christ Jesus will be persecuted" (2 Tim. 3:12).

In the final analysis, the world's approval means nothing. The way to true blessedness and joy is through obedience and identification with God in Jesus Christ. Jesus Himself made this plain when He said:

Blessed are those who are persecuted because of righteousness, for theirs is the kingdom of heaven. Blessed are you when people insult you, persecute you and falsely say all kinds of evil against you because of Me. Rejoice and be glad, because great is your reward in heaven, for in the same way they persecuted the prophets who were before you (Matthew 5:10-12).

There are a lot of people who spend their lives living for the approval of others. Too many believers are caught up in looking for "fans," too worried about what others think of them. We are not to be so concerned about who approves or disapproves of us, but remember that God's approval is what counts. Those whom God approves are approved indeed. Jesus warned, "Do not be afraid of those who kill the body but cannot kill the soul. Rather, be afraid of the One who can destroy both soul and body in hell" (Mt. 10:28).

 We are not to be so concerned about who approves or disapproves of us, but remember that God's approval is what counts.

Approval seekers get caught up easily in the "gang mentality," whose favorite word is "let's": "Let's do this," and "Let's do that." Anyone who is in "let's" has no personal identity anymore. Those who constantly seek other people's approval have no mind of their own. They do not control themselves from within, but are controlled and manipulated from without, by the very people they are trying so hard to please. Their desire to be liked causes them to surrender their will and self-determination. Proverbs 25:28 says, "Like a city whose walls are broken down is a man who lacks self-control." In other words, if we do not control our own lives from the inside, somebody else will control them from the outside.

The vain pursuit of the world's approval is like the story of two cats, one big and the other little. A big cat saw a little cat chasing its tail and asked, "Why are you chasing your tail so much?"

Said the kitten, "I have learned that the best thing for a cat is happiness, and that happiness is my tail; therefore I am chasing it. When I catch it, I shall have happiness."

Said the old cat to the kitten, "My son, I too have paid attention to the problems of the universe. I too have judged that happiness is my tail, but I have noticed that whenever I chase after it, it keeps running away from me, and when I go about my business without chasing it, it seems to chase me."

My point is this: The most well-liked people are those who don't run around trying to be liked, but who simply relax and concentrate on being themselves. If we have God's approval, we have all the approval we will ever need. Filled with His love, we have the capacity to love Him back, and to love ourselves as well. Winning the approval of other people is no longer of such great importance.

God's love sets us free from the need to seek approval. Knowing that we are loved by God, accepted by God, approved by God, and that we are new creations in Christ empowers us to reject self-rejection and embrace a healthy self-love. Being secure in God's love for us, our love for Him, and our love for ourselves, prepares us to fulfill the second greatest commandment: To love our neighbor as ourselves.

PRINCIPLES

1. We should love ourselves, not in a conceited manner, but simply by accepting for ourselves the value that God Himself places on us.

2. We are completely and absolutely accepted by God.

3. We are new creations in Christ, loved, accepted, and precious in His sight.

4. When we become believers, we become new creations in Christ, recreated in His image. The image of Christ in us will never change.

5. All who are believers, God has already approved; we do not need anyone else's approval.

6. If we have God's approval, we have all the approval we will ever need.

CHAPTER FIVE

Loving Your Partner

In relationships, as in anything else, knowledge is the key to success. Ignorance is dangerous. Whether we are talking about marriage or about less formal and less intimate arrangements, lack of knowledge is the fundamental and most frequent cause of failed relationships.

Conflict and tension arise in relationships most often because men and women simply do not understand each other. They fail to allow for the fact that males and females not only think and act differently from each other, but also perceive their environment in different ways. Much of this misunderstanding is due to the mistaken assumption that because males and females are equal in humanity and personality, they have the same needs as well.

As spiritual beings created in the image of God, men and women are indeed equal. They are equal as distinct persons; they are equal in finding complete spiritual fulfillment in relationship with God; and they are equal in authority and dominion over the earthly realm. As human beings with male and female bodies, however, their needs are distinctly different. This diversity of needs arises from their differences in design and function as males and females.

 Lack of knowledge is the fundamental and most frequent cause of failed relationships.

Function determines design and design determines need. An automobile's function is to provide motorized transportation. To perform that function, most cars incorporate an internal combustion engine as part of their design. That engine, also by design, requires gasoline for its operation. Design determines need. An automobile designed with an internal combustion engine *needs* gasoline in order to function. Kerosene won't work; neither will diesel fuel. Only gasoline will enable the car to fulfill its purpose.

It is the same with males and females: Function determines design and design determines need. Males and females have distinctly different needs because they are designed differently to perform different functions. Success in all human relationships depends on understanding and appreciating those differences.

Jesus said that we are to love God with all our heart, soul, and mind, and then to love our neighbor as ourselves. For the purposes of this chapter, "neighbor" is to be understood in the context of a "partner" of the opposite sex in a relationship, whether a spouse, fiancé(e), friend, or casual acquaintance. "Loving your partner" refers, of course, to *agape*, the divine and highest love which encompasses *phileo*, *storge*, and within the proper context of marriage, *eros*.

Loving our partner, whoever he or she may be and no matter what the relationship, requires that we understand the specific functions of male and female as designed by God as well as the distinctive needs that arise from those functions.

From Spirit to Flesh

In the beginning, God created a spirit being in His own likeness and image, a being that He called forth from Himself, and He called that being "man." Then God housed the spirit man in a physical body made from the dust of the ground. As it happened, that first human body was male in gender. A little later, God took a portion—a "pinch"—of that male body and fashioned from it a female body that also housed a spirit "man." This is exactly what the Scripture tells us: "When God created man, He made him in the likeness of God. He created them male and female and blessed them. And when they were created, He called them 'man' " (Gen. 5:1b-2).

God created "man" but He made "male" and "female." The natural question, though, is, "Why?" As we saw in Chapter Two, in the beginning God was all one—complete and sufficient within Himself. He was alone but not lonely. At the same time, God was love, and love must have an object in order to be fulfilled. Love has a compulsion to give; therefore God needed someone to give to. So, as the natural expression of His love, He created man to receive His love.

In order for love to be complete, the receiver must be like the giver. That is why God spoke to Himself when He created man; the receiver of His love needed to be just like Him. With the creation of man as a spiritual being in God's own image, the cycle seemed complete. God was the Giver, man was the receiver; God was the Lover, man was the loved; God was the Initiator, man was the responder.

Because God's purpose was for the spirit man to exercise dominion over the physical realm, and because spiritual beings cannot apprehend or appreciate physical realities, God had to clothe His spirit man in a physical body. "The Lord God formed the man from the dust of the ground and breathed into his nostrils the breath of life, and the man became a living being" (Gen. 2:7).

Now man was suited out in a physical body—a *male* body, a *human* body, formed from *humus*, the dirt of the ground—and this created a dilemma for him. Man was a receiver of and a responder to God's love, but because He came forth from God and was like God, this male "man" was also a giver and a lover just as God was. Yet, he had no one like himself to give to or to receive his love. Like God who created him, the male "man" was all one—he was alone. In order to be fulfilled and complete, he needed an object for his love.

I want to be clear on this distinction: "Man" as a spiritual being was complete and fulfilled in receiving and responding to God's love; the man as a male physical being was incomplete without another physical being like himself to receive and respond to his love. None of the other creatures God had made were suitable as objects for the human male's need to give and to love because they were not like him.

God recognized the need and knew what to do:

The Lord God said, "It is not good for the man to be alone. I will make a helper suitable for him."...So the Lord God caused the man to fall into a deep sleep; and while he was sleeping, He took one of the man's ribs and closed up the place with flesh. Then the Lord God made a woman from the rib He had taken out of the man, and He brought her to the man. The man said, "This is now bone of my bones and flesh of my flesh; she shall be called 'woman,' for she was taken out of man" (Genesis 2:18,21-23).

A "helper suitable for him" would be one who would be able to receive the male's love and respond to him. Therefore, this helper would be a receiver and responder for the male on the physical plane just as spirit "man" was a receiver and responder for God on the spiritual plane.

God put the male to sleep and took a "pinch" out of his side—the Hebrew word translated "rib" can also mean "side"—and made a female. She was, in the male's words, "bone of my bone and flesh of my flesh," made from the same stuff as the male himself. He called her "woman," the "man" with a "womb." Just as the spirit "man" came forth from God, so the female came forth from the male. Just as the spirit "man" was created to receive and respond to God's love, so the female was made to receive and respond to the male's love.

Another distinction is important here: Both male and female are "man" in the spiritual sense. Both relate directly to God as spiritual beings who have their source and end in Him, from whom they receive love, and to whom they respond in love. Both, therefore, are givers and lovers just as God is. In the physical sense, however, the male is designed to be a giver and lover for the female, and the female is designed to be a receiver and responder for the male. The male gives, the female receives; the male loves, the female responds.

Giving and Receiving

This is the fundamental principle of creation where God and man, male and female are concerned. God gives to man, male gives to female, man receives from God, and female receives from male. Many relationships fail because men do not realize they are to be givers rather than receivers (or takers) where women are concerned and because women do not realize that they are to be receivers rather than givers where men are concerned. In any relationship, when a man fails to give to his woman, he malfunctions. Likewise, when a woman cannot receive from her man, or is forced to give, she malfunctions.

 The male gives, the female receives; the male loves, the female responds.

The vast majority of relationship problems would be solved if every man and woman could only learn and apply this simple truth: Males are designed to give and females are designed to receive. This is evident even in the physical differences between male and female. A male's sexual organs are designed to give; a female's, to receive. That is one reason why homosexual and lesbian relationships are immoral and inappropriate. They violate God's design for the human species and His creation principle for human relationships. It is impossible to have a proper and truly fulfilling relationship between two givers or two receivers.

 The vast majority of relationship problems would be solved if every man and woman could only learn and apply this simple truth: Males are designed to give and females are designed to receive.

When God made a female from that "pinch" of the male's side, He made her the same as the male in almost every regard, except that He altered her chromosomes, making her into a receiver who would be physically compatible to the male. Her capacity to conceive and bear children came into being. The male's capacity to supply the seed already existed; he simply lacked a receiver. Just as God created man (not male) to receive from Him on the spiritual level, He made the female to receive from the male on the physical level.

I want to make it clear that this giving and receiving between male and female is much broader than just the sexual realm. According to the principles God established in the beginning, sexual expression outside the context of marriage is sinful, immoral, and inappropriate. Males are givers by nature and females are receivers by nature, and this is true in every arena of life and relationships.

God is not only a Giver; as Creator He is also an Initiator. Everything that exists came to be because God initiated it. In His sovereign will He chose to bring all creation into being. On the spiritual level, man (not male) is also an initiator, because he came from God. It is this quality that lies behind the great creativity of men and women in the arts, the sciences, and every other field of endeavor.

On the physical level, the male as a giver is also an initiator. As a receiver, a female is designed to respond to the male's initiation. Now don't get me wrong, women are sharp. God gave them just as much of a brain as men (often more!), but He also designed them as females to respond to proper and appropriate initiation and leadership by males.

Many men get frustrated when it seems as though the women in their lives can't make up their minds. Fellows, I've got news for you. As men, *we* are the initiators. The women may simply be waiting on us to make up *our* minds.

Here are a few important principles to remember with regard to the giving and receiving between males and females.

1. When a male *demands*, a female *reacts*; she doesn't respond.

2. When a male *gives*, a female *responds*.

3. When a male *commits*, a female *submits*. Nothing is more precious to a female than a committed male. Nothing is no more depressing to a female than an uncommitted male. Here's the secret, guys: If you want a submitted female, be a committed male. It's that simple.

4. When a male *abuses*, a female *refuses*. Whenever a man abuses a woman, she refuses to respond.

5. When a male *shares*, a female *cares*. If you find a man who is willing to share with the woman in his life, you will find a woman who is willing to care for her man.

6. When a male *leads*, a female *follows*. When a man carries out his God-given responsibility for leadership, a woman responds by following his lead. Leadership does not mean being bossy, always telling others what to do. No, leadership means going ahead, not putting others in the front. Good leaders lead by example, not by decree. Jesus led by example, and so did Moses, Peter, Paul, and all the other great leaders in the Bible. Leading by example means doing ourselves the things we wish others to do.

The Principle of Needs

God created everything to function by specific predetermined principles. Principles are fundamental rules, foundational laws or standards established by the Creator to govern and regulate the functions of His creations. All human beings were created to live by principles; without them, life would be nothing more than an unstable and unpredictable experiment.

Another word for principles is *needs*. Needs are principles that are created by the manufacturer as a predetermined component for the proper functioning of a product. In other words, a need is a requirement necessary for effective function. Every manufacturer designs his product to function in a certain way, and the requirements, or needs, for the proper function of that product are predetermined at the design stage.

Every product comes with inherent needs. A product does not determine its own needs, and neither does the user; those needs are built in. By design, an internal combustion engine comes with an inherent need for gasoline and lubricating oil. Otherwise, it cannot function.

In the same way, every man and woman, every male and female on the earth arrived with predetermined needs built in—needs necessary for proper functioning, a fulfilled life, and sometimes, even survival. More often than not, problems in relationships stem primarily from the fact that men and women do not understand each other's needs. Whenever a product or a relationship breaks down, it is a principle problem: Some need or other is not being met. Ignore the need and eventually the product will fail or the relationship will die. Take care of the need and you will take care of the problem. It really is that simple.

 More often than not, problems in relationships stem primarily from the fact that men and women do not understand each other's needs.

It is important, then, to understand how needs work in people's lives.

First of all, needs control and motivate behavior. Everything a person does is an attempt to meet their needs—everything. Needs determine behavior. People will even lay their lives down in order to have their needs met. For example, why do so many women stay in abusive relationships? The answer is complicated, but usually it is, at least in part, because that relationship, in spite of the abuse, is meeting a felt need in their lives. People's actions are motivated by their needs.

Secondly, needs determine fulfillment. We are fulfilled as people only when our needs are met. Until our needs are met, nothing else in life really matters. Our full attention, everything we do, will be focused on meeting those needs. That is why it is so vitally important in relationships for men and women to understand each other's needs. The life of any relationship is fulfilling the needs of the other person. As a matter of fact, that is one way to define love. Love is making a commitment to meet the needs of another person.

Thirdly, unmet needs are the source of frustration and lack of fulfillment. Frustration in a relationship is an indicator of unmet needs. A frustrated person is an unfulfilled person.

The key to life is meeting needs. It's that simple. When needs are met, creation functions. Satisfied needs produce fulfilled people, and fulfilled people are free to pursue and exercise their full potential as human beings. The primary goal, then, in any relationship should be the meeting of needs. We should not concentrate so much on meeting our own needs, but those of the other person in the relationship. A good test for the health of a relationship is to ask ourselves periodically whose needs we are meeting, ours or theirs? If we are focusing on our needs, the relationship is in trouble. In successful, healthy relationships, both parties put a priority on meeting the needs of the other.

 The key to life is meeting needs.

Another important dynamic of healthy relationships is that when we focus on meeting the needs of the other person, our needs will usually be met as well. It is the law of reciprocation. A person whose needs have been met is free to concentrate on meeting the needs of another.

The Five Needs of the Male and Female

There are five basic needs of males and females that highlight the differences between the two genders. How well we are able to love our partners depends to a large degree on understanding these needs and recognizing the differences.

The first basic need of a male is sexual fulfillment. Males are driven by this need. This drive is God-given and is so prominent in the male because he is the progenitor of the human family; he carries the seed. That's why men are always ready for sex. Their sex drive is not cyclical.

Of course, sexual expression by males or females is sinful and inappropriate outside the context of a marriage relationship. What is an unmarried mature male supposed to do about his sex drive? The same God who created that drive also provides, for those who seek it, the grace and ability to control that drive until they can fulfill it appropriately in marriage.

The number one need of a female is affection. Unlike a male, a female doesn't *need* sex. She can certainly enjoy sex if it's with her husband and accompanied by a lot of affection. A woman cannot function properly without affection. The male in the relationship needs to make sure her affection needs are met.

Affection means that he physically and verbally expresses his love, his care, and his support for her with both physical and non-physical activities: hugs, kisses, flowers, cards, gifts, extending common courtesies, showing little daily acts of thoughtfulness, and so forth.

The second most basic need of a male is recreational companionship. A man needs the woman in his life to be involved in his recreation. Most women do not recognize the importance of this need in a man's life. Find out what he likes to do and join him in it. Even if you do not like it yourself, at least take enough of an interest to have him teach or explain it to you. If he likes sports, watch games with him. If he likes to jog, go jogging with him. If he likes to listen to or perform music, take an interest in it with him. Remember, the key is meeting his needs, not yours.

A female's second greatest need is for communication and conversation. She wants—she needs—the man in her life to *talk* to her. Many men have a problem with this. Some have the mistaken notion that a *real* man is the silent type. A silent man is emotional starvation for a woman. She thrives on conversation. Usually, the end result or "bottom line" of conversation is not as important to her as is the *process* itself. So, men, talk to her. Listen to her. Take time to share with her, not just superficially but at the feeling level. The time invested will pay abundant dividends in a strong and healthy relationship.

The third basic need of a male in a relationship is an attractive woman. This is because men are stimulated visually; that's the way they are wired. Being "attractive" goes far beyond basic subjective opinions of beauty. An attractive woman is one who takes care of herself and seeks to dress and wear her hair and carry herself in such a way as to appeal to the man in her life, to enhance those aspects of herself that attracted him initially.

A woman's third basic need is for honesty and openness. Those two words make many men very nervous because they don't like to talk openly. Being open and honest means being willing to share candidly to the fullest degree that is appropriate for the level of the relationship. Husbands and wives, for example, would normally share at a deeper and more intimate level than would a man and woman who were merely dating. Here's a tip, guys: The more open and honest you are with her, the more she will trust you and be drawn to you, because she interprets openness as love.

The last two needs of the male and female apply more to married couples with established households than to unmarried couples, although the principles apply equally in all cases. Unmarried couples need to adapt these principles to fit their particular situations.

The fourth basic need of a male is domestic support. A man needs a haven, a safe refuge where he can come at the end of a day and find peace and serenity. In short, he needs a supportive home environment. Males are wired by God to be providers for the home. Remember that males are givers. When a man goes out and battles with life all day to support his family, the last thing he needs is to come home to family battles. With more and more women in the workforce now, this issue of domestic support is even more important—for both husband and wife. There are troubles enough in the "daily grind" without upheaval at home to add to the mix. Both husband and wife need to be sensitive to the issue of domestic support.

A female's fourth basic need is financial support. This may not be a major issue for a wife who works outside the home, but it is crucial for a wife who has chosen to stay at home, particularly if she is caring for children. These needs are interconnected. If the husband needs the domestic support of a comfortable home, the wife needs money to help make it that way. She needs to feel secure that the financial needs of her family are taken care of.

Finally, a male needs admiration and respect. The problem is that so many men, by the way they act and the way they treat the women in their lives, don't deserve admiration and respect. However, that does not change the fact that they need them. Men are wired with the need to know that the women they care about admire and respect them. They also bear the responsibility to behave in an admirable and respectable manner.

A woman needs family commitment. In other words, a wife needs to know that her husband is committed to their home and marriage, that he puts her ahead of any other women and puts their children ahead of any other children. She needs to know that he will be home at night and that he will give first priority to his family when making decisions on the commitment of his time.

No matter who we are, male, female, married or single, the greatest thing we can do to love our partner in any relationship is seek to understand his or her unique needs and then commit ourselves to meeting those needs. There are too many self-seeking and self-serving relationships in the world where people are interested only in what they can get, not what they can give.

Remember that *agape*—true love—gives by nature. When we commit ourselves to meet the needs of another we are expressing love in its truest and purest form, a love that gives with no demand or expectation of return, a love that reflects the very heart of the God from whom it came and who is Himself love.

PRINCIPLES

1. Just as the spirit "man" came forth from God, so the female came forth from the male. Just as the spirit "man" was created to receive and respond to God's love, so the female was made to receive and respond to the male's love.

2. God gives to man, male gives to female; man receives from God, and female receives from male.

3. Just as God created man (not male) to receive from Him on the spiritual level, He made the female to receive from the male on the physical level.

4. Males are givers by nature and females are receivers by nature, and this is true in every arena of life and relationships.

5. Whenever a product or a relationship breaks down, it is a principle problem: Some need or other is not being met.

6. Love is making a commitment to meet the needs of another person.

7. The first basic need of a male is sexual fulfillment; for a female, affection.

8. The second most basic need of a male is recreational companionship; for a female, communication and conversation.

9. The third basic need of a male in a relationship is an attractive woman; for a woman, honesty and openness.

10. The fourth basic need of a male is domestic support; for a female, financial support.

11. The fifth basic need of a male is admiration and respect; for a woman, family commitment.

~PART THREE~

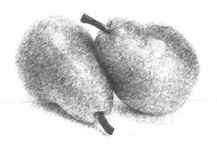

Understanding Love™
For a Lifetime

CHAPTER ONE

Marriage: A Roleless Relationship

$\mathcal{M}$arriage is an adventure. I think most newlyweds would agree that the process of getting married is at once exciting, intimidating, and at least a little scary. After all, leaving the comfortable familiarity of one's childhood home and family to begin a new home and family with the man or woman of one's dreams is emotionally kin to pulling up stakes in one country and sailing across the ocean to start over in another. Getting married has a certain pioneer spirit about it—the flavor of the frontier. Everything is new and different, somewhat raw at first, with even a vague hint of danger.

In those heady days of courtship and engagement, wedding and honeymoon, the very air itself seems charged with magic and wonder. Full of life and vigor, the newlyweds feel ready to take on the world. No door is closed to them. No goal is too high, no dream too lofty. The world is their oyster. Nothing is beyond their grasp.

Eventually, however, reality sets in. The lustrous glow of the honeymoon fades somewhat, and the "we can conquer the world" attitude gives way to more down-to-earth pursuits. One day the couple awakens to the knowledge of a new truth. Looking each other in the face they realize, "Okay, we're married. *Now what?*" Now that they have pledged themselves to each other in a lifelong commitment, how do they make it work? How do they get from here to the hereafter while building a successful marriage along the way? What must they do to fulfill their dream of a lifelong relationship characterized by love, joy, friendship, and fruitfulness? How can they build a successful life together?

These are not idle questions. Success in marriage is not automatic. Likewise, being married does not guarantee either fellowship or communication. As a matter of fact, being married actually exposes how much a husband and wife *do not know* about each other. During courtship and engagement it is easy and customary for the man and woman to try to impress each other by showing only their best side—always looking right, dressing right, and acting right. It is after the wedding when their less attractive and less appealing qualities show themselves. When that happens, it can be quite a shock. Each person begins to see in the other things that he or she never dreamed existed.

One of the first challenges married couples face is reaching a mutual understanding of expectations and roles in the marriage. Failure to do so is one of the major causes of marital problems. Husbands and wives need to work out together the decision-making mechanics in the family and clearly articulate their expectations of each other. How will decisions be made and who will make them? What is the husband's "role"? What is the wife's "role"?

Most couples enter marriage with some preconceptions regarding roles. For example, the husband empties the garbage while the wife takes care of the dishes. The husband cares for the yard and the outside of the house while the wife does the laundry and the cooking and cleaning. The husband works to provide for his family while the wife manages the home and the children.

 Husbands and wives need to work out together the decision-making mechanics in the family and clearly articulate their expectations of each other.

Preconceptions of marital roles are not always correct. Why? One reason is that they are sometimes based on outdated customs or cultural ideas. Another reason is that they often fail to allow for individual gifts, talents, or abilities that are not necessarily gender-based. A successful marriage depends in part on a proper understanding of roles. Part of this understanding involves knowing the sources of common role perceptions and being able to evaluate the validity of those perceptions.

Sources of Common Role Perceptions in Marriage

Perceptions of marital roles, in western culture at least, generally arise from any of four common sources: tradition, parents, society, or the Church. Each of these sources exerts a powerful influence over the way husbands and wives view themselves and each other.

Tradition. Many of our most commonly held views of marital roles have been passed down to us through tradition. We adopt particular roles because "that's the way it has always been done." Husbands work at the office or factory as the family's "breadwinner"; wives work at home cooking, cleaning, and taking care of the children. Husbands rule over everything and everyone in the home, including their wives; wives submit passively to their husbands. Husbands make virtually all decisions affecting the family; wives go along with those decisions.

Tradition is not necessarily a bad thing. Sometimes tradition is important for maintaining stability and order. At the same time, however, we need to recognize that just because something is traditional does not mean that it is correct. Traditions can be founded on error just as easily as they can be founded on truth. Even if they were correct at one time, traditions have a way of outlasting the circumstances that originally brought them into being. Married couples must be very careful about defining roles based solely on tradition.

 Traditions have a way of outlasting the circumstances that originally brought them into being.

Parents. Perhaps the most influential role perceptions in a marriage are those that the couple learns from their parents. Parents are, in fact, the primary channels through whom traditional role concepts are passed to the next generation. Most people adopt the role identities and relational methods they saw modeled at home while they were growing up. Whether those models were positive or negative, and despite their desire or intention to the contrary, most children grow up to be like their parents. One area where this is particularly true is in the raising and disciplining of children. Differing parenting philosophies and methods is a common point of conflict and disagreement for young married couples.

As with tradition, parental models of marital roles should be carefully evaluated because they may be wrong. Just because mom and dad did things a certain way for 40 or 50 years does not mean they did them right.

Society. Popular culture is another significant source for defining marital roles. This is distinct from tradition because where tradition remains unchanged for generations, social evolution is constantly creating new customs and trends. Modern society communicates its values and belief system primarily through the schools, through the entertainment industry (particularly television, movies, and popular music), and through the media. Throughout much of the western world these culture-shaping forces are dominated by a philosophy that is thoroughly rationalistic and humanistic in its worldview, allowing no place for either a Supreme Being or a truly spiritual dimension to life.

The pervasiveness of this influence makes it easy for anyone, even unwary believers, to easily pick up and internalize these values subconsciously. When believers bring worldly values and attitudes into their relationship, trouble always results. It is important that they keep their focus on the Word of God—the Bible—as their standard and source of knowledge.

When believers bring worldly values and attitudes into their relationship, trouble always results.

Church. Traditionally, the Church has been one of the primary shapers of marital role perceptions in Western culture. Although this is an appropriate function for the Church in society, it is an unfortunate fact that many of the "traditional" teachings of the Church regarding marital roles and male/female relationships in general have been negative, particularly where the woman is concerned.

For example, the Church in general has taught for many years that the woman is a "frail vessel," the "weaker sex," a fragile creature who must be handled with great care and not expected to perform any "heavy" tasks, either physical or mental. Modern research in biology and medicine has demonstrated conclusively that this is simply not true. Both physically and mentally, women are equal to men, although in different ways.

Another erroneous teaching is that women have little or nothing to offer spiritually to the overall life of a church. They are useful in service roles— the kitchen, the nursery, the choir—but not in *real* ministry like prophesying or laying hands on the sick.

The Church also has taught women to "submit" to their husbands no matter how they are treated. This is regarded as showing proper "respect" for their husbands. Wives who dare to strike back over harsh treatment are regarded as outcasts in the Church. Much of the traditional teaching on submission is based on a gross misunderstanding of the Scriptures, which has led to devastating results in the lives and relationships of countless women.

Much of the traditional teaching on submission is based on a gross misunderstanding of the Scriptures, which has led to devastating results in the lives and relationships of countless women.

Relating in Love

If the traditional sources for marital role perceptions are not always correct or relevant, what is to be done? Where can a married couple turn to find a reliable standard? Is there an "operating manual" for a successful marriage? Yes, there is. The best place to go for technical information on any product is the manufacturer. Marriage is no different. God created marriage and established it as the first and foremost of all human institutions and relationships. As the "manufacturer" of marriage, God understands it better than anyone else. It only makes sense, therefore, to refer to His "tech manual," the Bible, for information on how to make it work.

Surprisingly, many of the "traditional" marital roles are not specifically delineated in the Scriptures. There are no bulleted lists, no equations, and no formulas. What the Bible does provide are *principles*. Perhaps the most significant description of how husbands and wives are to relate to each other is found in the words of Paul, the first-century Jewish-Christian scholar, Church leader, and missionary:

Wives, submit to your husbands as to the Lord. For the husband is the head of the wife as Christ is the head of the church, His body, of which He is the Savior. Now as the church submits to Christ, so also wives should submit to their husbands in everything. Husbands, love your wives, just as Christ loved the church and gave Himself up for her to make her holy, cleansing her by the washing with water through the word, and to present her to Himself as a radiant church, without stain or wrinkle or any other blemish, but holy and blameless. In this same way, husbands ought to love their wives as their own bodies. He who loves his wife loves himself. After all, no one ever hated his own body, but he feeds and cares for it, just as Christ does the church— for we are members of His body. "For this reason a man will leave his father and mother and be united to his wife, and the two will become one flesh." This is a profound mystery—but I am talking about Christ and the church. However, each one of you also must love his wife as he loves himself, and the wife must respect her husband (Ephesians 5:22-33).

These verses mention nothing about specific, fixed "roles" for the husband and wife, but they do identify certain principles that should guide their relationship: submission, love, and respect. It is interesting to note that although Paul states four times that husbands should love their wives, he never once mentions that wives should love their husbands. Their love is implied in their submission to and respect for their husbands.

Clearly, Paul's emphasis here is on the attitude and behavior of the husbands: They are to love their wives "as Christ loved the church and gave Himself up for her." This focus on the husband is important for at least two reasons. First, by God's design the husband is the "head of the wife" and the spiritual leader of the home. His attitude and behavior will set the spiritual tone for the home and profoundly affect his wife's general and spiritual well-being.

The second reason is less evident to our modern-day social understanding. During the first century, when Paul wrote these words, women in both Jewish and Roman society were regarded as second-class citizens and had few rights of their own. Wives were viewed as little more than the property of their husbands. Paul's call for husbands to *love* their wives, particularly in the self-sacrificing way that Christ loved His Church, was a radically new concept, even revolutionary in its implications.

Love between a husband and wife was not itself new—ancient literature of every culture is full of love songs—but Paul's emphasis was. He was referring to a love in which a husband would serve his wife as Christ served the Church and would give his life for his wife as Christ gave His life for the Church. Sacrificial love is in itself a form of submission. Paul was talking about a love that would elevate a wife to *equal status* as a person in her husband's eyes.

 Sacrificial love is in itself a form of submission.

The closest this passage comes to defining marital roles is to say that a husband's "role" is to love his wife in a sacrificial, self-giving way, and a wife's "role" is to "submit" to her husband "as to the Lord" and to "respect" her husband. These "roles" are reciprocal. Any husband who is truly faithful to do *his* part will make it easy for his wife to do *her* part. Likewise, any wife who has a husband who loves her in this way will have no problem respecting him or submitting to his headship.

At the most basic level, then, a husband and wife should relate to each other through mutual love and submission rather than through a set of predefined roles, no matter what their source.

Relating without Roles

Essentially, marriage is a roleless relationship. It can be no other way if the marriage is truly grounded in sacrificial love. Sacrificial love is unconditional love—love without reason. True love has no reason; it just is. Unconditional love loves regardless of the behavior or "loveableness" of the ones loved, and whether or not they return that love. The New Testament identifies this kind of love with the Greek word *agape*. It is the kind of love that God exhibits toward a sinful human race, the kind of love that Jesus Christ demonstrated when He willingly died on the cross for that sinful race. As Paul wrote in his letter to the believers in Rome, "You see, at just the right time, when we were still powerless, Christ died for the ungodly. Very rarely will anyone die for a righteous man, though for a good man someone might possibly dare to die. But God demonstrates His own love for us in this: While we were still sinners, Christ died for us" (Rom. 5:6-8).

Sacrificial love is unconditional love—love without reason.

God does not need a reason to love us; He loves us because love is His nature. His love for us does not hinge on whether or not we "turn over a new leaf," "clean up our act," or love Him in return. *Agape* makes no demands, holds no expectations, and carries no guarantees except to guarantee itself. The Lord guarantees that He will love us regardless of whether or not we return His love.

The love of Christ is a roleless love based on responses rather than expectations. His death on the cross was His love *responding* to humanity's need for forgiveness. Jesus placed no expectations on us as a pre-condition to His sacrifice. He gave His life freely with no guarantee that any of us would love Him back. The only expectation Jesus had was His own joy and exaltation before His Father: "Let us fix our eyes on Jesus, the author and perfecter of our faith, who for the joy set before Him endured the cross, scorning its shame, and sat down at the right hand of the throne of God" (Heb. 12:2).

His is an unconditional, open invitation: "For God so loved the world that He gave His one and only Son, that *whoever* believes in Him shall not perish but have eternal life" (Jn. 3:16, emphasis added); "Yet *to all who received Him*, to those who believed in His name, He gave the right to become children of God" (Jn. 1:12, emphasis added). These words imply that Jesus had no guarantee. His love led Him to the cross, and He still would have died even if no one had believed in Him or received Him. *Agape* has no reason.

Love that looks for a reason is love with conditions attached. Conditions give rise to expectations. By expectations I mean those mundane and routine jobs, functions, or activities that husbands and wives automatically expect each other to do because it is their "role," such as washing the dishes, cooking the meals, cleaning the house, cutting the grass, making the bed, bathing the children, and so on. Expectations lead inevitably to disappointment. Disappointment leads to arguments, which strain the relationship, which then endangers fellowship.

What does all this have to do with a roleless relationship in marriage? Marital love is supposed to be like the love that Jesus has for His Church: unconditional, sacrificial, and without expectations or guarantees. Fixed roles create expectations, and expectations imply guarantees. For example, if a wife sees mowing the lawn as her husband's "role," that role creates in her mind the expectation that he will cut the grass when it gets tall. If he does not, he has violated the "guarantee." Her expectation turns to disappointment or even anger, and conflict results. If a husband believes that meal preparation is his wife's "role," he will be upset if supper is not on the table when he gets home from work. His wife has not fulfilled the "guarantee" implied in his expectation, which is based on his perception of her "role."

 Fixed roles create expectations, and expectations imply guarantees.

The upshot of all this is that love without reasons is love without expectations. If there are no expectations, there are no fixed roles. Marriage then becomes a relationship based on responding to needs rather than adhering to rigid preconceptions. If a husband and wife have no rigid role expectations of each other, neither will be disappointed. A response-based approach to marriage will bring a deep, fresh, and new dimension to the relationship. Married couples will experience greater success and happiness the more they learn how to relate without fixed roles.

Temporary Responsibilities, Not Permanent Roles

A roleless relationship in a marriage does not mean that nobody does anything or that the couple takes a random or haphazard approach to their home life. On the contrary, it is important for a husband and wife to come to a clear and mutual understanding of how things will be done. A relationship without fixed roles *does* mean that each partner will respond according to need, ability, and opportunity. Who regularly cooks the meals? That may depend on who is the better cook. Some husbands can cook better than their wives can. In that case, why should the wife be saddled with the responsibility to prepare the meals simply because that is her "traditional" role?

A role is a temporary responsibility that is based on the ability of the one who responds. As such, roles can change from one day to the next, from one minute to the next, and from one person to the other depending on the need of the moment. What needs to be done? Who can do it the best? Who is in the best position to do it right now? It is a matter of need, ability, and opportunity. That's why it would probably be better to refer to marital tasks as responsibilities rather than roles. Whatever the need, whoever is able and available at the time is responsible.

Relating without fixed roles is a natural outgrowth of a marriage based on *agape* and in which the husband and wife truly are equal partners. *Agape* seeks to serve rather than to be served. Jesus demonstrated this principle in a powerful example recorded in John 13:3-17. On the night before He was crucified, Jesus gathered with His followers to celebrate the Passover. As the disciples entered, no one was present to wash their feet (a task normally assigned to the most menial of servants) and none of them volunteered to do it. Their unspoken attitude was, "That's not my job!" Jesus Himself got up from the table, took off His outer clothing, wrapped a towel around His waist as a servant would, and proceeded to wash His disciples' feet. There was no question of roles. Jesus saw a need and responded to it. At the same time, He taught His followers a valuable lesson in humility and service.

Agape expresses itself in conscious response to recognized needs. It is not an automatic or unconscious reaction to stimuli based on conditioned habits or attitudes. A husband's anger at his wife's "failure" to wash the clothes may be simply a conditioned reaction to her violation of his role concept for her. An *agape* response would be to think before acting or speaking and evaluate the situation to see if there are mitigating circumstances—a legitimate reason why the laundry has not been done. Perhaps she has been caught up all day caring for a sick child. She may be under tremendous stress on the job or up to her eyebrows in homework for her night class. Whatever the reason, *agape* seeks to help with a need, not criticize a failure. Even if this husband and wife have a mutual understanding that she will normally take care of the laundry, in this instance the *agape* response—the roleless response—may be for him to wash the clothes and take some of the load off her. *Agape* doesn't look for roles; *agape* responds to needs.

 AGAPE *expresses itself in conscious response to recognized needs.*

Husbands and wives who approach their marriage from a roleless perspective assume full ownership of every aspect of their life together. There are no "his" and "her" roles, only "our" responsibilities. Who does what, and when, depends on the specific circumstances. Each couple should arrive at a mutual agreement as to which of them has the *primary* responsibility for each task or need, understanding as well that ultimately they share all responsibilities together.

Assignment of marital responsibilities may depend on each person's training, abilities, or temperament. Who should prepare the meals (primarily)? Whoever is the best cook. Who should manage the family finances (primarily)? Whoever has the best head for figures and bookkeeping. Who should do the house cleaning? Whoever lives in the house. Who should wash the dishes? Whoever dirties them. Who should make the bed? Whoever sleeps in it. Who should mow the lawn? Whoever has the time and the opportunity.

Clear assignment of primary authority and responsibility between a husband and wife establishes order and helps prevent chaos and confusion. At the same time, rather than producing rigidity in the relationship, it allows for flexibility so that either partner can do what is needed at any given time. Whoever can, does; whoever sees, acts. It's that simple.

Functioning in marital responsibilities also will be affected by whether or not both partners have jobs outside the home. A stay-at-home wife can reasonably be expected to regularly bear a larger share of the domestic responsibilities than can a wife who works a full-time job. Sharing responsibilities becomes even more important when both the husband and wife are away from home during the day. Each partner needs to take into account the schedule and obligations of the other, including those of work. Mutual understanding and cooperation are essential.

 Whoever can, does; whoever sees, acts. It's that simple.

So then, what is the husband's "role" in the marriage? He is the "head" of the home, the spiritual leader responsible for the spiritual direction of the family. He is to love his wife in the same way that Christ loved the Church, sacrificially and unconditionally. What is the wife's "role"? She is to respect her husband and submit to his headship. In the practical matters of home life they both should respond according to the need, their abilities, and their availability.

PRINCIPLES

1. At the most basic level, a husband and wife should relate to each other through mutual love and submission rather than through a set of predefined roles.

2. Essentially, marriage is a roleless relationship.

3. The love of Christ is a roleless love based on responses rather than expectations.

4. If there are no expectations, there are no fixed roles. Marriage then becomes a relationship based on responding to needs rather than adhering to rigid preconceptions.

5. A relationship without fixed roles *does* mean that each partner will respond according to need, ability, and opportunity.

6. A role is a temporary responsibility that is based on the ability of the one who responds.

7. *Agape* doesn't look for roles; *agape* responds to needs.

8. In a roleless marriage there are no "his" and "her" roles, only "our" responsibilities.

9. Assignment of marital responsibilities may depend on each person's training, abilities, or temperament.

CHAPTER TWO

The Question of Submission

*L*earning how to relate without fixed roles can be a major challenge for married couples, particularly if traditional role concepts are deeply ingrained in their minds. Successfully making the change will require significant adjustments in their thinking. Because most human cultures have operated for so long under the paradigm of a male-dominated social order, the concept of marriage as a partnership of equals characterized by a role-less relationship does not come easily to many people. Nevertheless, that is the biblical model.

In the beginning, God created man—male and female—in His own image and gave *them* dominion over the earth to rule it *together* (see Gen. 1:26). The first human couple enjoyed a marriage in which they were equal partners, sharing equal rights and equal responsibilities. They walked in open and continual fellowship with each other and with God.

The day came when Adam and Eve chose to disobey God. Immediately their circumstances changed. Their sin broke their fellowship with God and caused their equal-partnership marriage to degenerate into a shadow of its former self with the woman subjugated to her husband. This corrupted, male-dominated marriage became the "normal" pattern for male/female relationships in a sin-tainted world.

From the start God had a plan to restore mankind to fellowship with Himself. He sent His Son, Jesus Christ, to die on a cross for the sins of humanity, thereby breaking the power of sin and destroying its effects. Part of God's plan was to restore the institution of marriage to its original, pristine condition.

The first human couple enjoyed a marriage in which they were equal partners, sharing equal rights and equal responsibilities. They walked in open and continual fellowship with each other and with God.

A marriage between believers can and should be characterized by a role-less relationship in which both the husband and wife are equal partners. This, however, raises the natural question of how to reconcile the biblical concept of equal partnership in marriage with the equally biblical concept of a wife being in submission to her husband. On the surface these appear to be opposite and irreconcilable ideas. In the previous chapter we touched briefly on this subject, but understanding the question of submission is so critical to long-term success and happiness in marriage that we need to take a much closer look at it.

Husbands Should Act Like Jesus

We already have seen that mutual love, submission, and respect should characterize husband/wife relations in a biblical marriage, but what exactly does this mean? Consider once again the counsel that Paul gave to the Ephesians:

Submit to one another out of reverence for Christ. Wives, submit to your husbands as to the Lord. For the husband is the head of the wife as Christ is the head of the church, His body, of which He is the Savior. Now as the church submits to Christ, so also wives should submit to their husbands in everything. Husbands, love your wives, just as Christ loved the church and gave Himself up for her to make her holy, cleansing her by the washing with water through the word, and to present her to Himself as a radiant church, without stain or wrinkle or any other blemish, but holy and blameless. In this same way, husbands ought to love their wives as their own bodies. He who loves his wife loves himself. After all, no one ever hated his own body, but he feeds and cares for it, just as Christ does the church—for we are members of His body. "For this reason a man will leave his father and mother and be united to his wife, and the two will become one flesh." This is a profound mystery—but I am talking about Christ and the church. However, each one of you also must love his wife as he loves himself, and the wife must respect her husband (Ephesians 5:21-33).

Paul's first instruction concerns mutual submission: "Submit to *one another* out of reverence for Christ." Everything Paul says in these verses is in the context of mutual submission. A wife submits to her husband "as to the Lord" and the husband loves his wife "just as Christ loved the church and gave Himself up for her." This self-giving love on the part of the husband is itself a form of submission. It is this submission by the husband on behalf of his wife that is so often overlooked in teaching and in practice.

Throughout this passage Paul compares the husband to Christ. Wives are to respect and submit to their husbands "as to the Lord." The husband is "the head of the wife as Christ is the head of the church." Husbands are to love their wives "just as Christ loved the church and gave Himself up for her." In every case, the husband is to look to Christ as the example for his own behavior. What this means in practical terms is that a husband deserves and has the right to expect submission and respect from his wife to the extent and degree that he lives and acts like Jesus toward her. A husband deserves his wife's submission as long as he acts like the Lord. If he does not act like the Lord, then he has no right to expect his wife to submit to him "as to the Lord."

A husband deserves his wife's submission as long as he acts like the Lord.

Paul says that wives are to submit to their husbands "as the church submits to Christ." How does Jesus get His Church to submit to Him? What would happen if Jesus suddenly appeared and walked through your church swinging a baseball bat to see how many heads He could knock off, and yelling, "Listen up! You'd better do what I say, or else!" What if He started cursing His Church or kicking and spitting and bad-mouthing His Church? There would be an epidemic of backsliding, and I would be one of them. He would lose followers left and right. Who would want to follow that kind of "loving" Lord?

No, Jesus won the love, respect, and submission of His Church through His own submission to her in sacrificial love. Freely and willingly He gave His life for the Church. With His blood He cleansed the Church of sin and guilt and made her holy, blameless, and without any stain or blemish. Through His Spirit Jesus strengthens and sustains the Church, always loving her and showing compassion to her, always forgiving her, and always providing for her needs according to His riches in glory (see Phil. 4:19).

Jesus is the perfect example. If husbands want to learn how to win their wives' love, respect, and submission, they need to look at how Jesus treats His Church and follow His pattern.

If husbands want to learn how to win their wives' love, respect, and submission, they need to look at how Jesus treats His Church and follow His pattern.

Most Husbands Have Dropped the Ball

Unfortunately, the sad truth is that, measured against the standard set by Jesus, most husbands don't deserve submission. When it comes to loving their wives the way Christ loved the Church, most husbands have dropped the ball. This does not mean that the majority of husbands do not sincerely love their wives and want to do their best by them. The failure of husbands to measure up to Christ's standard reveals a fundamental flaw that lies at the heart of every man, a flaw shared also by every woman. The Bible calls this flaw "sin," and it has been a part of human nature ever since the first human couple defied God in the Garden of Eden and went their own way. Sin is the flaw that prevents husbands from measuring up to Jesus' example.

 Measured against the standard set by Jesus, most husbands don't deserve submission.

Although Adam and Eve enjoyed equal partnership and authority in the Garden of Eden, God had appointed Adam as the "head" of the family with the overall responsibility of teaching and guiding his wife in the ways of God. After Adam and Eve disobeyed God, sin became part of their nature. It destroyed their fellowship with God and made them fearful of Him so that they hid themselves. When God came looking for them, He sought out Adam first. Even though Eve was the first to disobey and then drew her husband in, Adam was the "head," and God held him primarily responsible.

> *But the Lord God called to the man, "Where are you?" He answered, "I heard You in the garden, and I was afraid because I was naked; so I hid." And He said, "Who told you that you were naked? Have you eaten from the tree that I commanded you not to eat from?" The man said, "The woman You put here with me—she gave me some fruit from the tree, and I ate it"* (Genesis 3:9-12).

As soon as he was confronted with his failure, Adam tried to shift the blame to his wife. Refusing to acknowledge his guilt, Adam tried to transfer responsibility to someone else—and men have been transferring responsibility for their failures ever since.

When Adam disobeyed God and sin entered his nature, four things happened immediately in his life. First, he knew he was guilty. He refused to acknowledge it, but he knew it. Second, he became afraid. Sin caused separation between man and God and that separation created fear. Third, he hid himself, and, fourth, he felt shame.

Refusing to acknowledge his guilt, Adam tried to transfer responsibility to someone else—and men have been transferring responsibility for their failures ever since.

All of these are the common experience of all men. Even today men know when they are wrong even if they never admit it. The thought of being exposed as a failure fills them with fear. Men still hide from their failures. Many hide behind their ego, their physical strength, or their position or status in the community. Others hide behind money, influence, political power, their jobs, sports—anything that helps them avoid having to deal with their failures.

Although few would readily admit it, when a man messes up he feels ashamed, no matter how tough he might act. He may disguise his shame with bragging talk or "macho" behavior with the "boys." He may try to drown it in liquor or act out his self-hatred by beating his wife and kids. The shame of a failed marriage may drive him into the arms of a mistress. He may seek to deflect his shame by blaming his wife for his failures.

Nothing destroys a man's ego like failure. Men have a great fear of being "naked"—of having their failure exposed for all the world to see. That's why so many men seek out false security in persons or environments that will affirm their manhood without bringing up their shortcomings. They would rather bask in the warmth of a false self-image than face the truth about themselves.

Husbands Should Shoulder Their Responsibilities

So here is the dilemma: Husbands are supposed to act like Jesus, yet few husbands do. Of course, no one is perfect; no husband can perfectly model the behavior of Christ. The problem is that so many husbands really have no clue how they are supposed to act or what they are supposed to do. They have been hiding from their true selves for so long that even if they realize that they need to change, they don't know how.

Husbands who are serious about following Jesus' example in relating to their wives must be willing to shoulder their responsibilities. They must be willing to accept responsibility for their actions without denying them, hiding from them, or shifting the blame to someone else, particularly their wives. They need to recognize that because they are human they will occasionally fail, but this does not have to be a cause of shame or disaster. A relationship established on *agape* will create an environment of forgiveness and support. Any husband who honestly tries to love his wife "as Christ loved the church" will find her at his side ready and eager to help him succeed. What reasonable woman could fail to respond to a man who truly loves her, covers her, protects her, provides for her, gives himself for her, and, humanly speaking, makes her the center of his world?

Within the overall context of loving his wife, a husband's first and primary role is to be the spiritual head and covering and teacher in the home. Through his words, lifestyle, and personal behavior the husband should teach the Word, the will, and the ways of the Lord to his wife and children.

One of the biggest problems in marriage and family life today is that in so many homes the husband has effectively abdicated his headship either by default or ignorance. In many believing households the wife knows more about the Lord and His Word and ways than her husband does because she spends more time exposed to them. She is in church while her husband is off somewhere else doing his own thing. Even if he is in church with her, the husband frequently is less engaged and involved in spiritual matters than his wife is. How can a husband teach what he does not know? How can he model for his family a lifestyle he knows nothing about?

One of the biggest problems in marriage and family life today is that in so many homes the husband has effectively abdicated his headship either by default or ignorance.

If more husbands were faithful in loving their wives as Christ loved the Church and in fulfilling their responsibility as head of the home, there would be little problem or confusion over the issue of wives being in submission.

Husbands Should Woo their Wives as Christ Wooed the Church

Just as Paul compares the husband to Christ, he compares the wife to the Church. Wives are to submit to their husbands as the Church submits to Christ. At the same time, husbands are to love their wives as Christ loved the Church. The two are reciprocal actions: As the husband loves his wife sacrificially, his wife submits to him.

Husbands must win their wives' submission by making themselves worthy of it. They do this by learning to love their wives in the way that Christ loves His Church. How does Christ love His Church? How does He draw His people to Him so that they submit to Him?

The two are reciprocal actions: As the husband loves his wife sacrificially, his wife submits to him.

Jesus wins us by wooing us. First He reveals Himself to us in some way and captures our heart with His love. Then He gently draws us to Himself: "I have loved you with an everlasting love; I have drawn you with loving-kindness" (Jer. 31:3b). He extends an open invitation for us to come to Him, be forgiven of our sins, and receive the gift of everlasting life. Once we understand how much He loves us and how much He has done for us, we realize that we would be crazy *not* to follow Him. That's when, in response to His gentle drawing, we decide *of our own free will* to come to Him.

Submitting ourselves to Christ is *our* choice. He never pushes His way in. Jesus never twists our arm or pressures us in any other way. He simply says, "Here I am. Come to Me." Submission is never forced from without. Submission is freely chosen and willingly given. Once we submit ourselves to Jesus, He becomes the center of our life. He has wooed us so well and we love Him so much that we are ready to go anywhere and do anything for Him.

In the same way, a husband should woo his wife. Always hold her in highest honor and regard her with utmost respect as a person. Cover her with prayer and protect her. Treat her with kindness, consideration, and compassion. Don't be afraid to show tender affection. Remember to do little acts of thoughtfulness. Buy her flowers. Take her to dinner at a fine restaurant. Surprise her with a weekend getaway just for two. In words, in deeds, and in every other way possible, let her know that she is loved, valued, and regarded above all others.

A Wife's Submission Is Voluntary

So far we have focused almost exclusively on the responsibilities of the husband. This is for at least two reasons: first, because the husband bears the greater responsibility since he is the head of the home, and second, because his responsibility is so widely misunderstood and therefore so rarely fulfilled.

The husband is the "head" of his wife; he is not her "boss." Neither is he the "boss" of the home. This is where so many husbands misunderstand. It may be a narrow distinction, but Christ *leads* His Church, He does not *rule* His Church, as with a heavy iron fist. Christ rules His Kingdom, but He *leads* His Church. He loves and cherishes His Church, and His Church submits to Him freely and willingly.

So what about the wife? What is her responsibility with regard to her husband? Consider again Paul's instructions in Ephesians: "Wives, submit to your husbands as to the Lord.... Now as the church submits to Christ, so also wives should submit to their husbands in everything" (Eph. 5:22,24). How does the Church submit to Christ, its Lord? Freely and willingly, out of love. Those qualities should also characterize a wife's submission to her husband.

Paul's words in these verses constitute a command: "Wives, submit to your husbands." Notice that this command is given to the wives, not to the husbands. Wives are commanded to submit to their husbands. Nowhere does Paul either command or give any authority to husbands to force their wives to submit. Forced submission is not true submission; it is subjugation. Submission is always freely chosen and willingly given.

Even though submission is commanded for the wife, her compliance is *voluntary*. She has the right to choose. As far as her husband is fulfilling his responsibility and seeking to love her with the same kind of sacrificial, self-giving love with which Christ loved the Church, a wife has the responsibility to submit to him "in everything." If she fails to do so, she is accountable not so much to her husband as to the Lord. Her failure to be in submission to her husband's headship is sin.

 Forced submission is not true submission; it is subjugation.

A wife's submission to a godly husband who strives to be like Jesus in his attitude and behavior toward her is not a demeaning or demoralizing act. Submission does not mean humiliation or abject subjection of a wife's personality and will to the whim and will of her husband. A husband who acts like Jesus toward his wife will not subject her to this kind of treatment anyway.

Submission means that a wife acknowledges her husband's headship as spiritual leader and guide for the family. It has nothing whatsoever to do with her denying or suppressing her will, her spirit, her intellect, her gifts, or her personality. To submit means to recognize, affirm, and support her husband's God-given responsibility of overall family leadership. Biblical submission of a wife to her husband is a submission of *position*, not person-hood. It is the free and willing subordination of an *equal* to an *equal* for the sake of order, stability, and obedience to God's design.

As a man, a husband will fulfill his destiny and his manhood as he exercises his headship in prayerful and humble submission to Christ and gives himself in sacrificial love to his wife. As a woman, a wife will realize her womanhood as she submits to her husband in honor of the Lord, receiving his love and accepting his leadership. When a proper relationship of mutual submission is present and active, a wife will be released and empowered to become the woman God always intended her to be.

Proper understanding and exercise of biblical submission by *both* the husband and wife are critical to the long-term success and happiness of any marriage. Without them, the couple will never realize their complete identity in Christ or release their full potential as human beings created in God's image.

PRINCIPLES

1. A husband deserves and has the right to expect submission and respect from his wife to the extent and degree that he lives and acts like Jesus toward her.

2. Sin is the flaw that prevents husbands from measuring up to Jesus' example.

3. Within the overall context of loving his wife, a husband's first and primary role is to be the spiritual head and covering and teacher in the home.

4. Husbands must win their wives' submission by making themselves worthy of it. They do this by learning to love their wives in the way that Christ loves His Church.

5. Submission is never forced from without. Submission is freely chosen and willingly given.

6. As far as her husband is fulfilling his responsibility and seeking to love her with the same kind of sacrificial, self-giving love with which Christ loved the Church, a wife has the responsibility to submit to him "in everything."

7. Biblical submission of a wife to her husband is a submission of *position*, not personhood. It is the free and willing subordination of an *equal* to an *equal* for the sake of order, stability, and obedience to God's design.

∼ CHAPTER THREE ∼

Mastering the Art of Communication

*A*mong the complaints that marriage counselors hear most frequently are statements like, "She just doesn't understand me," or "He never listens to me." The vast majority of marriages that are on the rocks today have run aground, either directly or indirectly, because of the couple's inability to communicate with each other.

Over my many years in ministry I have counseled hundreds of couples with marital problems. In all but a handful of cases the troubled relationship stemmed essentially from a communication breakdown at its core. Whenever I counsel a married couple, several ground rules apply. First, when the husband talks, the wife listens. Second, when the wife talks, the husband listens. Third, after both of them have talked, I talk and they listen. While one is speaking, no one else interrupts. It is always interesting to see the look of astonishment that so often appears on the face of each spouse while the other one is speaking. In many cases, this is the first time in months or even years that they have actually *listened* to each other, and they are absolutely amazed at what they hear.

Communication is an art that must be learned, a skill that must be mastered. It does not happen automatically, even in marriage. True communication can occur only in an environment conducive to honest self-expression. Many couples spend a lot of time talking *at* each other but very little time actually talking *to* each other. Just because they are talking does not mean they are communicating.

The only time some couples talk is when they argue. Sometimes critical statements and negative comments are virtually all a husband and wife hear from each other. Communication is best learned in an open, honest, and non-confrontational environment. Couples who do not learn how to communicate in such a low-key setting will never be able to do it in a confrontational situation.

Building the environment for effective communication must be deliberately planned. If I want to grow a nice garden, I cannot leave it to chance. I have to choose a spot for maximum sunlight, prepare the soil, plant the seeds, add fertilizer, pull weeds regularly, and make sure the plants get adequate water. In the same way, an environment conducive to communication must be built and nurtured deliberately and with great care. Couples who establish and maintain an atmosphere of openness, trust, and grace for talking about the good things also will find it much easier to talk about tough issues when they arise.

 Communication is best learned in an open, honest, and non-confrontational environment.

Communication is to love what blood is to life. Leviticus 17:11 says that life is in the blood. It is impossible to have any kind of healthy relationship without communication. This is true for anyone, whether regarding human relationships or a relationship with God.

Understanding Communication

Part of the problem with communication in marriage stems from the fact that many couples are confused about what it really means to communicate. Genuine communication requires both speaking and understanding. "Speaking" refers to any means by which thoughts, ideas, or feelings are expressed, whether by voice, gestures, body language, or facial expressions. Understanding involves not only hearing what was said, but also interpreting what was said according to the speaker's intention.

Communication between male and female or husband and wife is complicated by the fact that men and women think differently, perceive things differently, and respond differently. In general, men are logical thinkers and women are emotional feelers. Men speak what they are thinking while women speak what they are feeling. Men interpret what they hear from a logical frame of reference and women, from an emotional frame of reference. In other words, a man and a woman can hear the exact same message at the exact same time from the exact same speaker and perceive that message in two completely different ways. The same problem can easily arise when they are trying to communicate with each other.

Many people seem to equate conversation with communication. Just because two people talk to each other does not necessarily mean that they understand each other. What one says may not be what the other one hears, and what one hears may not be what the other one means. Two-way conversation does not guarantee communication. Once again, the key is understanding.

Understanding goes beyond simple acknowledgement of someone's spoken word. The verbal element is only a small part of the overall dynamic of human communication. Non-verbal elements such as gestures, facial expressions, and body language play an even greater part than the spoken word in determining how we interpret the messages we receive. Which would you believe, if I said, "I love you," with a warm smile, or through gritted teeth with a scowl on my face and fist clinched? Although the words are the same, the message conveyed is totally different.

 Non-verbal elements such as gestures, facial expressions, and body language play an even greater part than the spoken word in determining how we interpret the messages we receive.

Communication is a process by which information is exchanged between individuals or groups utilizing a common system of symbols, signs, or behavior. To communicate is to transmit information, thought, or feeling so that it is satisfactorily received or understood. It is a two-way interaction between people in which messages are both sent and received and where both parties understand what the other party means. If I speak to you and you speak back to me, confirming with me that what you heard and understood me to say is what I really meant, then true communication has taken place.

If the key to communication is understanding, the key to understanding is listening.

Listen Up!

In our fast-paced, high-stress modern society today, listening has become almost a lost art. Failure to listen is one of the most frequent problems related to communication. So often our natural tendency is to speak before we listen. We could avoid a lot of hurt, misunderstanding, and embarassment if we would simply learn to listen before we speak.

Epictetus, a first-century Greek philosopher, said, "We have two ears and one mouth so that we can listen twice as much as we speak." There is a great deal of truth in that statement. The Bible contains many similar words of wisdom. Throughout the Scriptures, listening is linked to knowledge and understanding. Over and over the Book of Proverbs calls us to *listen* to words of wisdom and learn. Time and again Jesus appealed to the crowds to *listen* to Him: "Jesus called the crowd to Him and said, 'Listen and understand'" (Mt. 15:10). Many are the times when Jesus said, "He who has ears, let him hear."

Perhaps the most direct reference to the balance between listening and speaking is found in the New Testament Book of James: "My dear brothers, take note of this: Everyone should be quick to listen, slow to speak and slow to become angry, for man's anger does not bring about the righteous life that God desires" (Jas. 1:19-20). James links the readiness to listen with the ability to avoid uninformed speech and unnecessary or inappropriate anger. How many times do married couples spout off and get angry with each other simply because they do not take the time to listen first? We could paraphrase James' counsel this way: "Listen first! Don't be in a hurry to talk, and even then be careful what you say and how you say it. Don't have a short fuse because explosive anger will only sabotage your spiritual growth."

Listening involves more than simply hearing or comprehending what someone says. Everything we hear passes through the filters of our own beliefs and experiences as well as our knowledge and impression of the speaker. These filters color how we interpret what we hear and can cause us sometimes to misunderstand the speaker's meaning. Good listening involves reaching beyond our filters to hear what other people are really saying, not only with their words, but also with their tone of voice, their facial expressions, and their body language.

Another problem related to listening is when we are more concerned about our own words than we are with the other person's words. Have you ever been talking to someone and found that rather than listening to them you are busy thinking about what you are going to say next? Have you ever felt that someone else was not listening to you for the same reason? This kind of thing happens all the time and we call it "conversation." It may be conversation, but it is not communication because no one is listening. There is no exchange of information with confirmed mutual understanding.

Part of the art of listening is learning to give the other person our full attention, taking a genuine interest in what he or she has to say with an honest desire to understand. If communication is our goal, we need to focus more on the other person's words, ideas, and values than on our own. Nothing in the world blesses a person like having someone listen—*really listen*—to him or her.

 Nothing in the world blesses a person like having someone listen—really listen—to him or her.

Proper and effective listening requires that we get our full faculties involved. In order for genuine communication to take place, we must learn to listen *fully*, engaging body, mind, intellect, emotions, eyes, ears—in short, everything. We need to listen *first* and set aside our own thoughts and words and agenda long enough to hear and understand the other person. Once we understand and the other person knows that we understand, then we can respond more appropriately from the context of that understanding. This establishes a clear channel for genuine two-way communication to take place.

Holistic Communication

Because communication is an art, it must be deliberately, patiently, and carefully learned over time. Effective face-to-face communication is always holistic in nature, involving all the senses and the full engagement of body, intellect, and mental energy.

Communication is an exchange of information—a message—between individuals in such a way as to bring mutual understanding. Every message contains three essential components: Content, tone of voice, and nonverbal signals such as gestures, facial expressions, and body language. When all three work in harmony, the probability of mutual understanding is very high. If any element is missing or contrary to the others, the likelihood of successful communication diminishes significantly.

In any communication where human emotions and personalities are involved, nonverbal elements are more significant than verbal. This is easily verified in life. A friend has just lost a loved one. You want to help, to express sympathy, but you don't know what to say. Quite often in a situation like this words are totally inadequate. Of greater value to your friend is simply your physical presence. A hug, a warm embrace, sharing quiet tears together—these simple nonverbal acts communicate your love and support for your friend much more clearly than could any number of fumbling words, no matter how well-intentioned they might be.

Research bears this out as well. Studies in communication have shown that the verbal aspect—the basic content—comprises only 7 percent of the total message that we send or that another person receives. Tone of voice accounts for 38 percent while the remaining 55 percent is nonverbal. In other words, how someone else perceives and understands us depends only 7 percent on *what* we say, 38 percent on *how* we say it, and 55 percent on what we are *doing* when we say it.

If we wish to avoid misunderstanding, hurt feelings, and arguments, we need to be careful to make sure that our tone of voice and our gestures, facial expressions, and body language send the same message as the words we speak with our lips.

This area of the nonverbal is where so many people—and so many married couples—have so much difficulty in communication. Problems arise between a husband and wife when there is a disconnection between *what* they say to each other and *how* they say it. The wrong tone of voice can be particularly devastating, causing an otherwise simple disagreement or misunderstanding to escalate into a shouting match or a hurtful barrage of sarcastic barbs fired back and forth.

Problems arise between a husband and wife when there is a disconnection between what they say to each other and how they say it.

For this reason, it would be good for couples to remember James' counsel to "be quick to listen, slow to speak and slow to become angry." Proverbs 15:1 provides another valuable bit of advice: "A gentle answer turns away wrath, but a harsh word stirs up anger." When trying to communicate with each other, a husband and wife should be careful to make sure their voices and faces agree with their words.

Five Levels of Communication

Most relationships never get beyond superficial interaction. Lasting relationships, however, move deeper. One sign of a healthy and growing relationship is a deepening level of intimacy in the interaction and communication of those involved in the relationship.

People interact for the most part at one or more of five different levels of communication, each level being deeper and more intimate than the previous one. At the lowest level is casual conversation. It is superficial and safe, such as the kind of talk we would have with a stranger in line with us at the supermarket. "Hello, how are you?" "I'm fine, and you?" "I'm fine, too. How are the children?" "They're fine. What do you think about this weather we're having?" There are no deep probing questions and no painful or embarrassing personal revelations, only polite, courteous, and inconsequential conversation. Everything is non-threatening and non-committal.

The next highest level of communication involves reporting the facts about others. This is the kind of conversation in which we are content to talk with others about what someone else has said or done, but offer no personal information or opinions on these things. This is the level of the objective journalist, reporting only the facts of a situation, and then usually only what someone else has said. It involves no personal element.

Level three is where true communication first occurs because we begin to express our ideas, opinions, or decisions with the specific intention of being heard and understood by others. This openness also places us for the first time at a level of personal risk. Anytime we reveal any part of our inner selves—thoughts, ideas, beliefs, opinions—we open the door to possible rejection or ridicule. Intimacy is growing at this level, but there is still a safety zone. Our personal beliefs and ideas are less vulnerable to injury than are our emotions and innermost being, which at this level are still safely tucked away.

At level four we feel secure and intimate enough to begin sharing our emotions. Although deep and serious communication occurs at this level, there is still a guarded quality to the relationship. We are not yet ready to open up completely and let the other person see us as we really are deep down inside.

The highest level of all is the level of complete emotional and personal communication, characterized by absolute openness and honesty. At this level there are no secrets and no "off-limits" areas. We are ready and willing to lay our hearts bare, to open up every room and every compartment and invite close inspection. There is no greater or deeper level of intimacy than when two people feel free and secure enough to be completely honest with each other. At the same time, the risks of rejection or ridicule are at their greatest as well. Risk is unavoidable where true intimacy is involved. One way to define intimacy is the willingness and trust to make oneself completely open and vulnerable to another. Vulnerability always involves risk, but there is no other path to true intimacy or genuine communication at its deepest level.

 Risk is unavoidable where true intimacy is involved.

Long-term success and fulfillment in marriage depends to a large degree on the scope and depth to which a husband and wife develop their art of communication. It is vitally important that they learn how to listen to and understand one another and feel comfortable sharing their deepest and innermost thoughts, feelings, joys, sorrows, hopes, and dreams. Marriage is a lifelong journey of adventure with surprises and challenges at every turn. Learning to communicate effectively is also the journey of a lifetime. It is neither quick nor easy, but it yields increasing rewards of intimacy and fulfillment through the years that are well worth the hard work required.

PRINCIPLES

1. True communication can occur only in an environment conducive to honest self-expression.

2. Genuine communication requires both speaking and understanding.

3. To communicate is to transmit information, thought, or feeling so that it is satisfactorily received or understood.

4. The key to communication is understanding, and the key to understanding is listening.

5. Good listening involves reaching beyond our filters to hear what other people are really saying, not only with their words, but also with their tone of voice, their facial expressions, and their body language.

6. Effective face-to-face communication is always holistic in nature, involving all the senses and the full engagement of body, intellect, and mental energy.

7. How someone else perceives and understands us depends only 7 percent on *what* we say, 38 percent on *how* we say it, and 55 percent on what we are *doing* when we say it.

8. One sign of a healthy and growing relationship is a deepening level of intimacy in the interaction and communication of those involved in the relationship.

9. One way to define intimacy is the willingness and trust to make oneself completely open and vulnerable to another.

CHAPTER FOUR

Don't Forget the Little Things

*U*nderstanding and practicing general concepts such as marital responsibilities, submission, and communication are key to a happy and successful
marriage. As critical as these principles are, however, ultimate success
depends also in giving attention to the "little things"—those simple, ongoing, daily courtesies and considerations that enhance communication and
add sweetness to a relationship. Because they are simple, the "little things"
can be easily overlooked amidst the clamor of more pressing concerns.

In marriage, as in any other endeavor, we cannot afford to underestimate
the importance of "little things" to overall success. The Great Wall of China
was built one brick at a time. The Great Pyramid on the Giza plateau in
Egypt rose up stone by stone. Ignoring little details may lead to serious consequences. As 17th-century English poet George Herbert wrote:

> For want of a nail, a shoe was lost;
> For want of a shoe, a horse was lost;
> For want of a horse, a rider was lost;
> For want of a rider, a message was lost;
> For want of a message, a battle was lost;
> For want of a battle, a kingdom was lost;
> All for want of a nail.

The Old Testament book, Song of Solomon, speaks of "the little foxes that
ruin the vineyards" (Song 2:15b). Many marriages get into trouble because
spouses ignore the little details, the day-by-day thoughtfulness that
strengthens their relationship as well as the "little foxes" of neglect, discontent, and unresolved issues that eat away at the "vineyard" of their happiness. Married couples need to give due attention to both in order to help
ensure the long-term success, health, and vitality of their marriage.

Rebuke but Don't Criticize

One of the most dangerous of the "little foxes" to be let to run loose in the marital "vineyard" is criticism. Nothing shuts down communication and disrupts the harmony of a relationship faster than harsh, sniping, negative comments. No one profits from criticism—neither the critic nor the person being criticized, or anyone else who may be within earshot. Constant criticism destroys a person's spirit. It breeds hurt, resentment, defensiveness, and even hatred. Criticism discourages openness and honesty, without which no relationship can remain healthy. By its very nature criticism is destructive because it focuses on finding fault with the intention of hurting rather than of finding a solution. People who are critical all the time usually have unmet needs or unresolved issues in their own lives, and these problems reveal themselves in the form of a critical spirit.

 Nothing shuts down communication and disrupts the harmony of a relationship faster than harsh, sniping, negative comments.

Every relationship at times faces interpersonal conflicts that must be dealt with for the good of everyone involved. Part of effective communication is establishing an environment in which problems can be resolved in a healthy manner. Hurtful criticism is never the answer. Rather, in such situations a rebuke may be in order.

Criticism and rebuke are not the same thing. A rebuke differs from criticism in at least two important ways: the spirit from which it comes and the purpose for which it is given. Criticism arises from a wounded and self-centered spirit that seeks to wound in return. It is not interested in either the welfare of the person being criticized or in finding a constructive solution to the problem. A rebuke, on the other hand, comes from a loving and compassionate spirit that not only recognizes a problem but also seeks a fair and equitable solution with a heartfelt desire for the good of the other person. In short, a rebuke is motivated by love, whereas criticism is not. A rebuke focuses on the solution while criticism harps on the problem. A rebuke seeks to correct while criticism only complains.

Watch out for the "little fox" of criticism that can nibble away at your relationship. Develop the discipline of thinking before speaking. Whenever a problem arises or a conflict flares up and you feel the urge to criticize, ask yourself if it is a legitimate problem for which rebuke and correction are in order, or only a personal gripe. Check your motivation: Are you acting out of love or out of anger?

Criticism profits nothing, but rebuke and correction do. There are two sides to this coin, however. Being willing and able to give correction is one side; being willing to receive correction is the other. Openness to correction is one of the most important elements of growth. People who are unwilling to receive correction will never grow. They will always be immature.

 Openness to correction is one of the most important elements of growth.

Don't Get Too Familiar

Another "little fox" to watch out for is the "fox" of familiarity. One of the greatest dangers to a marriage is for the husband and wife to become too familiar with each other. This is not the same as knowing each other. Spouses should know each other better and more intimately than they know anyone else in the world. A husband and wife should be each other's best friend. By familiarity I mean a comfortable complacency that causes a husband and wife to start taking each other for granted.

Familiarity reveals itself in at least three ways. First, it breeds ignorance. Couples feel so familiar with each other that they begin to ignore each other in lots of little ways that they may not even be aware of. Second, familiarity breeds assumptions. A husband and wife begin to assume that each knows what the other is thinking. The husband assumes not only that his wife knows what he is thinking but also that he knows what she is thinking. The wife makes the same assumptions. Third, familiarity breeds presumption. A wife will make a presumption regarding what her husband will say or do without even asking him first. A husband will make the same mistake with regard to his wife. If these three continue long enough the end result will be that as expressed in the old proverb, "Familiarity breeds contempt."

Here's a practical example of how this happens. Before marriage, when a couple is courting, they constantly tell each other how they feel. They don't assume anything. They pay attention to every little detail, every nuance of voice, every gesture and facial expression. They never presume to second-guess each other. They talk sweet things to each other on the phone for three hours and, meeting in person an hour later, spend two more hours saying more of the same. They compliment each other, give each other gifts, and spend every available moment together.

This constant attention to each other is good and necessary to building a strong relationship because it produces in each person a deep sense of security. They feel secure in each other's love and affection so that even when they are apart they still bask in the warmth of the knowledge that someone loves and cares about them. The more often we are told that we are loved, the more secure we feel.

For some reason, things begin to change after a couple gets married. It usually does not happen right away. Gradually the husband and wife start to assume things about each other. The husband stops saying to his wife, "I love you," as often as he once did. He assumes, "She knows I love her. I don't need to tell her all the time." This may not even be a conscious thought. They stop going out to dinner or on other dates. They stop giving "just because I love you" gifts or cards or flowers to each other. They have become comfortable together, and this comfort breeds a familiarity that can cause them to slowly drift apart without even realizing it.

When a married couple becomes too familiar with each other, a lot of the adventurous spontaneity goes out of their marriage. Marriage should be stable and strong so that both partners feel secure, but within that environment there should always be room for adventure. One excellent way to keep a marriage alive and vital and exciting is for the husband and wife both to be spontaneous at times—to do something unexpected. It may be something big, like a weekend away just the two of them, or something small and simple, like a candlelight dinner or a bouquet of flowers "just because." The key is to avoid familiarity and predictability by never taking each other for granted. Among other things, this means developing the practice of regularly expressing appreciation for each other.

 When a married couple becomes too familiar with each other, a lot of the adventurous spontaneity goes out of their marriage.

Express Honest Appreciation

Learning to appreciate people is one of the most effective ways to create an environment for open communication, as well as one of the most important nutrients for building healthy relationships. Appreciation involves being aware of what others do for us, letting them know that we recognize it, and thanking them for it. It also means praising someone for his or her accomplishments with sincere happiness at his or her success. It is very easy to be critical or to become jealous over another's achievements or attention. Most of us have to work at being appreciative because it goes against our selfish human nature.

One important thing that expressing honest appreciation does for us is to keep us mindful of our dependence upon each other. None of us ever achieves success or happiness by ourselves. There are people all along our path of life who help us on our way, and often it is easy to ignore or overlook their contribution. Nowhere is this truer than in marriage. Humanly speaking, a husband's greatest asset for success and happiness is his wife, and a wife's, her husband. They should be each other's greatest supporter, promoter, and encourager. No matter what happens in other circles, a couple's home should always be a place where they can find consistent love, appreciation, and affirmation.

Spouses who maintain a regular practice of expressing their love and appreciation to each other, even during good times when it is easy to take these things for granted, will discover that this deep sense of security will sustain them through bad times as well. Knowing that we are loved and appreciated by *someone* helps put in perspective the rest of life with all of its ups and downs. I can remember days when everything seemed to go wrong—nothing was working right at the office; some people canceled appointments while others did not follow through with what they said they would do. The car ran out of gas, then had a flat tire in the middle of a pouring rain. In times like those the only thing that kept me going was the secure knowledge that I had a wonderful woman at home—my wife—who loved me and cared about me.

Expressing honest appreciation regularly is so important to marital health that we cannot afford to leave it strictly to our emotions. Sometimes we don't feel like being appreciative. We may be tired or sick or angry or preoccupied. We must develop the habit of doing it anyway, based not on emotions but on knowledge. Emotions might say, "I don't feel like it," or "Don't bother me right now," whereas knowledge would say, "He *needs* to be affirmed right now," or "She *needs* me to reassure her that everything is all right."

Men generally have more of a problem with this than women do. For some reason, a lot of men have the idea that expressing their feelings openly and frequently to their wives is somehow unmasculine and a sign of weakness. On the contrary, there is nothing unmanly about a husband saying often to his wife, "Honey, I love you." A man who does this is displaying strength, not weakness. It takes more strength for a man to make himself vulnerable and expose his tender side than it does to put up a false "macho" façade that says, "I'm tough; I don't need to say that kind of stuff."

That's not acting tough; that's acting stupid because not even God takes that stance with us, and He is a lot bigger and a lot smarter than we are. Every day in many ways God tells us and shows us that He loves us. He does not leave it to chance. He knows we need to be reassured of it all the time. Those who are believers and followers of Christ know by experience that the Holy Spirit gives daily affirmation of God's love.

Husbands and wives need to get into the habit of expressing their love and appreciation for each other on a *daily* basis. Living under the same roof and sharing the same bed are no proof of love. Just ask any of the thousands of affection-starved men and women who endure unhappy marriages day after day.

Love is fed by love, not time. We need to get so used to expressing love and appreciation for each other that we feel uncomfortable whenever we *don't* do it. Honest love and appreciation are the lifeblood of a happy marriage. Don't take them for granted.

Husbands and wives need to get into the habit of expressing their love and appreciation for each other on a daily basis.

Don't Ever Assume Love

Love needs to be expressed regularly and often; it should never be assumed. Husband, never assume that your wife knows that you love her; *tell her*! Even if you told her yesterday, tell her again, today. She needs to hear it every day. Wife, don't assume that your husband knows that you love him; *tell him*! Even though he may never come right out and say it, he needs that reassurance from you. No matter how tough and strong he may appear on the outside, he still needs you to tell him that you love him. We humans have a built-in need to be affirmed in this on a daily basis. Where love is concerned, there is no room for assumption.

In this, as in everything else, Jesus provides us with a wonderful example. Ephesians 5:21-33 teaches that husbands and wives are to relate to each other the way Christ and the Church—His Bride—relate to each other. Verse 25 says that "Christ loved the church and gave Himself up for her." This is a reference to His death on the Cross. In John 15:13 Jesus told His followers, "Greater love has no one than this, that he lay down his life for his friends." Jesus' death on the Cross for us was the greatest expression of love in history. Even so, Jesus never assumed that the example of His death alone would be enough to keep us assured of His love for all time. He knew that we needed daily reassurance. This is one reason why after His resurrection He sent the Holy Spirit to dwell in all who believed in Him.

As recorded in the Gospel of John, Jesus refers to the Holy Spirit as a "Counselor" or "Comforter" (see Jn. 14:16,26; 15:26; 16:7 KJV). The Greek word is *parakletos*, which literally means "one who is called alongside." One important role of the "Comforter" is to "comfort" or reassure us on a daily basis of Christ's love for us. This is what Paul was referring to when he wrote, "God has poured out His love into our hearts by the Holy Spirit, whom He has given us" (Rom. 5:5b). For those who believe and follow Christ, the Holy Spirit resides permanently in their hearts and lives as a continual reminder of the love of God. Jesus gives us constant reassurance of His love; He never assumes that we know it.

Neither should we ever assume that our spouses know that we love them. Love may indeed "spring eternal," but our expression of it needs to be refreshed every day. We need to say it to our loved ones, and we need to hear them say it to us. Once, or even once in a while, is not enough. Here is an example.

Suppose a husband bought his wife a nice new car as an expression of his love for her. She is so excited and overjoyed with it, and he is pleased to be able to provide it. A few days later she asks, "Honey, do you love me?" A little surprised at her question, he answers, "I bought you that car, didn't I?" Several months later she asks again, "Honey, do you love me?" Again he replies, "I bought you that car, didn't I?" A year goes by, then another, and another, and it is always the same thing. Finally, 15 years later, the wife asks, "Honey, do you love me?" "I bought you that car, didn't I?"

 Love may indeed "spring eternal," but our expression of it needs to be refreshed every day.

Doesn't that sound ridiculous? Yet, this is not too far from the truth with many marriages. Some people go weeks, months, and even years with no tangible expression of love from their spouses, either verbal or otherwise. In our minds, yesterday's act of love does not necessarily carry over to today. We all need daily reassurance.

Although verbal expression accounts for only 7 percent of what we communicate when we interact with one another, it is still one of the most important elements for feeding and nurturing love, especially for women. Men thrive on what they see, women thrive on what they hear, and both thrive on what they feel. Words reinforce actions, and women need to *hear* words of love, affection, and appreciation from their husbands.

Most men don't spend enough time simply *talking* to their wives. Over the years I have counseled hundreds of couples who were on the verge of divorce over this very issue. I could not begin to count the number of times I have had a conversation with the husband that runs something like this:

"Do you talk to your wife?"

"Well, she knows I love her. I don't have to talk to her and tell her that. After all, I buy her rings and other nice things."

"I didn't ask you what you *bought* her. Do you *talk* to her?"

"She knows I love her."

"You're making an assumption."

"Look, I buy food for her and the kids, and…"

"I didn't ask you that. Do you *talk* to her?"

"Well, I bought her flowers on Mother's Day. I'm sure she knows I love her because of that."

"You're assuming again, and you're also presuming that your gifts equal your love, but that's not true."

Giving *things* is no proof of our love. We must give *ourselves* first. That's exactly what Jesus did; He gave Himself for us. Then we must verbalize our love. We must make our words match our actions. If we do not communicate our love verbally, we can end up confusing the difference between the thing and the person. We must learn to appreciate each other, communicate with each other, and talk to each other. Talking is the strongest way to attach meaning to our actions. We must be careful never to assume *anything* in our relationships, especially love.

Pay "Little Attentions"

Any happily married couple will be quick to agree that their happiness is due in large part to simple daily thoughtfulness—little attentions that they pay to each other on an ongoing basis. These can take many forms. Compliments are always in order, whether referring to a well-cooked meal, a promotion at work, a fetching new hairstyle, a completed painting or poem, or whatever it might be. Honest gratitude sincerely expressed is always a winner. What reasonable person could reject a heartfelt "thank you"? Unfortunately, because it is so easy for married couples to slip into the rut of taking each other for granted, compliments and thank-yous are often in short supply and overlooked in many households.

Usually, common sense is our best guide where daily thoughtfulness is concerned, coupled with consistent application of the "Golden Rule": "Do to others as you would have them do to you" (Lk. 6:31). In other words, treat others the way you would like to be treated. Show others the same thoughtfulness and consideration that you would want them to show you.

Don't wait for someone else to show consideration for you. Be proactive in this; set the example yourself. If you have agreed to pick your wife up at a certain time and find yourself running late, stop somewhere and give her a call, even if your tardiness is unavoidable and for a good reason. Don't assume that she knows that you have been unavoidably delayed. Be true to your word. If circumstances force a change in your plans, let her know. She deserves that courtesy. Besides, that little extra effort of consideration and communication will prevent misunderstanding and an unpleasant argument later.

Think about the kinds of things that make you happy or make you feel loved and secure, and do those same things for your spouse. Iron his shirts just the way he likes. Send her flowers "just because." Write secret love notes and hide them in his sock drawer or in his shirt or pants pocket, or in her jewelry box, or in other unexpected places around the house that your spouse will be sure to look every now and then. Sure, it takes time to write these notes, but the rewards reaped in marital harmony and happiness will be well worth the time invested.

Let your imagination go. Be creative. Find ways to surprise and delight your spouse with "random acts of thoughtfulness." Paying little attentions will help keep romance and the spirit of courtship alive in your relationship, even after many years of marriage.

 Find ways to surprise and delight your spouse with "random acts of thoughtfulness."

Always Show Courtesy

Above all, always be courteous. Everyone deserves to be shown basic human kindness and dignity because we are all created in the image of God. Spouses should extend more courtesy to each other than they do to anyone else, yet courtesy often is one of the first things to fall into neglect in a marriage once a couple has become "familiar" with each other.

Courtesy works both ways. Wives should be just as courteous toward their husbands as they desire and expect their husbands to be toward them. Husbands, open the car door for her. Pull out the chair for her at the restaurant. Always treat her as if you were still courting her. After all, why would the things that won her heart in the first place not still be appropriate to keep her heart? In every situation, both public and private, show her the utmost respect. She deserves nothing less, and you will lift her in esteem before the world, making it clear to everyone that she is more important to you than anyone else.

Wives, don't be too proud or too "liberated" to allow your husband to extend such simple courtesies to you. Otherwise you will destroy his ability and opportunity to bless you. God created the male to find his fulfillment in blessing and giving of himself to the female. Don't deny him the chance to fulfill himself by fulfilling you.

Always be courteous toward your husband, respecting him in speech and in action, especially in public. This is not a demeaning deference as a servant to a master, but the esteem of one equal partner toward the other. Men especially need to be esteemed in the eyes of their colleagues and peers, and no one can do that better than their wives. Take advantage of every opportunity to support him and lift him up and encourage him.

Whenever a husband and wife are together in public, there should never be any doubt in anyone's mind that the two of them share a relationship characterized by mutual love, esteem, and respect. These qualities are nurtured and strengthened by the little things—not criticizing, showing honest appreciation, clearly expressing love, paying little attentions, and extending common courtesies—that they build into their marriage from the beginning.

 Don't forget the little things. They are the building blocks for the big things.

Don't forget the little things. They are the building blocks for the big things—things like effective communication; growth of genuine love; and firm establishment of harmony, happiness, and lifelong success in marriage.

PRINCIPLES

1. Ultimate success in marriage depends largely on giving attention to the "little things"—those simple, ongoing, daily courtesies and considerations that enhance communication and add sweetness to a relationship.

2. By its very nature criticism is destructive because it focuses on finding fault with the intention of hurting rather than of finding a solution.

3. A rebuke comes from a loving and compassionate spirit that not only recognizes a problem but also seeks a fair and equitable solution with a heartfelt desire for the good of the other person.

4. One of the greatest dangers to a marriage is for the husband and wife to become too familiar with each other—to take each other for granted.

5. One excellent way to keep a marriage alive and vital and exciting is for the husband and wife both to be spontaneous at times—to do something unexpected.

6. Honest love and appreciation are the lifeblood of a happy marriage.

7. Love needs to be expressed regularly and often; it should never be assumed.

8. Paying little attentions will help keep romance and the spirit of courtship alive in the relationship, even after many years of marriage.

9. Above all, always be courteous.

CHAPTER FIVE

Kingdom Management Principles for Couples

*I*f there is any single area of married life that causes more problems for couples than any other, it would have to be resource management. Although it certainly includes financial matters, resource management goes far beyond simply the question of how a couple handles their money. Resource management impinges on every facet of a couple's life together: employment and job choices; spending, saving, and investing money; career, professional, and educational goals; future dreams; and even family planning.

Another word for resource management is *stewardship*. A steward is one who manages the assets and affairs of another person. Although not the owner of those assets, a steward generally has wide latitude and authority in managing them on behalf of the owner. Continued stewardship is contingent upon the steward's faithfulness and effectiveness in representing the owner's interests. Successful stewards bring growth and increase of the assets under their charge, leading frequently to their being entrusted with even more assets and greater responsibility.

This principle is clearly taught throughout the pages of the Scriptures. One of the best biblical pictures of stewardship is seen in the life of Joseph. Genesis chapters 37–50 tell how Joseph was sold into slavery by his treacherous brothers, yet rose to become the most powerful government official in Egypt, second only to the pharaoh. As a slave of the captain of Pharaoh's bodyguard, Joseph proved himself a faithful and effective administrator of his master's estate, which prospered greatly under his stewardship.

Even after he was falsely accused of trying to rape his master's wife and was thrown into prison, Joseph continued to be faithful. The chief jailer recognized Joseph's gifts and integrity and placed him in charge of all the other prisoners. Once again, Joseph ably managed all that was placed under his care.

Eventually, the day came when Joseph's gifts drew the attention of the pharaoh himself. Impressed with the young man's wisdom, integrity, and obvious administrative abilities, the pharaoh elevated Joseph from slave to prime minister of all Egypt. Joseph's skillful management in this position made the most of seven years of bumper-crop prosperity and carried the nation successfully through the seven years of severe famine that followed. During this time he was also instrumental in saving the members of his own family from starvation—including the brothers who had treated him so cruelly so many years before.

Joseph prospered as a steward because he was faithful to his God and because he was faithful in his management of the resources entrusted to him. Recognizing that God was the true owner of all things, Joseph took great care to discharge his responsibilities in an honorable manner.

What does all this have to do with success and longevity in marriage? Simply this: Good stewardship is a solid biblical principle for growth, prosperity, and happiness. Too many married couples struggle financially and in other areas because they have an inadequate understanding of the truth that, as Creator, God is the owner of all things and that they are merely stewards and responsible to Him for how they manage the resources He places in their charge.

Designed for Stewardship

Stewardship is woven into the very fabric of God's original design for human life and experience. When God created mankind—male and female—He gave them dominion "over the fish of the sea and the birds of the air, over the livestock, over all the earth, and over all the creatures that move along the ground" (Gen. 1:26b). The essence of dominion is rulership. God created men and women to rule over the created order as equal partners under His supreme sovereignty. He charged mankind with the responsibility of being stewards of the earth and all its resources. Even though in the garden context of creation this equal partnership is seen through the framework of marriage, the kingdom management principles revealed there apply in every setting and circumstance and to all persons, whether male or female, married or single.

 Stewardship is woven into the very fabric of God's original design for human life and experience.

To exercise dominion over the earth means to govern, control, or rule over it; it is to gain mastery over it. Mastery over the earth does not mean untrammeled exploitation and waste of resources but careful and wise management of them. Properly administered, dominion always involves management. Our dominion as humans extends throughout the earth and covers all the lower creatures, but it stops short of ruling over each other. Certainly, human society maintains governments, elected officials, and chains of command and authority to help sustain order, but these are legitimate only as far as they exercise their authority with the choice and consent of the people. God did not create any of us for the purpose of dominating anyone else, but He *did* create *all* of us for the purpose of dominating and managing the earth and its resources. We have dominion over *things*, not people.

There are schools of management today that teach us how to manage other people, but many of them actually focus on manipulating people, on "stroking" them and deceiving them into doing what we want them to do, regardless of their desires. This approach is motivated by a desire to control and even oppress other people, which is contrary to the will of God.

As humans, our original responsibility was administration; God built that capacity into us. He did not reserve dominion for a few specially favored and elite people, but opened it up for the entire human race. By God's express design, the seeds of greatness, the potential for leadership, and the basic capability for management and administration exist in each of us.

So God created man in His own image, in the image of God He created him; male and female He created them. God blessed them and said to them, "Be fruitful and increase in number; fill the earth and subdue it. Rule over the fish of the sea and the birds of the air and over every living creature that moves on the ground" (Genesis 1:27-28).

God never demands anything that He does not provide for. Whatever God commands us to do, He equips us to do. Before He said, "Be fruitful and increase in number; fill the earth and subdue it," He implanted the ability to do those things into the very fiber of our being.

The Lord of creation designed us for stewardship. Our original purpose was to rule over and manage the domain called Earth. Whenever we do not do what God created us to do, we suffer. Failure to fulfill our purpose often leads to poverty of spirit and mind, as well as of body. Apart from our divine design we fail to prosper. We may become frustrated, or even severely depressed.

 Failure to fulfill our purpose often leads to poverty of spirit and mind, as well as of body.

On the other hand, those who discover their God-given purpose and seek to live it out experience health, happiness, fulfillment, and satisfaction in every area of life, even in spite of hardships or challenges that come along the way. This is just as true for married couples as it is for individuals. Many marriages struggle and fail to prosper as they should because the couples have never understood their purpose as stewards of God's resources or learned to apply His Kingdom management principles.

God Is Looking for Managers

From the very beginning, the God of creation established management as a fundamental principle governing life on earth and the relationship of human beings to the rest of the created order. Growth and development are dependent upon effective management—upon stewardship. Without management there is no growth. This relationship is revealed in the second chapter of Genesis.

> *When the Lord God made the earth and the heavens—and no shrub of the field had yet appeared on the earth and no plant of the field had yet sprung up, for the Lord God had not sent rain on the earth and there was no man to work the ground, but streams came up from the earth and watered the whole surface of the ground—the Lord God formed the man from the dust of the ground and breathed into his nostrils the breath of life, and the man became a living being* (Genesis 2:4b-7).

Notice the progression indicated in these verses. Although God had already created the earth, no plants of the field had yet appeared for two reasons: no rain had fallen on the earth and "there was no man to work the ground." God withheld development until a manager was in place. Life could flourish fully only when a steward appeared to take care of it.

Poor management retards growth. God holds back progress until He has management. He allows no increase until He has someone who can manage the increase; no expansion until He has someone who is accountable for that expansion.

 Poor management retards growth. God holds back progress until He has management.

God created man not because He needed a "religious" creature—someone to sing or dance or pray to Him—but because He needed someone to manage the planet. What we do during our worship services does not excite or interest God as much as what we do *afterward*. He wants to see how well we manage our affairs: how we spend our time, what we do with our money, how wisely or how foolishly we use the resources at our disposal. He is looking for increase because good management always produces increase.

Wise management attracts God. If we are faithful with a little, God will entrust us with more. This too is a biblical principle. One day Jesus told a story about a wealthy man who went away on a long trip, leaving a different sum of money with each of three servants, according to their abilities (see Mt. 25:14-30). The first two servants went out immediately and, through careful management and wise investing, doubled their money. The third servant, however, did nothing except hide his money until his master returned. Upon his return, the master praised the first two servants for their faithfulness and increase, but he condemned the third servant for his poor stewardship. Ordering that the third servant's money be taken from him and given to the first servant, the master said, "For everyone who has will be given more, and he will have an abundance. Whoever does not have, even what he has will be taken from him" (Mt. 25:29).

 Wise management attracts God. If we are faithful with a little, God will entrust us with more.

If we hope to become effective and successful in life, ministry, and especially marriage, we have to learn to be good managers. Stewardship means being accountable to God for every resource under our care. Effective managers do more than simply keep things running; they add value to everything they have responsibility over. Under a good manager, resources will appreciate in value. The third servant in Jesus' story was punished not because he lost his master's money (he didn't; he still had it) but because he did nothing with it. He was judged because he added no value—brought no increase—to the resources entrusted to him.

All married couples should examine themselves periodically and ask, "What have we done with the resources God has given us? How are we handling His blessings? Are we spending our money wisely? Have we progressed over the past year? Are we moving in the direction God wants us to go? Are we obeying His will? Is He pleased with our management? What does He want us to do next?" These are important questions for growing in stewardship.

Dominion Is a Result of Stewardship

One key to growth in this area is for couples to understand that effective stewardship is not static but a developing process. This is how it was with the first human couple in the Garden of Eden. Genesis 1:28 reveals the progression: "God blessed them and said to them, 'Be fruitful and increase in number; fill the earth and subdue it. Rule over the fish of the sea and the birds of the air and over every living creature that moves on the ground.'" God's purpose for mankind was for them to rule over the created order, but to fulfill that purpose they first had to be fruitful, increase, fill, and subdue. Only then would humanity attain full dominion. Essentially, dominion is not a goal as much as it is the *result* of the fourfold process of fruitfulness, increase, filling, and subduing.

The first thing God did was to *bless* mankind—the male and female He had created. To bless means to release ability. By blessing them God released their ability to become what He had created them to be. He released them to be stewards of the earth and its resources. Then He instructed them on *how* to exercise dominion.

 Dominion is not a goal as much as it is the result of the fourfold process of fruitfulness, increase, filling, and subduing.

Be fruitful. God's command in Genesis 1:28 is most often understood as referring to procreation, but filling the earth with people is only part of the meaning. The Hebrew word for *fruitful* means more than just sexual reproduction; it refers to being fruitful in either a literal or a figurative sense. Fruitfulness can be qualitative in nature as well as quantitative. Mankind has never had a problem being procreative—a current global population of over six billion is proof of that—but we do have a problem with being fruitful in the other ways God desires.

Essentially, being fruitful means releasing our potential. Fruit is an end product. An apple tree may provide cool shade and be beautiful to look at, but until it produces apples it has not fulfilled its ultimate purpose. Apples contain the seeds of future apple trees and, therefore, future apples. However, apples also have something else to offer: a sweet and nourishing food to satisfy human physical hunger. In this sense, fruit has a greater purpose than simply reproducing; fruit exists to bless the world.

Every person is born with a seed of greatness. God never tells us to go find seed; it is already within us. Inside each of us is the seed potential for a full forest—a bumper crop of fruit with which to bless the world. We each were endowed at birth with a unique gift, something we were born to do or become that no one else can achieve the way we can. God's purpose is that we bear abundant fruit and release the blessings of our gift and potential to the world.

 Every person is born with a seed of greatness.

The tragic truth is that cemeteries are filled with unreleased orchards—people who died with their gift still locked inside of them in seed form. This is where the human race so often fails to fulfill God's command to "be fruitful." The world is forever poorer because of the countless millions who died without releasing their blessings.

Don't ever make the mistake of telling God that you have nothing to offer. That simply is not true. God does not create any junk. Every one of us is pregnant with seed, and God wants us to let our seed sprout, grow, and produce abundant fruit. He wants us to develop our seed to an edible phase, where the world can partake and be nourished and blessed.

What is your seed? Can you cook really well? Can you paint? Can you write? Do you have good business sense? Consider your combined gifts as a married couple. What financial and other physical or material resources has God entrusted to you? Do you have the gifts and abilities to start your own business? Are you equipped to work together in a unique or much-needed ministry? What professional and personal resources can you bring to bear to fulfill the purpose God placed in you when you were born? You have something the world needs. Be fruitful. Let the Spirit of God bring out of you what your Creator put in you.

Increase. Being fruitful is a good and necessary start, but it should grow into the next phase, *increase*. Once again, even though the idea here is to multiply or reproduce, sexual procreation is only part of the meaning. The Hebrew word for *increase* also can mean "abundance," "to be in authority," "to enlarge," and "to excel." It carries the sense of refining your gift until it is completely unique. It is impossible to reproduce what you have not refined.

In this context, then, to increase means not only to multiply or reproduce as in having children, but also to improve and excel, mastering your gift and becoming the very best you can possibly be at what you do. It also means learning how to manage the resources God has given you and developing a strategy for managing the increase that will come through refinement. By refining your gift, you make room for it in the world. The more refined your gift, the more in demand you will be. Proverbs 18:16 (KJV) says, "A man's gift maketh room for him, and bringeth him before great men."

 By refining your gift, you make room for it in the world.

What is your fruit—your gift? What are you known for? What do you have that is reproducible? What quality or ability do you have that causes people to seek you out? What brings you joy? What are you passionate about? What do you have to offer the world, even just your little part of it?

Fruit must be reproducible or else it is not genuine fruit. "Be fruitful" means to produce fruit; "increase" means to reproduce it.

Fill. The third phase of dominion is to "fill" or "replenish" the earth. Bearing fruit, refining our gift, and mastering the use of our resources create demand and lead naturally to wider "distribution." To "fill the earth" means to expand our gift, our influence, our resources, just as a growing business would by continually improving its product, opening new outlets, and hiring more employees.

Another way to look at it is to think once again of an apple tree. A single apple seed grows into an apple tree, which then produces apples, each of which contains seeds for producing more trees. Planting those seeds soon turns a single apple tree into a whole orchard.

This expansion to "fill the earth" is a joint effort between the Lord and us. Our part is to be faithful with the resources He has given. He is the one who brings the expansion. The more faithful we are with our stewardship, the more resources God will entrust to us. That is a biblical principle.

Subdue. Fruitfulness, increase, and filling lead naturally to the end result of subduing. To *subdue* means "to dominate or control," not in the negative sense of oppression, but in the positive sense of administration. Using business terminology, to subdue means to dominate the market. As we learn to manage our resources, God expands those resources and enlarges our influence. He increases our "market share," so to speak.

There is no limit to what the Lord can do in and with and through any individual or any married couple who surrender themselves and their resources completely to His will and His way. He wants to cover the world with His "orchards" of human fruitfulness. Habakkuk 2:14 says, "For the earth will be filled with the knowledge of the glory of the Lord, as the waters cover the sea," and the Lord is fulfilling that promise one person at a time and one couple at a time.

There is no limit to what the Lord can do in and with and through any individual or any married couple who surrender themselves and their resources completely to His will and His way.

Two Important Financial Principles

Basic stewardship of resources for married couples who are believers centers around understanding and practicing two fundamental financial principles: tithing and budgeting. Herein lie the seeds of dominion—the secrets of fruitfulness, increase, and filling. Tithing recognizes God as the source of our resources while budgeting recognizes our responsibility to God to manage those resources wisely.

Rather than a rigid, legalistic designation of 10 percent of "our" income to God performed out of a sense of duty, tithing at its heart is a freely given offering of "firstfruits" in recognition that God is the Creator and true owner of *everything* that we have. It reminds us not to hold on to our possessions too tightly because we are merely stewards, not owners. It helps us keep our priorities in proper perspective, so that we do not make the mistake of allowing our possessions and pursuit of prosperity to supercede our relationship with the Lord as first place in our lives. Indeed, tithing reminds us that God is the source and giver of our prosperity: "But remember the Lord your God, for it is He who gives you the ability to produce wealth" (Deut. 8:18a).

Tithing is an expression of seed faith that operates on the principle of blessings and returns. It demonstrates our trust in God's ability and promise to meet our needs day by day. For married couples who desire God's blessings and prosperity on their home and to see His power at work in their lives and daily influence, a commitment to tithing is indispensable. God has made His promise clear and unambiguous: "'Bring the whole tithe into the storehouse, that there may be food in My house. Test Me in this,' says the Lord Almighty, 'and see if I will not throw open the floodgates of heaven and pour out so much blessing that you will not have room enough for it'" (Mal. 3:10). This principle is operable at every level, in individuals, couples, families, and churches.

 Tithing is an expression of seed faith that operates on the principle of blessings and returns.

Although giving is important, the attitude of the giver is more important. The amount we give is not as important to God as the spirit in which we give it. Jesus taught this lesson to His followers one day as they watched different people place their offerings in the temple treasury (see Mk. 12:41-44). Many who were wealthy gave large amounts of money while a poor widow dropped in only two coins, worth about a penny. Jesus commended the widow for her attitude of trust in God: "I tell you the truth, this poor widow has put more into the treasury than all the others. They all gave out of their wealth; but she, out of her poverty, put in everything—all she had to live on" (Mk. 12:43b-44).

 The amount we give is not as important to God as the spirit in which we give it.

God desires that we give freely from a joyful heart rather than out of a sense of obligation, acknowledging Him as the source of our blessings. Paul, the great first-century missionary and New Testament writer, had this to say to the believers in the city of Corinth: "Each man should give what he has decided in his heart to give, not reluctantly or under compulsion, for God loves a cheerful giver" (2 Cor. 9:7).

Unfortunately, no matter how hard they try, many couples fail to achieve even the most basic level of prosperity or financial stability. More often than not, the primary reason for this is that they have never under-stood or settled within themselves the basic issue of tithing and the princi-ple of blessings and returns.

God's program of prosperity does not operate on the world's principles. As long as we act as if we own our resources, we will tend to be very pos-sessive of them and unwilling to release them for God's use. This will shut us off from His greater blessings, both the blessing of being used for His purpose and the blessing of being entrusted with greater resources. If as stewards we hold lightly to them, however, we can release them for the Lord's use as He leads and, by proving ourselves faithful with a little, He will entrust us with much.

Tithing should be one major facet of a couple's overall financial plan. Every household should operate on a budget, or financial plan. Budgeting is a basic principle of resource management. A household budget should be no more complex than needed to manage the family's resources effectively. Depending on a couple's circumstances, a simple ledger to keep track of income and expenses may be all that is necessary. Generally, the more com-plex a couple's assets, the more detailed their plan for managing them will need to be.

 A household budget should be no more complex than needed to manage the family's resources effectively.

The complexity of the family budget also will depend upon the dreams and plans of the couple. Do you want to buy a house? If so, you will need to initiate a clear plan for saving money regularly, as well as being very careful with your credit and with managing debt. Do you plan to invest? These plans need to be set out specifically in your budget or financial plan and you need to agree together as to how you are going to pursue your goals.

Don't neglect to budget "fun" money. Leisure and recreation are important for overall physical, mental, and emotional health, and they should be provided for in the budget. These do not have to be expensive, and a couple should certainly keep these costs in line with their financial means. Whether or not both the husband and wife work outside the home, each should have a regular "allowance" of money to spend entirely on their own.

The type or complexity of your financial plan is not as important as the fact that you have a plan of some kind in place and operating. As long as your budget is adequate for your needs, it doesn't matter what form it takes. A working budget represents good management and an honest effort at wise stewardship. God honors both.

PRINCIPLES

1. Good stewardship is a solid biblical principle for growth, prosperity, and happiness.

2. God charged mankind with the responsibility of being stewards of the Earth and all its resources.

3. We have dominion over *things*, not people.

4. By God's express design, the seeds of greatness, the potential for leadership, and the basic capability for management and administration exist in each of us.

5. Stewardship means being accountable to God for every resource under our care.

6. Being fruitful means releasing our potential.

7. To increase means not only to multiply or reproduce as in having children, but also to improve and excel, mastering our gift and becoming the very best we can possibly be at what we do.

8. To "fill the earth" means to expand our gift, our influence, our resources, just as a growing business would by continually improving its product, opening new outlets, and hiring more employees.

9. To subdue means to "dominate the market."

10. Tithing recognizes God as the source of our resources.

11. Budgeting recognizes our responsibility to God to manage those resources wisely.

~ CHAPTER SIX ~

Sexual Intimacy in Marriage

*A*lthough effective resource management may be the most practical challenge that the majority of married couples face, achieving fully satisfying sexual intimacy is probably the most personal. Many couples are confused about their sexuality, not so much with regard to their sexual identities as with understanding how to properly relate to each other sexually. Sexual dysfunction is a significant source of frustration, conflict, and unhappiness in many marriages. Often dissatisfaction with sex is one of the root causes of spouses entering into extramarital affairs. What they are not getting at home they look for elsewhere. Quite often, this sexual confusion stems from a basic lack of understanding of both the true nature and purpose of sex as well as the proper conditions for fulfilling sexual expression.

Unfortunately, conscientious couples looking for solid answers oftentimes have trouble finding them. Our modern sex-saturated society is certainly not much help. Although we live in a time when sexuality issues are discussed more openly and frankly than ever before, much of the popular discussion of sex is based on dreams, fantasy, and human ideas rather than on truth, reality, and the wisdom of the ages.

Everywhere we turn we are bombarded by sexual images and messages. Sex drives both the entertainment and the advertising industries. It fills the airwaves and the movie theaters. It is used to sell everything from shaving cream to automobiles. Even our everyday speech is peppered with sex talk. Some people seemingly cannot hold a conversation unless it is laced with sexual references. Yet, for all of our talking and thinking about sex, much of society remains largely ignorant of the subject because so much of our dialogue is based on error and misconceptions.

Another sad truth is that the modern Church typically has little to add to the discussion. This is especially tragic because believers, who know and follow the God who created sex and established its proper parameters, should be able to speak more intelligently and confidently about it than anyone else. Yet the community of believers is often silent in the public forum regarding sex, whether because of embarrassment, confusion,

timidity, or a sense that the subject of sex is either too personal or not suf-
ficiently "spiritual" for the Church to weigh in on publicly.

Sex is not a side issue with God. The Bible has much more to say on the
subject of sex and sexual relations than most people are aware of. Sexuality
is fundamental to God's design and plan for humanity. "So God created
man in His own image, in the image of God He created him; *male and female*
He created them" (Gen. 1:27 emphasis added). "Male and female" are gender distinctions that imply sexuality. Sex also lies at the very core of God's
initial instructions to the first human couple to "be fruitful and increase in
number; fill the earth and subdue it" (Gen. 1:28b). Although, as we saw in
the previous chapter, this command deals essentially with dominion and
the stewardship of resources, it certainly also includes sexual activity as a
fundamental principle.

  Sex is not a side issue with God.

Because of its importance to human experience and because of the widespread confusion that exists on the subject today, it is crucial that we come to
a biblical understanding of sexuality in order to counter the errors and misinformation that are so prevalent in our society. We need to understand what
sex is *not*, what it *is*, and what its purpose is, as well as establish guidelines
for acceptable sexual activity within the context of a biblical marriage.

Sex Is Not Love

In the eyes of the world, sex and love are synonymous. Even the most
casual perusal of today's newspapers, magazines, books, movies, and television programs will make this clear. Much of the material in these media
treats sex and love as if they are inseparable, as if there is no difference
between them. The logical outflow of this view is the philosophy that says,
"If you love me, you'll let me." After all, if sex and love are the same, how
can you claim to love someone and yet decline to have sex with him or her?

Closely related to this is the view that sex is proof of love. How often do
we encounter this scenario in books or on film: A man meets a woman and
they hit it off well. The next thing we know, they are in bed together. This is
our "tip off" that they are "in love." They must be in love; they're having
sex, aren't they? It may be an adulterous relationship with one or both of
them married to someone else, but that doesn't matter. All that matters is
that they are in love. They go to bed, have their fling, get up the next morning, and everything is fine.

That's the picture the world paints. What these books and films rarely if ever reveal is the negative side to these kinds of encounters. In real life, sexual liaisons of this type produce in most people feelings of guilt, shame, and a sense of being dirty, not to mention a deep absence of fulfillment. It may be "fun" for a moment, but it leaves them feeling empty, and often they don't know why.

The idea of sex as love is one of the biggest lies with which the world has perverted God's original design for sexual expression, enjoyment, and fulfillment.

The idea of sex as love is one of the biggest lies with which the world has perverted God's original design for sexual expression, enjoyment, and fulfillment.

Sex Is Not Spiritual

Love—*true* love—is spiritual in nature. Sex is not. Sex is 100 percent physical and chemical. That is why we run into problems whenever we try to equate love with sex. Love is a spiritual union between two people—a joining of spirit to spirit. Sex is a physical coupling of two people—a joining of flesh to flesh. In its proper use, sex is a beautiful and fulfilling physical expression of the spiritual joining that is true love.

Love is a spiritual union between two people—a joining of spirit to spirit. Sex is a physical coupling of two people—a joining of flesh to flesh.

Understanding this distinction will help us guard against falling prey to a lot of the weird ideas floating around out there that try to convince us that sex is (or can be) some fantastic kind of "spiritual bonding" or getting in touch with the spiritual realities of life. It is nothing of the sort. Sex is an exhilarating physical experience, but in and of itself there is nothing spiritual about it. Sexual activity never bonds us spirit to spirit with another person. Nowhere does the Bible teach that a sexual experience will cause us to see God or be brought close to Him. Sex is a product of the human part of our makeup and has nothing to do with our spirit. Rather, our God-given sexual drive is an appetite that must be brought into subjection to and controlled by our spirit. Our spirit is to rule over our flesh.

Sex Is an Appetite

Sex is an appetite, one of many appetites that God built in to us when He created us. Whether we call them drives, cravings, hungers, passions, or whatever, they are still appetites. We have an appetite for food, an appetite for water, an appetite for sleep, an appetite for sex, an appetite for God—you name it. All of these are perfectly normal. God designed us for appetites.

The strength of any appetite is determined by the degree to which the capacity for that appetite has been activated. All appetites begin at a capacity level of zero. The ability for an appetite is always present, but its capacity will be zero until it is activated. A baby develops an appetite and capacity for food even before it is born as nourishment flows to it from the mother through the umbilical cord. That's why the very first thing a baby wants to do after it is born is to feed—its food appetite has been activated.

Although a newborn infant knows food hunger, its capacity is still low. A baby is hungry only for what its appetite has been activated for. Infants accustomed to liquid nourishment through the umbilical cord before birth and breast milk or formula and bland baby food afterwards have no craving for salt or other spices, or for sugar or any other kind of sweets. Those appetites are dormant until they are activated. Parents activate those appetites in their children by introducing them to seasoned foods and to cake, candy, and other sweet treats. Until then, a child has no appetite—and therefore no desire—for them.

The reason we get hungry is because chemicals in our stomach and digestive tract become active and signal our brain that we need food. Depending on how long it has been since we last ate, and other factors such as the kinds of foods we crave, our appetite capacity rises accordingly. Our sense of hunger will continue to grow until we satisfy it by eating. Once satisfied, our appetite falls off until it is reactivated when it is time to eat again.

An interesting thing happens, however, to an appetite that is left unsatisfied: Eventually it falls off anyway. People who enter into an extended fast quickly discover this. The earliest days of a fast are the hardest because our appetite for food has to be readjusted. After our body adapts, the fast is easier.

My point is this: Not only can we *satisfy* our appetites, we also can *control* them. *Every* appetite is like that. Our hungers and cravings are subject to our will. This is just as true for our sexual appetite as for any other. Paul made this clear in his first New Testament letter to the believers in the Asian city of Thessalonica when he wrote: "It is God's will that you should be sanctified: that you should avoid sexual immorality; that each of you should learn to control his own body in a way that is holy and honorable" (1 Thess. 4:3-4). What makes this passage even more interesting is that the Greek word *skeuos* ("body") also could be understood to mean "wife." In this sense, then, Paul would be saying that husbands should learn to "live with their own wives in a way that is holy and honorable." Either way, the emphasis is on controlling one's sexual appetite, reserving it for expression exclusively in the context of a marriage relationship.

 Our hungers and cravings are subject to our will. This is just as true for our sexual appetite as for any other.

God's Purposes for Sex

God created us as sexual beings, as male and female. Sexuality is built into our very core as humans. You could say that we are "hardwired" for sex. Appropriate and truly fulfilling sexual expression can occur only within the careful and specific limits that God has established. Outside those limits there is trouble—guilt, shame, fear, sorrow, disappointment, and heartache. Within those limits, however—the limits of one husband and one wife devoted exclusively to each other—there is great freedom, flexibility, and joy.

From the pages of the Bible we can glean three primary purposes for human sexual activity: procreation, recreation and release, and communication.

Sex Is for Procreation

As we have already seen, procreation lies at the very heart of God's original charge and command to mankind. "God blessed them and said to them, 'Be fruitful and increase in number; fill the earth and subdue it. Rule over the fish of the sea and the birds of the air and over every living creature that moves on the ground'" (Gen. 1:28). God created man to exercise dominion over the created order, and one way of accomplishing that goal was through procreation: to reproduce and populate the earth.

It was to this end that God created man in two genders, a male "man" and a female "man." The man and the woman were of the same spirit and the same essence—they were made of the same "stuff," as it were. First, God created the man, Adam. Then He made a woman—Eve—from part of Adam's side, and presented her to him. "The man said, 'This is now bone of my bones and flesh of my flesh; she shall be called "woman," for she was taken out of man.' For this reason a man will leave his father and mother and be united to his wife, and they will become one flesh" (Gen. 2:23-24). The phrase "one flesh" is a sexual reference relating to the physical union between a husband and wife.

The Bible contains many other references that indicate that human reproduction is a fundamental part of God's plan for mankind. In its proper place, sex is both honorable and a source of blessing from God.

> *If you pay attention to these laws and are careful to follow them, then the Lord your God will keep His covenant of love with you, as He swore to your forefathers. He will love you and bless you and increase your numbers.* **He will bless the fruit of your womb**, *the crops of your land—your grain, new wine and oil—the calves of your herds and the lambs of your flocks in the land that he swore to your forefathers to give you. You will be blessed more than any other people;* **none of your men or women will be childless**, *nor any of your livestock without young* (Deuteronomy 7:12-14 emphasis added).

Here God actually makes a commitment to His people that if they are faithful and obedient to Him, none of them will be barren or childless. God wants His people to procreate. He wants to populate the world with His children so that His glory will fill the earth.

> *Sons are a heritage from the Lord, children a reward from Him. Like arrows in the hands of a warrior are sons born in one's youth. Blessed is the man whose quiver is full of them. They will not be put to shame when they contend with their enemies in the gate* (Psalm 127:3-5).

Children are a heritage from God. The Hebrew word *ben* ("sons") has a wide variety of meanings and can refer to all children, not just males. Heritage means "property." God takes the conceiving, birthing, and raising of children very seriously because they are His heritage. That's why abortion and physical and sexual abuse of children are such serious sins—they are messing with God's heritage.

God takes the conceiving, birthing, and raising of children very seriously because they are His heritage.

There are many other passages that could be cited but these should be sufficient to demonstrate clearly—if there was any doubt—that one of the primary purposes of sex is for procreation.

Sex Is for Recreation and Release

If procreation is the practical, necessary side to sex, then recreation and release make up the "impractical" side. We have sex not only to reproduce the race but also for the sheer joy and pleasure it affords. Let's be frank: Sex is fun. God meant for us to enjoy sex; otherwise, why would He have designed it to be so pleasurable?

Some people, including many believers, are uncomfortable with such frankness where sex is concerned. They feel even more ill at ease at the thought of parts of the Bible—God's Word—being sexually explicit. Nevertheless, it is true that the Word of God contains some "racy" sections, particularly the book called the Song of Solomon (Song of Songs in the New International Version). This Old Testament book is so open and frank in its language that many believers have felt more comfortable allegorizing its content into a symbolic story about Christ's love for His Church. Perhaps it does indeed have that meaning as well, but at heart the Song of Solomon is a frank and explicit love song that celebrates the joy and bliss of married love.

God meant for us to enjoy sex; otherwise, why would He have designed it to be so pleasurable?

One example will be sufficient to show how the Bible presents sex in marriage as a recreational pleasure apart from any reference to procreation.

How beautiful you are, my darling! Oh, how beautiful! Your eyes behind your veil are doves....Your lips are like a scarlet ribbon; your mouth is lovely....Your two breasts are like two fawns, like twin fawns of a gazelle that browse among the lilies....You have stolen my heart, my sister, my bride; you have stolen my heart with one glance of your eyes, with one jewel of your necklace. How delightful is your love, my sister, my bride! How much more pleasing is your love than wine, and the fragrance of your perfume than any spice! Your lips drop sweetness as the honeycomb, my bride; milk and honey are under your tongue. The fragrance of your garments is like that of Lebanon. You are a garden locked up, my sister, my bride; you are a spring enclosed, a sealed fountain. Your plants are an orchard of pomegranates with choice fruits, with henna and nard, nard and saffron, calamus and cinnamon, with every kind of incense tree, with myrrh and aloes and all the finest spices. You are a garden fountain, a well of flowing water streaming down from Lebanon. Awake, north wind, and come, south wind! Blow on my garden, that its fragrance may spread abroad. Let my lover come into his garden and taste its choice fruits (Song of Songs 4:1a,3a,5,9-16).

This is frank and intimate sex talk between two lovers, but the passage also makes it clear that they are husband and wife. Three times the man refers to his lover as "my sister, my bride." These verses describe the husband's relaxed, loving inventory of his wife's physical beauty. In verse 12, the phrases "a garden locked up," a spring enclosed," and "a sealed fountain" refer to the bride's virginity on her wedding night. In the eyes of her husband she is a garden of beauty, an orchard of "choice fruits," "incense," and "all the finest spices." Verse 16 is actually the bride's response to her husband's love talk, inviting him, her lover, to "come into his garden and taste its choice fruits."

If the explicit and intimate nature of this language shocks you, keep in mind that it does not shock God. God invented sex, and He wants us to experience its joys. *In the proper context of a loving marriage relationship*, there is nothing shameful, wrong, or immoral about sex. Sex is a pleasure meant to be enjoyed between a husband and wife for its own sake.

Sex Is for Communication

The third purpose for which God designed sex is communication. Sex is no substitute for open and honest conversation between a husband and wife, but in a loving environment that encourages communication, sexual consummation provides a degree of intimacy and communion that goes far beyond words. No one should be more intimate or more "connected" physically, mentally, or emotionally than a husband and wife. Their friendship should have no rival; no other earthly relationship should have higher priority. This is the essential meaning behind Genesis 2:24: "For this reason a man will leave his father and mother and be united to his wife, and they will become one flesh."

Under God's standard, sexual activity is restricted to marriage. The husband/wife relationship is a singular relationship, and sexual foreplay and intercourse provide a unique form of intimate communion and sharing that they should reserve exclusively for each other.

Be Responsive to Each Other's Sexual Needs

Sexual dysfunction and dissatisfaction in marriage often stem not so much from a husband's or wife's inability or unwillingness to "perform" sexually as to the couple's failure to be sensitive, aware, and responsive to each other's sexual needs. As with effective communication, remembering the little things is important where sex is concerned also.

We have to be willing to look beyond our own feelings and perspective to those of our spouse. Just because we may or may not desire sex at a particular moment does not necessarily mean that our spouse feels the same way. It would be unhealthy to our relationship to make that assumption. This is where mature, effective communication skills are very important.

Sexual fulfillment and happiness in marriage depend on an open, loving, accepting, and affirming environment in which each spouse feels comfortable making his or her needs and desires known to the other.

Although there have been some significant changes in recent years, particularly in the West, it is still quite common in most societies for wives to feel very inhibited when it comes to initiating sex with their husbands. In some cultures it is unheard of for the wife to be so bold. In others, women are raised to believe that if they initiate sex, they are being "loose" or throwing themselves at the man. Whatever the reason, even if they crave sexual intimacy, wives often wait passively for their husbands to be the aggressor.

For his part, a husband may interpret his wife's passivity as disinterest and leave her alone because he does not want her to feel that he is forcing himself on her. As a result, both of them suffer through days, weeks, or even months of wandering in a sexual desert simply because they have failed to make their needs known to each other. If their uncommunicated needs go unmet long enough, they may seek sexual satisfaction outside their relationship.

It is very important that husbands and wives, and especially wives, learn to speak up regarding their sexual needs. Wives, as far as your husband is concerned, it is all right for you to be as "loose" as you want to be! If *you* are not "loose" with him, some other woman will be. Your husband has legitimate sexual needs and if you do not meet them, someone else will. Use your imagination! Be bold! Do something daring! Don't be afraid to initiate a sexual encounter occasionally. Surprise your husband with your aggressiveness! Remember that as a man your husband is "hardwired" for visual stimulation and arousal. Give him something to be stimulated about!

By the same token, husbands, keep in mind that as a woman your wife is "hardwired" for tactile and aural stimulation and arousal. She craves your touch. Embrace her and hold her close. She needs you to *tell* her how beautiful she is, how sexy she is, and how much you love her, how much you desire her, and how much you need her! She loves to hear you whisper "sweet nothings" in her ear.

 It is very important that husbands and wives, and especially wives, learn to speak up regarding their sexual needs.

These may sound like small things, but they are the things that will keep the fire burning in a marriage. Husbands and wives have a responsibility to love each other at all times and to express that love sexually often enough to keep each other satisfied. Of course, how often is enough will depend on the couple. Sexual relations are a normal part of marriage that each spouse has the right to expect from the other as well as the responsibility to give to the other. Here is what the New Testament writer Paul had to say in this regard:

> *The husband should fulfill his marital duty to his wife, and likewise the wife to her husband. The wife's body does not belong to her alone but also to her husband. In the same way, the husband's body does not belong to him alone but also to his wife. Do not deprive each other except by mutual consent and for a time, so that you may devote yourselves to prayer. Then come together again so that Satan will not tempt you because of your lack of self-control* (1 Corinthians 7:3-5).

It is clear from the context of this passage that "marital duty" refers to sexual relations. Both the husband and the wife have the responsibility—the duty—to respond to each other sexually. Duty often takes precedence over feelings. Understanding this can help on those occasions when one partner is "in the mood" and the other is not. There are times when, regardless of our personal feelings, we will need to respond to our spouse out of love and responsibility.

Sexual relations are a normal part of marriage that each spouse has the right to expect from the other as well as the responsibility to give to the other.

Sometimes we forget that the little things in our sexual relationship are what make the whole marriage a complete fellowship and union. The little things are important to communicating our love to our spouse, and sometimes it has nothing to do with our feelings.

Does It Edify?

There is one final question we need to consider regarding sexual intimacy in marriage. Amidst the multiplicity of ideas and attitudes about sexual activity that exists in the world, many married couples today, especially believers, are confused to some extent as to what does and does not constitute appropriate sexual behavior for husbands and wives. What is moral, right, and proper, and what is not? This confusion is understandable since so many people come into marriage from a worldly background that promotes an "anything goes" approach to sex. In the eyes of secular society, nothing is taboo anymore. Masturbation, oral sex, anal sex, group sex, pornography, pedophilia, homosexuality, bestiality, sado-masochism—you name it—the world says, "If it's right for you, do it!"

The question we need to ask, however, is, "What does the Word of God say?" God invented sex. He designed it and established the guidelines, parameters, and limits under which it can be morally exercised. One fundamental principle of creation is the "fitness" principle. God created everything to "fit" in its proper place and in relation to everything else. This is just as true with human sexuality as with any other area of life. The male and female sexual organs were designed to "fit" and are ideally suited for their mutual function. Any activity that goes beyond the bounds of design function violates the "fitness" principle and amounts to perversion. Perversion simply means the abuse, misuse, or misrepresentation of the original purpose of a thing. This is why homosexuality, for example, is such a sin; it is a perversion of the original design function of human sexuality.

What constitutes inappropriate sexual behavior? Some people would say that for married couples, anything that they agree upon is okay. What goes on in a couple's bedroom is their private affair, but nothing is hidden from God. I think it is safe to say that there are certain types of behavior that are always inappropriate. Aside from those acts that violate the "fitness" principle, inappropriate sexual behavior would include anything that is deliberately physically painful, harmful, or unhealthy, as well as any sexual act that one partner forces on the other, particularly if the second partner feels uncomfortable with it.

A solid biblical guiding principle for all of life, including sexual behavior, is to ask the question, "Does it edify?" That's the point Paul made to the believers in the city of Corinth. "'Everything is permissible'—but not everything is beneficial. 'Everything is permissible'—but not everything is constructive. Nobody should seek his own good, but the good of others" (1 Cor. 10:23-24). Paul's point is that although Christian believers are not bound under the law, and therefore "everything is permissible," not everything is helpful or constructive. Another word for "constructive" is *edifying*. To *edify* means "to build up" something or to "strengthen" it.

When we evaluate the rightness or wrongness of actions or behavior, we need to ask ourselves if that behavior will edify—build up—ourselves or someone else, or if it will tear down. The question is not what we can get away with, but what is healthy and edifying. When it is all said and done, are we edified spiritually? Have we been built up and strengthened in our relationship with the Lord or with our spouse, or have we been weakened? Do we come away encouraged or discouraged, confident or filled with a sense of guilt or shame? Is our conscience clean?

The question is not what we can get away with, but what is healthy and edifying.

The measure of whether or not a sexual behavior is appropriate for us is whether or not it edifies us. Whatever we can do and be edified afterwards is lawful and appropriate. If it does not edify, it is inappropriate. God has provided in His Word solid principles to guide our behavior, and those principles are always a reliable standard.

PRINCIPLES

1. Sex is not love.

2. Sex is not spiritual.

3. Sex is 100 percent physical and chemical.

4. Sex is an appetite.

5. Sex is for procreation.

6. Sex is for recreation and release.

7. Sex is for communication.

8. Sexual fulfillment and happiness in marriage depend on an open, loving, accepting, and affirming environment in which each spouse feels comfortable making his or her needs and desires known to the other.

9. A solid biblical guiding principle for all of life, including sexual behavior, is to ask the question, "Does it edify?"

Family Planning

*I*n recent years, no matter where I travel in different parts of the world to meet with government officials and religious leaders alike, when I ask them what the number one problem is in their society, I routinely get the same answer: the condition of the family. I hear this in the Caribbean, in South America, in the United States, in Israel—everywhere I go. The deterioration of the family is a universal problem.

It should come as no surprise to us that the institution of the family is under such attack from the enemy. Destruction of the family will lead to the breakdown of civilization. The family is the first and most basic unit of human society. Families are the building blocks with which every society and culture is constructed. In essence, the family is the prototype of society. A prototype is the first of its kind and demonstrates the basic characteristics of all the "models" that follow. In other words, the condition of society reflects the condition of the family. Just as a building is only as strong as the materials used to construct it, so any society is only as strong as its families.

God invented the family right at the very beginning, and it is still His ideal institution for establishing human society. Therefore, the cure for all of the social, psychological, emotional, spiritual, and civic problems that we face in our communities lies in rediscovering, restoring, and rebuilding the family.

 The condition of society reflects the condition of the family.

Everything that exists has a purpose. As Creator, God had a specific purpose in mind for everything He made. This is as true for the family as for anything else. Humanity's first family was established when God made Eve from a portion of Adam's side and presented her to him (see Gen. 2:21-24). The Book of Genesis is specific regarding God's purpose for the family: "So God created man in His own image, in the image of God He created him; *male and female He created them.* God blessed them and said to them, *'Be fruitful and increase in number';* fill the earth and subdue it. Rule over the fish of the sea and the birds of the air and over every living creature that moves on the ground'" (Gen. 1:27-28 emphasis added). God's desire was to fill the earth with human beings made in His image, and the family was the avenue He chose for accomplishing it.

Another clue to God's purpose for the family is found in the Book of Malachi, the last book in the Old Testament. The people of God were upset because He seemed to no longer answer their prayers. Malachi explained why:

> Another thing you do: You flood the Lord's altar with tears. You weep and wail because He no longer pays attention to your offerings or accepts them with pleasure from your hands. You ask, "Why?" It is because the Lord is acting as the witness between you and the wife of your youth, because you have broken faith with her, though she is your partner, the wife of your marriage covenant. **Has not the Lord made them one?** In flesh and spirit they are His. **And why one? Because He was seeking godly offspring**. So guard yourself in your spirit, and do not break faith with the wife of your youth (Malachi 2:13-15 emphasis added).

Children are dear to God's heart. The growth and perpetuation of human society both depend on children. From the beginning God established a firm foundation upon which to build society. Stage one was the creation of man—male and female. Stage two was marriage, a spiritual union in which two individual humans are fused into one and that is consummated physically through the act of sexual intercourse. Marriage leads naturally to stage three—a family unit consisting of a father, a mother, and one or more children. This is the traditional definition of the word *family*. Although single-parent households and unmarried individuals living alone certainly qualify as families in a broader sense, the traditional understanding is more significant when we are talking about perpetuating human society and "filling the earth" with people.

A husband and wife together build a marriage. Marriage establishes a family. Children are born, grow to maturity, and establish their own families. Multiplication of families creates communities; multiplication of communities gives rise to societies; and multiplication of societies results in nations.

If there is any command of God that mankind has faithfully obeyed, it is the command to "be fruitful and increase in number." We humans have followed that instruction so diligently that in the twenty-first century the global population has reached the danger point, and millions live with the daily threat of malnutrition and starvation. In the face of this crisis, now more than ever before, conscientious people of God have a responsibility to give careful consideration to the need for deliberate family planning.

To Beget or Not to Beget

Depending on their culture or how they were brought up, many believers are uncomfortable talking about family planning. Some are confused on the subject because of inadequate or inaccurate teaching, while others have an uneasy feeling that there is something sinful about trying to "plan" such an intimate and "holy" undertaking as having children. This being the case, it is important to understand what family planning means and what it does not mean.

Simply stated, family planning involves making deliberate decisions *in advance* to avoid unwanted pregnancies and to limit the size of one's family to the number of children that the parents can adequately love, provide for, nurture, train, and protect. Carrying out these decisions requires specific, concrete actions aimed at *prevention*. In other words, family planning includes birth control. The most common means of birth control today are the condom, the diaphragm, and the birth control pill, all of which prevent pregnancy by preventing sperm cells from the male from fertilizing the ovum from the female. Birth control prevents the *conception* of a new human being.

Family planning focuses on prevention and *advance* control of child bearing. It has nothing to do with the *deliberate termination* of pregnancies. Therefore, abortion is *not* family planning. Neither is it birth control or health care. Abortion is immoral and a sin because it is the deliberate destruction of an existing human life. As such, it goes against the direct design and intention of God.

There was a time when large families were the norm and even necessary for survival, particularly in agriculturally based societies. Infant and child mortality rates were so high due to disease or injury that parents needed to produce many children in order to ensure that some would reach maturity to help work the farm as well as carry on the family line. In today's industrialized society and current economic realities, family planning and birth control simply make good sense. This is also true in many third-world cultures with pervasive poverty and malnutrition where population runs rampant because of ignorance and lack of access to legitimate birth control options.

 Family planning focuses on prevention and ADVANCE control of child bearing. It has nothing to do with the DELIBERATE TERMINATION of pregnancies.

There are at least three questions regarding family planning that every couple need to answer together, preferably before they get married, but certainly no later than in the early months of their marriage. First, "Do we want children?" For a variety of reasons some couples opt not to have any children. Whether it is for career reasons, concern over health risks, the danger of passing on hereditary health problems, or whatever, this is a decision that each couple must make for themselves.

If a couple decides that they do want children, the second question they must answer is, "When?" This is a very important question. There are several major factors to consider in determining the timing for starting a family, such as maturity, whether one or both partners are in school, and whether a steady job and income are in place. In order to grow up healthy, children need a home environment that is stable financially, emotionally, and spiritually.

A third question a couple needs to answer with regard to children is "How many?" One of the most significant factors to consider here is the couple's financial means. Very simply, the more children a couple has, the more it will cost to raise and care for them properly. For example, a household that brings in an income of $300.00 a week cannot reasonably expect to provide for ten children. It is the parents' responsibility to determine not only how many children they want, but also how many children they can realistically support.

Raising children is a serious and important matter to God, and parents are accountable to Him for how they treat and care for their children. "If anyone does not provide for his relatives, and especially for his immediate family, he has denied the faith and is worse than an unbeliever" (1 Tim. 5:8). God is not opposed to the idea of couples having a lot of children, but He does expect and require them to love, support, and provide for those children in a responsible manner.

 It is the parents' responsibility to determine not only how many children they want, but also how many children they can realistically support.

Birth control can be a blessing, especially for young newlyweds who need time to adjust to each other and establish their household before bringing children into the picture. For couples who desire no children or who have all the children they want, procedures are available to prevent further conception: a vasectomy for the man or a tubal ligation for the woman. All of these are blessings of technology that are invaluable for helping married couples make wise and informed decisions concerning the size of their families.

Children are a Heritage from the Lord

Married couples who decide to have children desire a good thing. The Bible is full of passages that describe the blessings related to bearing and raising children. In Old Testament times, parents who had many children were considered to be extraordinarily blessed by God. At the same time, women who were unable to bear children were thought to be under God's curse. Although we recognize today that there is no link between the size of one's family and the blessings of God, this attitude reveals just how valuable and important children were to the people of ancient times, and particularly to the Hebrews, the children of God.

> *Sons are a heritage from the Lord, children a reward from Him. Like arrows in the hands of a warrior are sons born in one's youth. Blessed is the man whose quiver is full of them. They will not be put to shame when they contend with their enemies in the gate* (Psalm 127:3-5).

As I stated in Chapter Six, the Hebrew word for "sons" in verses 3 and 4 also can be translated as "children." The word *children* in verse 3 is a translation of two Hebrew words that literally mean "fruit of the womb." Children are fruit, the product of their parents' fruitfulness. Thus, married couples who have children fulfill one of God's purposes for marriage: "Be fruitful and increase in number" (Gen 1:28a).

 Married couples who decide to have children desire a good thing.

Verse 4 in Psalm 127 compares children to arrows in a warrior's hand, and verse 5 states that a man whose "quiver" is full of children is blessed. Arrows are not made to stay in the quiver, however, but to be shot from a bow at the target. As long as an arrow rests in the quiver it cannot fulfill the purpose for which it was made. The same is true with children. Children rest for a time in the "quiver" of their home and family while they learn and grow to maturity, but the day eventually comes when they need to be released into the world. Only then can they fulfill the purpose and unleash the full potential that God has implanted in them. It is the role of the parents to prepare their children to leave the quiver.

God is looking for godly offspring (see Mal. 2:15), and godly offspring come about best through godly parents. His goal is for His children to have His nature and His character—to be like Him. The best way to become like

God is to imitate Him. Only believers and followers of Christ can truly become like God because to do so requires the indwelling presence of the Holy Spirit. Writing to the body of believers in Ephesus, Paul had this to say: "Be imitators of God, therefore, as dearly loved children and live a life of love, just as Christ loved us and gave Himself up for us as a fragrant offering and sacrifice to God" (Eph. 5:1-2).

Jesus Christ Himself is our model. As Jesus is toward us, so we should be toward our children. One of the goals of parenting is to raise children who act like their parents, who share similar beliefs and values. Example is the greatest teacher of all, and children learn more from the lifestyle modeled by their parents than from anything their parents say. Actions really do speak louder than words.

Proverbs 20:11 says, "Even a child is known by his actions, by whether his conduct is pure and right." Where do children learn pure and right conduct if not from their parents? For better or for worse, the attitudes and behavior of children reflect the parenting they have received. In the vast majority of cases, behavioral problems in children and adolescents can be traced back to poor parental modeling.

 As Jesus is toward us, so we should be toward our children.

Good parenting is no accident. It cannot be done passively or from a distance, either physically or emotionally. Effective parenting is focused, intentional, and deliberate. Parents must *plan* for success, and godly offspring is the goal. If our children grow up sharing our moral, ethical, and spiritual values, we have succeeded as parents. If they learn to love, worship, follow and serve the Lord, we have succeeded as parents.

Who of us would not take the greatest care to protect and preserve a treasure in our possession? There is no greater treasure on earth than our children. They are a heritage from God, and as godly parents we have a responsibility and an obligation under God to treat them as such. Our goal is to produce godly offspring who will glorify and honor their heavenly Father.

Foundational Principles of Parenting

In a very real sense God was the first parent because He produced "children" designed to be like Himself. This is revealed in the very first statement He made regarding mankind as recorded in the Book of Genesis. "Then God said, 'Let us make man in our image, in our likeness...'" (Gen. 1:26a).

Contained in this verse are three foundational principles of parenting, wrapped up in the two words *image* and *likeness*. An image is a direct resemblance of an original and represents its nature or character. The word *likeness* means to look like, act like, and be like someone or something else.

God created humans to be a direct resemblance of Him; they would live, behave, and be like Him in every essential way. This truth carries clear implications for parents.

Foundational Principle #1: *Parenting should reproduce the nature of the parent in the child.* God is holy, and He created man to be holy. Sin corrupted man's holiness and distorted the divine image in him. Ever since, God's purpose and intent have been to restore man to his original holy nature. That is the very reason He sent His Son, Jesus Christ, to live in the flesh. By His life, Jesus showed us what God is like and, by His death for our sins, made it possible for His image and holiness to be fully restored in us.

By the same token, if we as parents desire godly children, we must live godly lives as an example. God is holy and righteous by nature, and He wants children who exhibit the same nature. Parenting should reproduce the nature of the parent in the child. Only the Spirit of God can reproduce the nature of God, whether in us or in our children. That is why we must depend completely on the Lord and walk closely with Him as we seek to parent our children wisely and effectively.

 If we as parents desire godly children, we must live godly lives as an example.

Foundational Principle #2: *Parenting should reproduce the character of the parent in the child.* Nature and character are very closely related. Our character is determined by the nature that controls us. It reveals who we *really* are, regardless of how we present ourselves to others. Closely akin to our reputation, character refers to our moral excellence and firmness (or lack thereof) and touches on the mental and ethical traits that mark us as individuals. Character is the person we are when no one else is around.

From a parenting point of view, this is very important. One way to measure our effectiveness as parents is by how our children act in our absence. What do they say and do when we are not around to approve or disapprove or to commend or correct? Whether we like it or not, our children very likely will become like us. It's a part of nature—children turn out like their parents. If we want to produce children of high character, we must be parents of high character.

Character is the person we are when no one else is around.

Foundational Principle #3: *Parenting should reproduce the behavior of the parent in the child.* Nature determines character, and character determines behavior. When parents focus on their children's behavior alone, they are doomed ultimately to failure and frustration because behavior is linked to character.

As with character, parents who desire good behavior *from* their children must model good behavior *for* their children. The old "do as I say, not as I do" approach, besides being hypocritical, simply will not work. Children can see right through hypocrisy, and they quickly lose respect for people who say one thing and do another.

If we are good and godly parents, our children will have a good and godly nature. If we are upright in all our dealings, our children will develop strong character. If we behave ourselves as parents, our children will learn to behave themselves.

We must always look not just to our children, but to *their* children as well. The final test for our effectiveness as parents is how our grandchildren turn out. If we have done our job, our children will internalize our nature, character, and behavior and pass them on to their own children. In this way, righteousness can be passed from generation to generation. This fulfills God's plan, for He is looking for godly offspring.

 The final test for our effectiveness as parents is how our grandchildren turn out.

Parental Mandates

Parenting is a great joy, but it is also a great responsibility. God has made clear in His Word, the Bible, what He requires and expects of parents and holds them accountable for. His mandate is simple: Parents, train your children.

Train a child in the way he should go, and when he is old he will not turn from it (Proverbs 22:6).

The rod of correction imparts wisdom, but a child left to himself disgraces his mother (Proverbs 29:15).

He who spares the rod hates his son, but he who loves him is careful to discipline him (Proverbs 13:24).

Discipline your son, for in that there is hope; do not be a willing party to his death (Proverbs 19:18).

These commandments that I give you today are to be upon your hearts. Impress them on your children. Talk about them when you sit at home and when you walk along the road, when you lie down and when you get up (Deuteronomy 6:6-7).

Proverbs 22:6 illustrates the importance of training children while they are still very young: When they are old (or grown), they "will not turn from it." Reputable studies have shown that a child's basic character is formed by the age of seven. What we fail to teach and impart to our children during their first seven years of life, they will learn later only with great difficulty, if at all. Early training establishes the foundation for later life. Even when older children and adolescents test their boundaries (as they always do), they generally return to the beliefs and values they learned in their earliest years, if those lessons were taught with integrity and consistency and by parental example.

 A child's basic character is formed by the age of seven.

Good parenting always involves training. This is so because, first of all, *children need training.* Training is not the same as counseling. Some parents try to counsel their children regardless of age. Generally speaking, the younger the child, the less effective counseling will be. Young children need to be trained to obey first and later to understand why. This is for their own protection. As they grow in reasoning and analytical skills, they are better able to understand the "why" of their training. We must be careful not to make the mistake of trying to counsel our children before they are ready.

 Good parenting always involves training.

Secondly, *children cannot train themselves.* This should go without saying, yet there are still many parents who basically let their children make all of their own decisions and generally fend for themselves, even at very early ages. Training of the children is almost non-existent. When questioned, these parents often defend their actions (or inaction) by claiming that they don't want to force their own beliefs on their children or restrict their children's freedom to choose their own path. This is sheer folly and a recipe for disaster because children have not yet developed the capacity to make wise and mature choices. They need the clear and steady guidance of adults who can show them the way. They need the training of parents.

Thirdly, *training must be intentional.* The raising and teaching of children is too important a job to be approached haphazardly or left to chance. Parents must willingly and deliberately shoulder this burden. We are the first line of defense for our children, the first and primary source for their training and example. Good or bad, right or wrong, our children will take their lead from us. Our training and example must be fair, consistent, and unified. In matters of household rules, routine, and discipline, parents should always present a united front so that their children do not learn to play one parent against the other.

 Good or bad, right or wrong, our children will take their lead from us.

Fourthly, *training focuses on the long term.* We must not expect our children to be good instantly or to learn everything the first time they are told. Training is a developmental process. Maturity does not come overnight. As parents we must always look far ahead to our children's future and to their children's future. Where training and discipline are concerned, short-term pain means long-term gain. It may break our heart to inflict the pain of discipline on our children and to see their tears, but the long-term goal of preparing them to live responsibly as adults justifies the short-term pain of disciplining them while they are young.

Finally, *failure to train is a commitment to destroy the child.* Remember Proverbs 19:18: "Discipline your son, for in that there is hope; do not be a willing party to his death." That verse tells us that our failure to discipline our children makes us a party to their destruction. If our children go wrong and mess up their lives because we did not teach them properly, then we bear the greatest burden of responsibility. We become unwitting accomplices to their destruction, in cahoots with those forces in the world that seek to destroy our children.

Be the Engine, Not the Caboose

I have one final word of counsel for parents or hope-to-be parents: *Be the engine, not the caboose.* The engine provides power for a train and determines both the direction and pace that the train will travel. Like all the other cars, the caboose follows the engine; it never leads. Wherever the engine goes the caboose goes. If the train is an analogy for the family, then the parents are the engine and the children are the caboose. Children should follow where their parents lead. Parents go ahead of their children, determining the route and speed. As long as the engine arrives safely at its destination, the rest of the train will also.

One of the big problems in many families is that the parents have allowed themselves to become the caboose. Their children have seized control of the engine and are off and running with no sense of direction or purpose, and all the parents can do is be pulled along as the "train" of their family goes careering down the track. Eventual derailment and destruction are virtually certain. Whatever else we do as parents, we must never allow our children to run the train.

The engine determines which track the train runs on. In the same way, we as parents determine where our children go and what they become by the track that we put our own lives on. Ahead of us lies a fork in the track, and we can switch our train onto one or the other. One leads to life and health and prosperity, while the other leads to death and destruction. The choice is ours: Which way will we go?

 Whatever else we do as parents, we must never allow our children to run the train.

God is seeking godly offspring. He wants us to choose life for ourselves and for our children. In the words of Moses, the "friend of God":

This day I call heaven and earth as witnesses against you that I have set before you life and death, blessings and curses. Now choose life, so that you and your children may live and that you may love the Lord your God, listen to His voice, and hold fast to Him. For the Lord is your life, and He will give you many years in the land He swore to give to your fathers, Abraham, Isaac and Jacob (Deuteronomy 30:19-20).

Children need the love, guidance, training, discipline, and protection that only parents can provide. The strength and health of the next generation depend on the faithfulness and diligence of the parents of this generation. Married couples who decide to have children choose a good thing. Yes, raising children is an awesome responsibility that carries with it a sizeable portion of frustration, heartache, and stress. More than that, however, parenting is a wonderful privilege that is accompanied by great joy, deep satisfaction, and abundant hope for the future.

PRINCIPLES

1. Family planning involves making deliberate decisions in advance to avoid unwanted pregnancies and to limit the size of one's family to the number of children that the parents can adequately love, provide for, nurture, train, and protect.

2. Family planning involves answering three questions with regard to children: "Do we want children?"; "When?"; and "How many?"

3. In order to grow up healthy, children need a home environment that is stable financially, emotionally, and spiritually.

4. Example is the greatest teacher of all, and children learn more from the lifestyle modeled by their parents than from anything their parents say.

5. Effective parenting is focused, intentional, and deliberate.

6. Parenting should reproduce the nature of the parent in the child.

7. Parenting should reproduce the character of the parent in the child.

8. Parenting should reproduce the behavior of the parent in the child.

9. God's mandate is simple: Parents, train your children.

10. Parents should be the engine, not the caboose.

CHAPTER EIGHT

Living Under AGAPE

*M*arriage that lasts a lifetime must be built on a solid foundation that will not rot, erode, or wear away over time. A successful, happy, and fruitful marital relationship must be founded on principles that are permanent, not temporary; forged from things that last, not fade away.

Physical attractiveness won't do it. External beauty fades over time. Hair turns gray or white or falls out, skin wrinkles, muscles turn flabby, waistlines enlarge, teeth come out, eyesight dims, hearing diminishes. If you have built your marriage relationship on physical attraction, what will you do when the physical attributes that initially drew you together disappear?

Sex won't do it. Moods and attitudes change and evolve. With increasing age both the ability to perform sexually and the interest in sexual activity decline. In the meantime, an appetite that is 100 percent physical and chemical is insufficient by itself to nourish and sustain a relationship that is essentially spiritual in nature.

Finances won't do it. Due to economic downturns, job loss, physical disability, long-term illness, or a host of other factors, financial status can change drastically very quickly. A marriage based solely or primarily on economic factors or earning potential is a recipe for failure.

Possessions won't do it. As permanent and substantial as material things appear, they are only temporary and can fly away with the morning breeze. Just ask anyone who has suddenly lost everything in a disastrous fire or a hurricane. What's more, centering our life or marriage around the accumulation of possessions simply creates an insatiable hunger for more, a craving that can never be satisfied.

Upon what, then, can a married couple build a happy, secure, and lasting relationship? What foundation will stand the test of time as well as the storms of adversity? I hope I have made it clear throughout this book that the only sure foundation for a lifelong marriage is *agape*, the self-giving love that has its source and origin in God alone. Only that which derives from God Himself will last; everything else is transitory. Writing to the community of believers in Corinth, Paul had this to say about the lasting quality of agape:

> *Love never fails. But where there are prophecies, they will cease; where there are tongues, they will be stilled; where there is knowledge, it will pass away. For we know in part and we prophesy in part, but when perfection comes, the imperfect disappears....And now these three remain: faith, hope and love. But the greatest of these is love* (1 Corinthians 13:8-10,13).

In the end, faith, hope, and love will remain. All of these have their origin in God, and love (*agape*) is the greatest of the three. This is so because faith and hope arise from God's love and can exist only in the environment of His presence. Because God is eternal and *agape* is His very nature, His love can never fail. Prophecies, tongues, and knowledge—all the things that seem so permanent to us—will someday disappear. These things also have their origin in God, but they are by His design temporary in nature. When they have fulfilled their purpose, they will pass away. It is different with love. *Agape* is eternal; it will never pass away.

 AGAPE *is eternal; it will never pass away.*

Love Is an Ongoing Debt

In Chapter One we learned that *agape* is unconditional love—love without reason—the sacrificial, self-giving kind of love that Jesus demonstrated when He died on the cross for our sins. Love without reason means loving regardless of the loveableness of the people involved and whether or not they reciprocate in that love. *Agape* sets forth no conditions, makes no demands, and holds no expectations. It carries no guarantee except to guarantee itself.

A marriage based on *agape*, then, is a roleless relationship because spouses love each other unconditionally, sacrificially, and without fixed expectations of each other. Fueled by love, their relationship is characterized by responding to needs rather than conforming to fixed roles.

For believers, *agape* should be the guiding and motivating force behind all relationships, marriage or otherwise. Simon Peter, one of Jesus' closest friends and followers, had this to say about the unconditional, non-expectant nature of *agape*: "Above all, love each other deeply, because *love covers over a multitude of sins*" (1 Pet. 4:8 emphasis added). *Agape* does not overlook or ignore sin; it *covers over* sin, just as the blood of Jesus covers our sin to put us in a right relationship with God. In marriage, *agape* means that spouses, rather than overlook each other's faults and weaknesses, relate redemptively to each other and allow love to overcome each other's short-comings and not allow them to become points of strife and conflict.

Love is an ongoing debt that we owe each other, a debt that should never be paid off. Paul made this clear when he wrote to the believers in Rome, "Let no debt remain outstanding, except the continuing debt to love one another, for he who loves his fellowman has fulfilled the law" (Rom. 13:8). If we get into the habit of thinking of ourselves as always owing a debt of love to our spouses, we will be less inclined to take offense when they say or do something that we do not like. The implication of Paul's words is that we are to love others *always*, regardless of their attitude or response toward us.

 If we get into the habit of thinking of ourselves as always owing a debt of love to our spouses, we will be less inclined to take offense when they say or do something that we do not like.

Love Lived Out

What then are the practical implications for married couples living under *agape*? Understanding the answer requires first of all a good working definition of *agape* in practical terms. I believe we could find no better definition than the one found in the thirteenth chapter of Paul's first letter to the believers in Corinth:

> *Love is patient, love is kind. It does not envy, it does not boast, it is not proud. It is not rude, it is not self-seeking, it is not easily angered, it keeps no record of wrongs. Love does not delight in evil but rejoices with the truth. It always protects, always trusts, always hopes, always perseveres. Love never fails* (1 Corinthians 13:4-8a).

Let's consider each of these points briefly with regard to the relationship between husbands and wives. At all times in all things we should be careful to heed Jesus' words, "Do to others as you would have them do to you" (Lk. 6:31).

Love is patient. Always remember that no one is perfect. We all have our own faults and flaws, our own particular idiosyncrasies and annoying habits or mannerisms. Everyone enters marriage with a certain amount of emotional, psychological, and spiritual baggage. Adjusting to each other's uniqueness takes time and *patience*. The King James Version often uses the word *longsuffering* for patience, which really captures the idea of what we're talking about here. Patient love makes allowances for individual differences and seeks to understand before speaking or judging. In our marriage relationships we all need healthy allowances of grace, not only that which we extend toward our spouses, but also that which they extend to us. Patient love is full of grace. Rather than finding fault, it seeks to help the other person reach his or her full potential and personhood in Christ.

 Patient love is full of grace.

Love is kind. The Greek word for "kind" in verse 4 literally means "to show oneself useful" or "to act benevolently." Kind love is always seeking after the best interests of the other person, actively looking for ways to help, comfort, encourage, strengthen, and lift up. This is where remembering the little things comes into play—a compliment, a card, a bouquet of roses. There is more involved here than just thoughtfulness, however. Kindness is active, deliberate engagement in pursuing the welfare of another. It is gentle and tender, yet firm and tough when necessary, refusing to stand idly by and allow loved ones to engage in self-destructive behavior. Sometimes the greatest act of kindness is to forcibly intervene to prevent someone we love from heading down the path to ruin. Kind love is also tough love.

 Kindness is active, deliberate engagement in pursuing the welfare of another.

Love does not envy. *Agape* is a love that rests secure in itself and its relationships. When we live under *agape*, we will be comfortable with who we are and with our status and relationships with others. We will not feel threatened by their success or envious over their happiness. On the contrary, we will actively and sincerely rejoice with them over these things. To envy means to be zealous, eager, or anxious, either for or against someone, and it is closely akin to jealousy. Secure and confident as it is, *agape* pulls the fangs out of envy and jealousy, leaving them powerless. Non-envying love means that when a wife receives a nice promotion at work, her husband won't feel threatened by or in competition with her success, but honestly rejoice with her. It means that when a husband is honored by his colleagues, his wife will sincerely take pride in his recognition and not fear that any attention is being taken away from her. Love that does not envy is love that has learned to be content, whatever the circumstances.

 AGAPE is a love that rests secure in itself and its relationships.

Love does not boast. Literally, to boast means to play the braggart. A braggart is someone who is always sounding his own praises or "tooting his own horn." He wants to make sure everyone knows about his gifts and accomplishments. In reality, braggarts usually accomplish little of use to anyone else because they spend all their time boasting. Love, on the other hand, is always too busy *doing* good to spend time talking about it. Those who live under *agape* have no need or drive to boast because they find their fulfillment and purpose not in the praise and recognition of men but in the opportunity to serve the needs of others in the name of Christ. If we feel a need to boast about or broadcast our love, that is a sure sign that no love is present. *Agape* neither needs nor seeks fanfare. True love reveals itself by its actions, and when it is present, everyone knows it.

Love is always too busy DOING *good to spend time talking about it.*

Love is not proud. Pride is the great sin of mankind, the sin of Adam and Eve that brought their downfall in Eden. The Greek word literally refers to a pair of bellows pumped up with air. A proud person is arrogant, with an inflated ego that is puffed up in vain self-confidence, smugly reliant on his own powers, talents, and knowledge. Love is the exact opposite: humble, gentle, never forceful. Families who live under *agape* treat each other always with dignity, honor, and respect because they know that they are equally dependent upon God for all things and equally indebted to Him for their forgiveness and righteous standing with Him through Christ. Pride always focuses on the self; *agape* never does, focusing instead on God and on other people. *Agape* destroys pride because where love fills all, there is no room for pride.

AGAPE *destroys pride because where love fills all, there is no room for pride.*

Love is not rude. In many segments of modern society, rudeness seems commonplace, even expected. Nonetheless, polite behavior has never gone out of style. Good manners are always appropriate. Rudeness means to act unbecomingly, improperly, or indecently, and in a manner deserving of reproach. Love seeks always to act properly and becomingly in every cir-cumstance and relationship of life. This means showing due honor and respect for the place and opinions of others, whether higher or lower in rank. All persons, regardless of status, are worthy of respect and decency.

People living under *agape* are careful to maintain proper respect and behavior in all the relationships of life: husband, wife, parent, child, brother, sister, son, or daughter. Love that is not rude also acts to prevent anything that would violate decency.

 Good manners are always appropriate.

Love is not self-seeking. This is another way of defining a roleless love—love without conditions or expectations. *Agape* has no ulterior or selfish motives; it is unconditional. Conditional love sets limits; *agape* sets none. This kind of love seeks the welfare of others even at the cost of self-denial and personal sacrifice. Living under *agape* means that we are not concerned primarily with seeking our own happiness, but the happiness of others, and that we will not pursue our happiness at the expense of others. People who live under *agape* live for the purpose of doing good, just as Jesus did (see Acts 10:38).

 People who live under* AGAPE *live for the purpose of doing good, just as Jesus did.

Love is not easily angered. This means that it takes a lot to provoke us. We do not rise to the bait and let anger overcome us. The Greek word carries the idea of irritation or sharpness of spirit. Agape, although it is not soft or gullible, also has no "rough edges." If we are ruled by agape, we will not be prone to violent anger or provocation, always keeping our temper in check. We will not be quick to judge or be hasty in drawing conclusions, but give others the benefit of the doubt. We will not "fly off the handle" or "go off half-cocked" whenever any little thing does not suit us. Instead, we keep in mind the words of James, Jesus' half-brother: "Everyone should be quick to listen, slow to speak and slow to become angry, for man's anger does not bring about the righteous life that God desires" (Jas. 1:19b-20).

Love keeps no record of wrongs. Two ideas are in mind here. First, love does not "keep inventory" of wrongs, hurts, insults, or offenses with a view to returning the same in kind. In other words, love has no interest in "getting even." The desire for revenge is one of the most destructive impulses in the entire realm of human relationships. People guided by *agape* will not keep bringing up past wrongs to throw in the face of the offender. The second idea is that *agape* always imputes the purest and highest motives to the actions of others. This does not mean being gullible or a pushover, but it does mean looking for and thinking the best about every person. It means neither receiving nor passing on gossip or hurtful information about another person. *Agape* never plays the "blame game" and holds the highest opinion of others until and unless clear evidence indicates otherwise.

Love does not "keep inventory" of wrongs, hurts, insults, or offenses with a view to returning the same in kind.

Love does not delight in evil. The psalmist wrote, "Blessed is the man who does not walk in the counsel of the wicked or stand in the way of sinners or sit in the seat of mockers" (Ps. 1:1). That is the thought that is in mind here. Not only does *agape* refuse to associate itself in any way with wickedness and evil, but it also mourns their presence in the affairs and lives of men. If we are under the rule of *agape*, we will find no pleasure in sin, either our own or anyone else's. News of the misfortune of others, even of enemies, will sadden us because *agape* desires the best for everyone, and especially the repentance and salvation of those who are alienated from God.

If we are under the rule of agape, we will find no pleasure in sin, either our own or anyone else's.

Love rejoices with the truth. Psalm 1 continues describing the "blessed" man: "But his delight is in the law of the Lord, and on His law he meditates day and night" (Ps. 1:2). There is no greater truth than the Word of God, and those who live under *agape* will take genuine delight in it. We will read it, study it, discuss it, share it, teach it to our children, and proclaim it to a dark and dying world. Rejoicing with the truth also means being genuinely happy with the honest and honorable success of others, even people who disagree with us or with whom we have trouble getting along. It means celebrating when justice prevails and injustice is overturned. Rejoicing with the truth means being happy when people come out of restrictive, self-limiting ignorance into the light of knowledge. *Agape* is active rejoicing that gets personally involved in serving and working for the truth.

Love always protects. The Greek word for "protects" literally means "to cover," as with a roof, and "to hide or conceal." In this sense, then, *agape* is always careful to hide the faults or failings of others rather than broadcast them to the world. With regard to marriage and the family, this means that a husband "covers" his wife, and both of them cover and protect their children, depending all the while on the protecting and covering *agape* of God over their lives, their circumstances, and their welfare. *Agape* is the shield or barrier that insulates a family from the harsh onslaughts of life and the arid, desiccating values of a godless world.

Love always trusts. This is true, first of all, with regard to God. Since *agape* has its source in God alone, its very life is wrapped up in Him alone. If we are guided by *agape*, we will trust the Lord in all things and will look to Him for wisdom, leadership, and discernment in every affair of life, whether at home, on the job, or elsewhere. Trust in God will permeate our conversation as well as every relationship with both family and friends. In addition, love that always trusts means having faith in other people, not to the point of gullibility, but believing the best of them unless there is irrefutable evidence to the contrary. In this sense, it is similar to the quality of keeping no record of wrongs. *Agape* delights in and assumes the virtue and good feeling of others.

Love always hopes. What is meant here is not the dreamy, wishful thinking type of hope that the world understands. *Agape* hope—biblical hope—is grounded solidly in accomplished fact and the promises of God. Because of this, if we are living under *agape*, we can have a confident and assured expectancy that our lives will turn out well. We are in the capable hands of a loving Father who promised us: "For I know the plans I have for you...plans to prosper you and not to harm you, plans to give you hope and a future" (Jer. 29:11). *Agape* always sees the bright side of things in both the physical and spiritual realms, not through denial that refuses to acknowledge pain, sorrow, and hardship, but through an optimism that refuses to despair because it is grounded in the unfailing nature and promises of God.

 AGAPE *hope—biblical hope—is grounded solidly in accomplished fact and the promises of God.*

Love always perseveres. When all else fails (or seems to), love never gives up. It hangs on to the end. Loving parents never give up on their children, never stop loving them, never stop praying for them, no matter how rebellious and wayward they may be. God is eternal, and since agape has its source in Him, it too is eternal. Therefore, by nature and definition, agape always perseveres. *Agape* bears up under persecution, slander, hardship, abuse, false accusations, ingratitude—anything. The persevering quality of *agape* is what Jesus displayed when He prayed from the Cross for His enemies and executioners: "Father, forgive them, for they do not know what they are doing" (Lk. 23:34.)

Love never fails. This statement sums up all that has gone before. The word *fails* here is used in the sense of something giving way, falling off, or ceasing to exist. Love is eternal. Prophecies, tongues, and knowledge will someday pass away but agape will never fail. This world we live in, as well as the entire physical universe, will eventually disappear, but *agape* will never fail. *Agape* is a little bit of Heaven on earth right now, and it will remain to characterize life for all of God's people in the new Heaven and new earth that are to come. Though all else may pass away, love will remain. *Agape* never fails.

Learning to live under *agape* is the primary key to understanding love that lasts a lifetime. Every married couple faces the question, "Okay, we're married, now what?" Modern society offers them many different options, a multiplicity of voices that offer counsel and advice. The world has a lot to say about love—good and bad, right and wrong—but no one understands love the way God does, because God *is* love (see 1 Jn. 4:16). If we want to understand love, we need to go to the source. If we want to grow and live a successful, lifelong marriage, we need to consult the manufacturer.

Marriage is an adventurous journey, and every traveler on that road needs a reliable Guide and a trustworthy handbook. Whether you are newlyweds just starting out on your journey together or experienced veterans seeking to enrich and refresh yourselves along the way, commit your lives and your marriage to the Lord. Live for Him and follow His Word, and He will bless your journey, bring you success, and fill you with joy and contentment along the way. Consider the words of the wise man:

> *Trust in the Lord with all your heart and lean not on your own understanding; in all your ways acknowledge Him, and He will make your paths straight* (Proverbs 3:5-6).

PRINCIPLES

1. The only sure foundation for a lifelong marriage is *agape*, the self-giving love that has its source and origin in God alone.

2. Love is an ongoing debt that we owe each other, a debt that should never be paid off.

3. *Agape* is patient.

4. *Agape* is kind.

5. *Agape* does not envy.

6. *Agape* does not boast.

7. *Agape* is not proud.

8. *Agape* is not rude.

9. *Agape* is not self-seeking.

10. *Agape* is not easily angered.

11. *Agape* keeps no record of wrongs.

12. *Agape* does not delight in evil.

13. *Agape* rejoices with the truth.

14. *Agape* always protects.

15. *Agape* always trusts.

16. *Agape* always hopes.

17. *Agape* always perseveres.

18. *Agape* never fails.

Bahamas
Faith Ministries
International

The Diplomat Center
Carmichael Road
P.O. Box N-9583
Nassau, Bahamas

TEL: (242) 341-6444
FAX (242) 361-2260

Website:
http://www.bfmmm.com

Other books by Myles Munroe

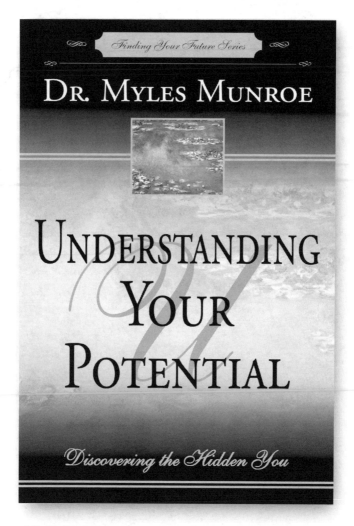

UNDERSTANDING YOUR POTENTIAL

This is a motivating, provocative look at the awesome potential trapped within you, waiting to be realized. This book will cause you to be uncomfortable with your present state of accomplishment and dissatisfied with resting on your past success.

ISBN 1-56043-046-X

Available at your local Christian bookstore.

For more information and sample chapters,
visit www.destinyimage.com

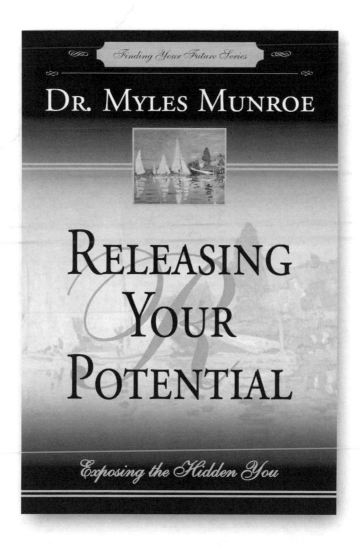

RELEASING YOUR POTENTIAL

Here is a complete, integrated, principles-centered approach to releasing the awesome potential trapped within you. If you are frustrated by your dreams, ideas, and visions, this book will show you a step-by-step pathway to releasing your potential and igniting the wheels of purpose and productivity.

ISBN 1-56043-072-9

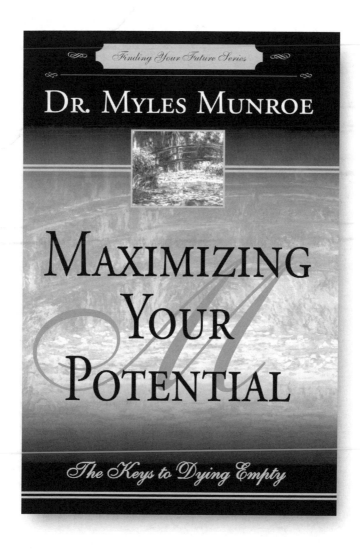

MAXIMIZING YOUR POTENTIAL

Are you bored with your latest success? Maybe you're frustrated at the prospect of retirement. This book will refire your passion for living! Learn to maximize the God-given potential lying dormant inside you through the practical, integrated, and penetrating concepts shared in this book. Go for the max—die empty!

ISBN 1-56043-105-9

THE PURPOSE AND POWER OF PRAISE & WORSHIP

God's greatest desire and man's greatest need is for a Spirit-to-spirit relationship. God created an environment of His Presence in which man is to dwell and experience the fullness of this relationship. In this book, Dr. Munroe will help you discover this experience in your daily life. You are about to discover the awesome purpose and power of praise and worship.

ISBN 0-7684-2047-4

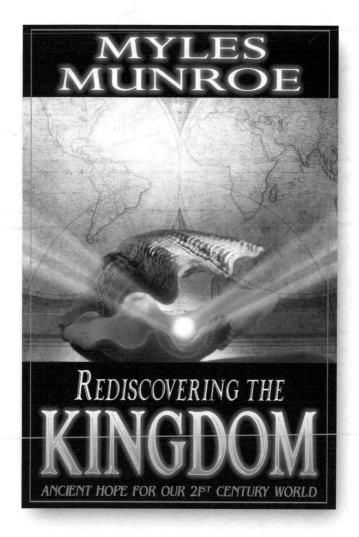

REDISCOVERING THE KINDGOM

As Dr. Munroe unveils the reality and power of the Kingdom you will be challenged to the core of your religious soul as you are exposed to realities that few are declaring in these days. *Rediscovering the Kingdom* will defy almost every concept you have about *religion*, as he shifts the focus away from religion toward *the* ultimate issue—the Kingdom of God.

Hardback ISBN 0-7684-2217-5   **Paperback ISBN 0-7684-2257-4**

Available at your local Christian bookstore.

For more information and sample chapters, visit www.destinyimage.com